THE DAMNED DON'T CRY

Pages From The Life of a Black Prisoner & Memoirs of an Organizer

By Frank Edgar Chapman, Jr.

Changemaker Publications

THE DAMNED DON'T CRY:

Pages from the Life of a Black Prisoner and Memoirs of an Organizer

By FRANK EDGAR CHAPMAN, JR.

Changemaker Publications
Pittsburgh 2019

Layout & Design: Carl Davidson

ISBN: 978-0-359-70571-9

Order online at:

http://www.lulu.com/spotlight/changemaker

A Blurb And Two Quick Reviews

Angela Davis in a note for my memoirs wrote:

"This extraordinary memoir from a seasoned communist organizer is also the riveting account of a prisoner's unrelenting journey toward freedom. Combining a close analysis of movement building – from battles against police violence and political repression to successful election campaigns – with a personal story of the effects of mass incarceration, Frank Chapman reveals what it means to generate optimism amid circumstances where all hope would seem to be obliterated. In these neoliberal times, Frank is cautious about presenting his account, including his struggle with personal demons, as an individual triumph. Instead, he shows us the potential of a political engagement so profound that it has the power to save many lives, including his own."

Bill Ayers, who was cast by Barack Obama's opponents in 2008 as a former leader of the Weather Underground, wrote this short review:

"Frank Chapman's life story is entirely compelling, and his memoir-riveting, trembling, and real-is a foundational American narrative, illuminating the flip side of the mythical American Dream: the agonizing, painful, and sometimes horrifying American Nightmare.

"The Damned Don't Cry" is the heartfelt personal account of one Black man sentenced to life plus fifty years in prison when he was just 19-years-old, and his life-long struggle for truth and reconciliation, redemption and justice.

On a deeper level this is the story of our country in full, including the violence and the pain, the tragedy and the shame. The after-life of slavery is made manifest on every page, vivid illustrations of oppression and predation, thunderous echoes of genocide, torture, and terrorism. The education of Frank Chapman contains a curriculum for the country, and for all of us.

Teacher, organizer, long-time inmate and jail-house lawyer, intellectual and writer-Frank Chapman is, above all, a class warrior and a freedom fighter. As a young man he chose to storm the heavens in pursuit of human liberation, and he never quit. In this essential book we hear the adult voice, the mature voice, both reflecting on that long-ago revolutionary commitment, and urging us to build an unstoppable social movement for peace and justice-for a world in balance and powered by love.

Aislinn Pulley, a leader of Black Lives Matter Chicago wrote in her review:

This is an incredibly timely and important book about a leader who continues to offer wisdom and guidance and inspiration to today's movement. Frank's lived experiences illustrate the torturous reality of US imprisonment that has only increased with the rise of mass incarceration.

What is most inspiring is Frank's intellectual pursuit and intellectual curiosity that broke through the shackles of prison, a life sentence, solitary confinement, prison guard beatings, to produce liberatory and revolutionary mobilization while inside the current day manifestation of slavery that is the current US prison system!

His analysis and commitment to justice and the oppressed enabled him to see through the carefully disguised use of prison segregation- to disguise the brutal reality of prison and the torture it wages on all prisoners- and instead fought for integration. He engaged in this fight not because of some naive conception of unity, but because he understood the forces of the prison system benefitted from segregation in order to foster racial animosity between Black and white prisoners to keep the animosity on the source that waged brutality on them all, the prison system itself.

The most eye-opening example of this was when Frank details the warden's attempt to create a "race riot" by caging the Black radicals with the white supremacist prisoners together, beat them and maced them, in order to get the groups to enact violence upon each other. Instead this ended up uniting them by exposing the true arbiter of violence, and exposing the true intent of racial division. What a truly remarkable real life example exposing one of the most important functions of US white supremacy,

which is to mask the brutality, inequity and class exploitation that is a required function of the US capitalist colonialist empire.

Frank continues to inspire, motivate and teach not only me but a whole layer of people who have newly become radicalized through today's popularly called Black lives matter movement. It is integral and necessary that we study lessons and struggle with those who have had the fortune of amassing great experience and wisdom so that we lessen the chance of making needless mistakes and increase our ability to carry the torch of liberation forward. We are lucky to count Frank among us. We are privileged to struggle alongside him. Amandla!

Dr. Gerald Horne, *Black historian, prolific writer and author of over 30 books had this to say:*

"Move over Malcolm X and George Jackson and make room for Frank Chapman. His riveting and astonishing book is a monumental contribution to the literature on the struggle of Black prisoners and how they overcome, which in turn is a worthy successor to that other formidable corpus: the slave narrative. Cinematic in scope and drama this is the first Great Book of the 21st Century."

ACKNOWLEDGEMENT

Special thanks to Mary Baker for transcribing from my voice to
the written word the midsection of the book. Thanks to Hatem,
Joe, Nerissa, Sarah and Steve for taking time to read
the manuscript and giving me feedback.

SPECIAL DEDICATION

To my two beautiful daughters Naima and Jamilya and their
courageous mother Maria Ramos. To my beautiful step daughter
Corlita Mahr and her wonderful ever-caring mother Coraminita
Mahr. To my present wife Dorice Smith and step children, Tanya
and Jason. They all continue to show me nothing but love.

DEDICATION

A Short Journey Into the Night of a New Day

*Written November, 2017 while visiting
prisoners in Jefferson City, Missouri*

I entered the Missouri Department of Corrections November
3, 1961 with a sentence of Life and Fifty Years. I was charged
with murder and robbery and the sentencing Judge said I
should be isolated from society for the rest of my life. I was
19 years old.

Thanks to the movement led by Charlene Mitchell, Angela Davis,
Esther Cooper Jackson, Hershel Walker and others I came home in
1976. In the same prison, in 1969, I met a young 17-year-old prisoner who had been certified as an adult when he was 16 and sentenced to two Life Sentences. His name was Larry Thomas and he

was an outstanding boxer on his way to becoming the middle weight champion in the prison.

I gave him a book *(Ghetto Rebellion to Black Liberation,* by Claude Lightfoot) along with this message: "Read this because you can't box your way out of prison." He did, and he also joined our Marxist-Leninist collective and founded the prisoner advocate group called "Lifers Incorporated". Larry went on to get out of prison and graduated from Lincoln University with a Master of Arts Degree

A Reunion

Well today Larry and I had a reunion. What was the occasion? A prison branch of the NAACP in Jefferson City, Mo. Invited us to their annual awards dinner because they wanted to thank us for the founding of Lifers, Inc. and the first State Prison Branch of the NAACP in the nation in 1973. They saluted us for leading struggles inside the prisons to desegregate, and end the overcrowdedness which was causing Black prisoners to live four and six men to a cell; for getting 32 illegally held juveniles released; for litigating for our first amendment rights to read Black literature and literature on national liberation and socialism; for winning the right to continue to pursue our education at the college level and for getting started in 1972 a community college at the prison in Moberly, Missouri. It was a very moving experience having young prisoners telling us "what you brothers did then, over forty years ago has inspired us to continue the struggle for our human rights and for reforms that will end mass incarceration...."

It was an emotional experience that defies verbal expression to see these brothers fighting now with the same tenacity and revolutionary fortitude we had over forty years ago. They called us in as honored guests not to share a simple success story of how we beat the unbeatable odds but to acknowledge and carry forward a legacy of struggle that refuses to surrender to oppression period. They called us in to remind us that we have a duty to make freedom ring for those imprisoned Now. After Larry and I spoke Marcus Granger, the prison chapter of the NAACP President, handed me a brochure with this message from W.E.B. DuBois:

"Now is the accepted time, not some more convenient season. It is today that our best can be done."

Today unlike yesteryear 1961 I took a short journey into the night of a new day where prisoners themselves (once again) are taking the helm and demanding our support. We must and will help them in whatever way we can.

I dedicate this book to them and to Theodore Taylor (Sleeves), Leon Dent (Black Liberator) who were murdered by the prison guards, and to those like Ronnie Jones, Virgil Pearson, Jerry Spraggins, and Henry (Shasha Black Panther) Brown who survived the prison experience only to perish in the dog eat dog existence of capitalism and of course to determined survivors like Robert Arnold Jameson, Danny Boy Jackson, Joseph Stalin Reynolds, Thomas McCreary (Black Panther), Larry Thomas and Lorenzo Petty,I also dedicate this book.

There is another whole army of people in the movement to whom I owe my existence and so much more. Let me name them in the order that they came into my life:

Esther Cooper Jackson, James Jackson, Jack O'Dell, Herschel Walker, Dr. Betty Lee, Leo Fichtembaum, Myrna Fichtembaum, Pearly Evans, Assemblywoman Daverne Calloway, Ernest Calloway, Senator Gwen Giles, Corminita Mahr, Virginia Brodine, Claudia Zaslavsky, Beatrice Lumpkin, Charlene Mitchell, Angela Davis, Lew Moye, Kenneth Jones, Jay Ozier, James Robnette, Bob Williams, Alice Windom, Percy Greene, Margaret Phillips, Rev. Milt Stoh, Rev. Paul Beams, Rev. Sterling Belcher, Rev. Bill Stickney, Jim Wilkerson, Frank Wilkerson, Sheila and Gus Lumpe, Harold Gibbons, Steve Hollis, Steve Mitchell, Anne Mitchell, Mattie Jones, Judge

Claudia Marcum, Llenda Jackson, Lenny Polletta Carol Pittman, Mayor Eddie Carthan, Ted Basset, Grace Basset, Joe Sims, Mayor Gus Newport, Mina Baraka, Amiri Baraka, Joseph Jazz Hayden, Dharuba bin-Wahad, James Robnette, Horace Smith, Walle Amusa, Kenneth Jones, Jay Ozier, Brenda Jones, John May, Pam Talley, Zenobia Thompson, Michael Myerson, Henry Winston, Maria Ramos, Anne Braden, Scott Douglas, Sylvia Woods, Beatrice Lumpkin, Ishmael Flory, Clarice Durham, Mildred and Willie Williamson, Camile Williamson, Dr, Linda Murray, Josephine Wyatt, Lennox Hinds, Llenda Jackson, Claudia Morcom, Dr. Jim Tate, Deacon Alexander, Franklin Alexander, Kendra Alexander, Evalina Alarcon, Rudy Lozano, Lupe Lozano, Emma Lozano, Margaret Burnham, Dorothy Burnham, Claudia Loftis, Kay Anderson, Carl Bloice, Kendra and Franklin Alexander, Deacon Alexander, Lisa Brock, Josephine Wyatt, Sylvia Woods, Clarice Durham, Dr. Peter Orris, Dr. Jim Tate, Dr. Mary Charlston, Fania Davis, Rita Anthony, Judy Hand, Joy Portugal, Louise Patterson, Mary Louise Patterson, Jarvis Tyner, Joe Sims, Margarette and John Pittman, James Wilkerson and so many more whom I will hopefully mention in this book.

Prefatory Note

I believe biography and autobiography are part of the narrative history of humankind and as history they reveal the personal human drama of the times in which we live; they are obviously of human interest and they teach us how people are shaped by history even as they make it; and in our own peculiar ways we are all born to make history.

I believe human beings play a significant role in creating themselves. There are those who are known and unknown, sung and unsung but in the simple terms of life and death no human being is greater or lesser than the other; nature stamps us all with her own brand of equality which is independent of human convention and covenants.

We are born, we live and struggle through life for better or for worse and then we die. People can be born into society deaf, dumb and blind, like a Helen Keller, and still become conscious human beings sharing in human culture. We are born like all natural beings but we become conscious as humans through the associated productive activity of human beings. Animal behavior is explained by instinct, human behavior is explained by consciousness. What we dread is death, the fact that consciousness will cease to exist as soon as we as natural beings cease to exist. Those who are remembered and endeared in the hearts and minds of humanity are those who fought the good fight so the least of us could have a better day. Our egos come and go in this endless ebb and flow of humanity.

My first hero was my father who was a jazz musician of the be-bop school. Unlike my mother he was like a thorn thrust into the heart of my youthful existence. He was not a frustrated genius as far as I could tell, but a frustrated man who couldn't find a way to express his genius in a society in which his people were the pariah. I guess the same could be said of Charlie Parker and other more widely known jazz artists, and let me quickly add that they too were my heroes. Following in my father's footsteps was my choice because I thought it was the hip thing to do and only after it nearly cost me my life was I willing to reconsider.

I moved on to find new heroes like Frederick Douglass, Wendell Phillips, Thomas Paine, Victor Hugo, V. I. Lenin, Karl Marx, Patrice Lumumba, Kwame Nkrumah, Nelson Mandela, et al; and sheroes like Harriet Tubman, Sojourner Truth, Ida B. Wells, Rosa Luxemburg, Elizabeth Gurley Flynn, Claudia Jones, Rosa Parks, Charlene Mitchell, Angela Davis, Assata Shakur and the list goes on. Where I came from in the first place was never a matter of choice but now I march to the beat of a different drummer and how this came about is what my life story is all about.

My mother, who joined the ancestors three years ago, was the unsung shero of my life. She was there helping us as best she could through the pains and agonies of children abandoned by their father. But let me not get ahead of myself by reflecting on the story before it is told.

My Family Background

I will no doubt have to do some research in this area. But in general here is what I know. On my mother's side of the family my ancestry is mostly West African and Ethiopian, a dash of Irish, a pinch of Anglo-Saxon and a flood of Native American Indian.

On my father's side West African, French, East Indian and Native American Indian. Just to show how eminent this genealogy is my mother's father (they called him Kato) was an Ethiopian (born in Ethiopia) and my father's father John was of black West African heritage but born in Troy, France.

My grandmother on my mother's side was named Margaret. She was killed in a car accident before I was born. But I remember Margaret's mother, whom we called Granny, and who lived to be 113 years old. Granny's name was Mattie White Eagle and she was full blooded Chiricahua Native American. She was 34 years old and part of the Chiricahua Removal in 1877 when her people were forced into concentration camps called "reservations". I was 14 when Granny died in 1957.

My great grandmother on my father's side was dead before I was born but my father's mother, Adelaide Kelts Chapman (we called her Addie or affectionately Mama Chapman). Granny gave birth to 14 children and Mama Chapman 7. On both my mother and father side we had large families. Mama Chapman had 4 boys and 3 girls and Granny had like 9 girls and 5 boys. Here are my siblings listed in the order they were born from 1943-61: Yvonne, Kathleen, Sharon, Devoid, Rita, Chris, Linda, Ace, Craig, Fontina and Daryll.

Childhood and Adolescence

I was born in St. Louis, Missouri on September 12, 1942 to Frank Edgar Chapman and Katherine Roberts. I was baptized a Catholic in October 1942. My sister, Yvonne was born eleven months later in 1943, and then came Kathleen in 1944 and Sharon in 1947.

I started Catholic school in September, 1947. I had brain surgery at the age of seven in 1949. I stayed in a coma for two weeks. The operation involved removing a benign tumor and it was successful.

After about three weeks of hospitalization I was returned home to my mother and father. Shortly thereafter my mother and father separated for the first time probably due to my father being arrested and imprisoned by the federal authorities. He was charged with drug possession and drug addiction.

At the age of eight I began running away from home and hanging out with street urchins who like me also came from broken homes. We became a little band of thieves, stealing out of grocery and department stores. Yet I still managed to go to school.

Somewhere between ages nine and ten I started playing hooky from school and getting arrested by the cops on a regular basis.

Soon after I turned nine a new addition to the family was born. His name was Devoid and we called him Dee Dee. My first baby brother who I took care of for the eighteen months of his life and then he was killed by electrocution after he bit a live wire protruding from the wall in our tenement. I became very angry with my mother, myself and everyone else. And I started living in the streets. Running away from home was running away from tragedy or so I thought.

1953 was a turning point in my life for two reasons, my brother's death and my father returning home from prison. Like I stated earlier my father went to prison for possession of a controlled substance (heroin) and for being an addict. I was hoping that my mother and father would get back together; and they did for a minute but then dad was back in the streets and so was I. This time I stayed with him and in so doing I got exposed to the life style of hustlers, thieves, pimps, prostitutes and heroin addicts. After about six months my father was back in the slammer with a five-year sentence for using and peddling drugs.

I followed in his footsteps drinking wine and getting my first stint in reform school in 1953 for playing hooky and grand larceny (that is, stealing over fifty dollars). I stayed in reform school for 16 months during which time I had 47 escapes and attempted escapes combined; I was released on June 16, 1954.

My mother had moved to the west end of St. Louis to a much better neighborhood, She was able to do this because she had, through the Catholic Charities, placed my sisters in a "boarding school for Negro girls" called Saint Francis. My mother was endeavoring to help them get educational opportunities she missed, primarily due to race and poverty. She also sent me to the Catholic Charities.

The Catholic Charities assigned me a caseworker named Ms. Randolph. I can't remember her first name for the life of me but she was very kind and caring. She would say to me things like: "Frank please don't waste your intelligence, you owe it to yourself, your family and the Negro people. If I can get you in Saint Joseph's School for Boys please stay and make something of yourself!" And I could tell that these words came from her heart. Then she was a young Black woman in her thirties, now I have no idea of where she is or when or where she died.Ms. Randolph pulled it off for me. I was enrolled in St. Joseph's in July 1954 two months before the fall semester. It was really a school for white kids covering grades five through the first semester of high school.

But for me it was almost like living in a fantasy. We lived like I imagined rich kids lived. We had the best of food and clothing, study time, leisure time, lots of recreation and sports and games; we went to nice schools in the well-to-do neighborhoods and we got a weekly allowance. For a while I was very happy with my new surroundings. But being that there were only three African Americans on the campus it was difficult getting along with our peers. And being fresh out of reform school it was a hard fit for me. These kids knew nothing of drinking wine, hanging out on the corner and having fun. I couldn't make the adjustment because as silly as it seems I missed my street buddies, so I kept running away until finally they put me out.

Back in the streets again and turning 13. Back with the fellows drinking wine, smoking cigarettes and stealing. We took it up a notch, this time we were stealing cars and selling car body parts. One night I stole a car drunk, had a wreck and got busted by the cops. This was very serious said the juvenile Judge and he gave me an undetermined sentence in The Missouri State Training School for Boys. Now I had to go up state and do some time with the "bad boys" for real. We called this place Booneville because it was located in a town by that name.

I don't know about now but back then in 1955-56 Booneville was a rough joint in terms of both the guards and inmates. We were treated mean and brutal by the guards and so we reacted in the same manner. There were lots of fist fights and they were always bloody. If you learned anything you had to learn how to fight and how often you fought depended on how good you could fight and if you could fight well then you didn't have to fight often. My partner, Peter "Rabbit", and me were street fighters and in the streets we used weapons as well as fists. A lot of our fellow inmates especially the Sarah and Finney gang were pissed off at Peter because he had shot at them on the streets. Here we had to learn how to use our fists and we did.

I was in Booneville for about fourteen months before making parole. I was released in January 1957. I was fourteen years old and six feet tall. My mother couldn't believe how I had grown.

Because of my excellent grades while in reform school my mother took me, and my report card to Soldan High School, to a Mr. DeSheilds, who was the principal. He was so impressed with my grades that he enrolled me immediately into a college prep program. I proceeded to assume the normal life of a teenager. I got me a girlfriend named Joyce whom I fell in love with. I participated in sports (basketball) and acquired new friends. These were ghetto kids who in spite of all odds were trying to become productive members of society; they were working for their dreams and I was starting to work for mine as I found myself getting exposed to new ideas through literature, science and history. History was my favorite subject; but back then all it meant to me was reading wonderful stories about all the great things human beings had done. What I liked about history is that it was not merely a chronicle of events but the story about how individual men and women actually made history.

This brief respite of two months was interrupted when the police came to my mother's house and arrested me. Someone had apparently implicated me in a car theft. The police came in the still of the night with their pistols and flashlights, handcuffed me and took me off to the twelfth district police station. Once at the station the interrogation was intense and they used every trick in the book, including physical violence, to try to get me to confess to something I did not do. There were times when I almost broke down but I all could do was cry out "I didn't do this so why are you beating on me? Is it because I'm colored?" And of course they would really get brutal after I called out their racism.

In spite of my denials I was booked and sent to the juvenile home. They said I violated my parole so I was promptly returned to Booneville. And needless to say I was heartbroken. In one fell swoop I lost my girlfriend, and the confidence I had with my new friends and Mr. DeSheilds. I returned to Booneville bitter and angry.

I immediately got involved in an escape plot with my old comrades there. We jumped the house guard, took his keys (car keys included) locked him in the basement of the cottage, stole his car and took off to the freeway. There were four of us. I was the designated driver. It was raining so the visibility wasn't good. We took the bridge over the Missouri River and headed for a town called Columbia. As soon as we hit the highway the state troopers were chasing us. They forced us off the highway into a roadside ditch. We were caught and returned to the reformatory. But that brief moment of freedom had us all feeling good and kind of proud of what we had done. They said we were the first inmates to ever do something like this. It even made the local newspapers and radio stations. Our enthusiasm was short lived. For being the first we got a first class, brutal ass whipping and while still bleeding thrown into isolation cells called "the hole." Now there was talk of certifying us as adults and sending us to Algoa, a prison camp for young adults from ages 17 to 21. Four or five days later, just when I had resigned myself to my fate, a guard told me to come out of the cell because I was leaving. I didn't believe him so at first I wouldn't move. "Come on you fucking hooligan," he shouted, "you're aunt is here to take you back to the Judge in St. Louis!" After hearing this I moved rather quickly.

My Aunt Lola was my father's oldest sister and a Pentecostal Minister. She told me she had talked to her friend Judge McMillan (a very liberal Black Judge in St. Louis who is well known today because he was the first Black Judge to be appointed to the Missouri Supreme Court Bench) and told him all about how I had brain surgery in 1949 and that because of the years of neglect that followed my release from the hospital that I needed special care. Aunt Lola, who was doing well for herself (she owned a Cadillac, her own home and pastored a church) told the Judge she was willing to be my guardian and help me to get on the right path. Apparently Judge McMillan thought she was perfectly suited for the task and by some legal maneuver unknown to me secured my immediate release.

I stayed with Aunt Lola for almost two years. She got me back in Soldan High. But it was too late for Joyce and me; her parents didn't want her messing with no jailbird. I got over it real soon. Aunt Lola spoiled me with fine clothes (I was one of the sharpest cats in my school and she didn't buy cheap stuff), riding me to school every morning in her Cadillac and even giving me an allowance. This really gave me the edge with the girls and made me the envy of the in-crowd guys who came from working class families with bourgeois aspirations. I was a downtown Negro from the heart of the ghetto and I was dressing better than them. I had one fight and the guy was heavier than me but he was not a pugilist like me, he hadn't been to Bonneville! It was an easy win. After that the in-crowd backed off unless they caught me at a house party where they could gang up on me. So I went to school in one neighborhood and hung out in another. The bad thing about being with Aunt Lola is that she lived in the old hood. So guess what? I would go down to the corner of Compton and Laclede in my fine clothes flash my little bankroll and talk shit. Before long I was back into crime based strictly on association and the desire to be with my old friends or running buddies. They were also my drinking buddies, for by this time I was really hitting the jug.

The year was 1958 and I remember giving up on ever being a square or being what Ms. Randolph and Aunt Lola wanted me to be. I figured that I kept ending up in the streets because I belonged in the streets. Let's face it I was attracted to the criminal, easy money life. I guess I got this from my father but I really don't know where it came from. All I know is when you grow up a certain way, being subjected to the indignities of racism and watching cats on the corner like T.J. Ruffin, who was a true live gangster that stayed clean, talked trash and kept plenty of money then that's who you wanted to be like. I wasn't expecting nothing from the system (which we called "The White Man" or simply "The Man") other than what I always got. So, I jumped back into the life feet first and started supporting myself by hustling and stealing.

However, it also needs to be said that Ms. Randolph and Aunt Lola offered me a way out of crime. I did not take the way out that they offered because of my "sick" thinking. I knew that crime was wrong but I liked it because I wanted to take things and not work and sacrifice for them. In other words, I rationalized being selfish and reckless and in doing so I hurt the people who loved me as well as myself. At this stage of my life I had no appreciation for the integrity of working people who selflessly sacrifice, through hard work, for their families and their community. I saw nothing heroic about the men who worked at Scullins Steel Mill 12 hours a day to provide for their families.

Youth and into the Night

I was sixteen years old playing the role of an adult. Eddie Walls (who was an orphan in the streets) and we were probably the only young cats in the hood with cribs. (A crib was wherever you lived, boarding room, apartment or house). My crib consisted of a one-bed room joint just big enough for a dresser, the bed and me. But I was proud of it because it was mine and I paid five dollars a week rent for it. Later on I teamed up with a hustler out of Detroit and we got a two-bedroom place for fifteen dollars a week. (Now that same apartment would cost about two hundred and fifty dollars a week).

Here's how it happened: We had just pulled off a nice caper on the Southside that put about seven hundred dollars in our pockets. I told my partner, "Damn, I can pay off the Landlord for the year and still have some money for clothes, food and fun." He had a better idea. We could go in together for a two-bedroom crib for $7.50 apiece, pay three months rent, and have more money left. This would give us more time to lay low for a while. We would cut back on the risk of getting caught and going to jail if we lay back a little.

Who could disagree with this? So that's how we got down together; we got the two-bedroom joint and started hustling together on a regular. But things didn't quite work out as planned. For the next three months we did more partying than hustling. We went from drinking sneaky Pete wine to smoking reefer and snorting dope. Weeks before our three months of living off of advance rent was up we were broke and back hustling again.

Doing alcohol and drugs almost every day gave our hustling a different edge. Now we felt desperate for money because we needed drink and drugs. We hastily planned an armed robbery of two white landlords in the West end. We were caught but my partner got away and that is the last I saw or heard of him. The juvenile

officer promised me that I would be certified as an adult and probably get twenty-five years in prison. Well I thought like the song
says, "This is it!" My ass was really in the slingshot this time. I sat
locked up in the Juvenile Jail waiting for a decision.

My mother pleaded with my juvenile probation officers, Mr. Ed
Trip, and Ms. Billie Boykin, a female officer, to stop my certifi-
cation as an adult. My mother told Mr. Trip that I was seeing a
psychiatrist at Barnes Hospital but that my care kept getting interrupted by me running away and staying in jail. So, Mr. Trip had me
examined by one of the jailhouse shrinks and I was sent by court
order to The Missouri State Hospital for the Mentally Disturbed for
six weeks observation.

I believe it was the winter of 1958 when I was sent to the state
hospital. I was horrified by the very idea of going to a nut house
for any reason. I didn't think I was "crazy" or "nuts" and neither
did Mr. Trip. He thought I was simply a sociopath who needed reform but he was willing to let the experts decide. Upon my arrival
I was placed on the diagnostic ward, which had these nice, little,
spacious rooms with two beds, a cafeteria-style dining room and
a large solarium that could accommodate about 30 people. I was
assigned a young, white female student nurse who took me off
the ward for x-rays, physical checkups, and psychological exami-
nations during my first two weeks. Every morning after breakfast
they would call my name and she would be there waiting with a
wheel chair ready to wheel me off to my appointments for the day.

The appointments always involved a long wait so Ms. Smith and I
always had plenty of time to chat. And boy did we talk! She asked
lots of questions pertaining to my life style as a criminal and she
was truly fascinated; but the funny thing about this is that I actually trusted her and told her the truth about why I committed
crimes not about how I committed crimes. I guess I wanted to
trust somebody at this point in my life and so she was the one.
The main value of this experience for me was that it proved to me
that white people who didn't have the power of life and death over
you could be decent human beings like anyone else. Ms. Smith
took a big chunk out of my socially instinctive fear and hatred
of white people. I became attracted to her and she liked me too,
the way one likes exotic things, but we were both aware of our
environment. Even now I still appreciate having had such a young,

sensitive and intelligent woman in my life. Without even knowing it she helped me to step outside my narrow racial thinking that categorically condemned all white people. But this brief episode didn't produce any radical change in my perspective on race. I still thought most white people were die in the wool racists in search of a black victim.

While the doctors and Ms. Smith were exploring my mind my libido was running wild. Without getting too graphic let me just say that I was having sex with my hand but really preferred a female partner, and I'll be damned if one didn't come alone.

The men and women lived on separate wards but every Friday we got together to socially mingle at a dance. The first time I went I met this deep, dark chocolate beauty called Anna Marie Collins. But she was about five feet seven and built like a brick house. She had just turned seventeen and of course I told her I was eighteen, given my size who could doubt it. Any way we danced, held hands and talked about everything under the sun.

After four weeks I was allowed a pass to go home. Anna had been there a year so she got passes every week. We made arrangements to meet one another while on pass. We tried acting normal, you know going to the movies and such. This happened a few more times and then she told her doctor about me and that's how it ended.

After my escapades with Anna had been exposed I was placed on restrictions and confined to the ward. I was a little shaken by this because I thought they were getting ready to send me to jail because my six weeks were just about up.

Also, it was apparent that this was a racially segregated ward yet all the attendants were white. The attendants were openly racist brutes. They told me that they didn't like me being friendly with white nurses and the young Jewish guy I had befriended name David Jacobs. I can't explain why David was in a state hospital because he came from a family that had plenty of money. We hit it off good because he was really into jazz and Black music, and as far as I could tell he was not a racist.

Every time I looked around I was accused of breaking some rule. The punishment was quite severe. We were forced to lie down on a gurney covered with an ice-cold sheet and then they would take frozen sheets out of a freezer, beat the stiffness out of them and then methodically wrap them around your naked body until you looked like a mummy. Everything but your head and feet would be wrapped in ice cold sheets.

Then you would be strapped down and forced to lie like this for two agonizing hours. At first your body would be shivering and teeth clattering from the cold and then your body would get warm and you'd start to feel drowsy but you couldn't sleep because as the ice on the sheets melted the sheets tightened up on your body causing every joint to ache with excruciating pain. It was torture but they called it treatment.

When I finally was let out of this frigid hell I felt real light headed for several hours. It was almost like a high. And oddly enough I was calm instead of pissed. I had no idea about what these racist creeps had done to me but I knew I wanted no more of it. This is when I started seriously thinking about escaping.

We were allowed off of the ward to get commissary even while under restrictions. On our day I went to the commissary. I asked the nurse who accompanied us could I use the rest room and she said, "yes but hurry back" That was all the leeway I needed. Instead of going to the rest room I sneaked into another hallway and walked out of the building as if I had a pass.

I couldn't go to my mother's house because I knew the police would be expecting me to go there. I really didn't have anywhere to go except back to my old running buddies and hide out in the hood. And so, I got in touch with Tuck, who was about five years my senior, and told him I needed a hideout. He told me that no one was using the clubhouse in the alley behind his house and that he had no problem with me hiding out there. I had to turn this coal shed of a clubhouse into something livable. I put in a bed and electric heaters, which I could only use at night. It took hours to heat this place up when it was very cold. On those real bitter, cold nights Tuck would let me sleep in the house on the couch; and there were plenty of cold bitter nights. My friend had a young wife and a newborn baby girl. He never complained or anything but I was very uncomfortable with this whole situation. Besides feeling like I was imposing on Tuck and his family I was suffering from asthma and had contacted pneumonia as a result of sleeping in the clubhouse. My hitting the jug didn't help. I ended up in Homer G. Phillips Hospital.

The staff at Homer G. Phillips routinely contacted the police. The cops told me that they had no warrant for my arrest but that they did have orders to return me safely to the state hospital. I think they were lying because as soon as the hospital released me they hand cuffed me and then proceeded to return me to the hospital. I believe it was August 1959 when I was readmitted to the State Hospital. More cold sheet therapy, and one month later I ran away again never to return. When I ran away for the last time I was forced to live in extreme destitution. Not only did I have to elude the police, but due to lack of money I had to sleep in abandoned cars, cold and damp basements, and occasionally at my sister Yvonne's house. Unexpectedly I got word from two friends of mine (Joe and Osborn) who had moved to Chicago. They contacted me through our mutual friend Tuck. They suggested that I catch the first thing running out of St. Louis and come to Chicago. I borrowed some money from my sister, Yvonne and headed out for Chi Town.

I never will forget that first night I arrived in Chicago on the Greyhound bus. I had on this blue navy coat and a little winter cap. When I got off the bus I was so cold until I felt like I didn't have anything on. I mean it was bone cold and the wind coming off of Lake Michigan was sharp as a razor. I got off the bus at Jackson Park, 63rd and Stony Island. It must have been about two o'clock in the morning. I called my father just to say hello. I have no idea why I did this. At any rate he was too surprised to get angry. "Boy what are you doing here!?" he shouted. I quickly explained to him that I would be staying with some friends and could check back with him later.

In a few days I was settled. We stayed in an apartment on the South side on 43rd and Drexel. There were three of us living in a large kitchenette with a bed that came out of a wall closet. During the day we just had a large living room with a sofa and a small kitchen and bathroom. At night we would let the bed out of the closet transforming the living room into a large bedroom. We took turns of two on the bed and one on the floor. Osborne and Reed helped me get some honest work at a hospital out in Roger Park on the North side.

While working at this hospital I met a young woman (she was 19) whom I later married. Her name was Altamease Johnson. When I met her in the dining room of the hospital I learned that she had just broke up with her former husband, who later became a famous band leader. She was cute and giving me "That I really go for you look". Finally we got together and bingo she was in love and wanted to get married. I wasn't in no hurry to get married but she kept pressing me. My roommates and I got a bigger, three-bedroom apartment and before I knew it Altamease had quietly moved in and we were sleeping together every night. This was my first lengthy sexual experience with a woman so emotionally I was out to snacks.

On May 17, 1960 we got married in a Barber shop in East St. Louis, IL. Altamease was 19 and I was 17, so my mother had to sign consent papers. My father strongly disapproved. After I got married I wanted to make it work. I got a job (through my brother in law Ernest Williams) in Evanston, Illinois working as an apprentice printer for a white printer at Wieboldts Dept. Store. He was a nice man but he taught us very little about printing. What we (the Black workers) did was mostly menial labor around the shop and errands. But it was a stable job and paid eighty dollars every two weeks. Our rent was $14 a week and we spent about $20 a week for groceries. So that meant that every two weeks $68 came out of my check just for rent and food leaving just $12 for transportation, clothes and recreation. This was just enough money to ward off starvation and get shelter and get back and forth to work. Beyond this there was nothing.

So I started hustling with my uncle Fuquay (who was married to my father's sister, Aunt Rose). Fuquay was a junk hustler, which means he went up and down alleys in rich, white neighborhoods salvaging throw away furniture, newspapers or anything else he could sale to a junk yard or people who dealt in used furniture. I could only do this on the weekends and very rarely did I make enough money to raise an eyebrow. It was hard times and as young people full of energy we suffered dearly. Under these conditions bickering and heated arguments casting blame upon each other for our troubles was inevitable. For a moment we lapsed into drugs, music (I was into bebop and my wife was more of an R&B person who loved dancing), doing partying we could ill afford and more intense sex for emotional release. Of course, the drugs made matters worse with, to use the words of Balzac, wretchedness wearing a smile and misery looking decorous. We separated. Separation had very little to do with how we really felt about each other. It was about surviving. On the night we separated I felt total despair. This was the one thing in life I really wanted and it left a wound in my heart that never quite healed and as much as I hate to admit it Altamease was the last woman to leave me because every woman I got close to or married after her I made sure I was the one to get out the door first. After we separated I remember literally walking the streets and sleeping on el trains for two days. I was utterly depressed. Then I got the idea that I would return to St. Louis and get money the best way I knew how and return to Chicago with enough money to get my family back.

I returned to St. Louis penniless and desperate in January 1961. My plans were to start a stick candy crew (that was the name for arm robbery back then) and do some loan companies, pawnshops and check cashing joints so we could stack a lot of money fast. For some reason there were lots of stick candy artists robbing white people in St. Louis at that time. I heard about some guys I knew who were reportedly getting a lot of money. I found them and presented to them my ideas and they suggested that we start with pawnshops. I guess they wanted to check my nerve out before we try anything big. I teamed up with another guy that I hardly knew and went to do the job.

Without going into graphic details at this time let me just say that I was accused of robbing a shoe repair shop were some one was murdered. The headlines of the infamous "Whirl" newspaper (which was a scandalous crime rag at that time) screamed "Wanted For Murder, Frank String Bean Chapman". According to the Whirl I was a dangerous eighteen-year-old Negro male weighting about 170 pounds and six feet tall, brown eyes and light brown skin color. The police described me as armed and dangerous, which meant in those days to shoot on sight.

When these headlines came out I was in Chicago. I was not really running. I knew I would get caught because I didn't have the money or resources to run and hide for long. I just wanted to see my wife one last time to explain to her what had happened. The occasion for me telling her what happened in St. Louis was a strange one. We went to see this movie called "*Odds Against Tomorrow*" at one of the local neighborhood movie houses. Harry Bellefonte and Robert Ryan stared in this movie, based on a novel by John Oliver Killens, about three guys down on their luck robbing a bank. It was a kind of surrealist experience sitting there watching that movie and then having to tell my wife that I was wanted for arm robbery and murder. And after hearing my story she looked at me teary-eyed and said, "Damn Frank, it's like the movie except this is real!" A few days later I was arrested in Evanston for possession of drug paraphernalia. Shortly thereafter the police learned that I was wanted for murder and I was extradited back to St. Louis, MO.

On the long ride back to St. Louis with detectives Oscar Farmer and Fred Grimes I was repeatedly urged to confess to the charges against me if I wanted to live. I mostly set quietly staring out the window at the boring flat, featureless landscape, occasionally saying, "The man I'm accused of killing was white, so if I get convicted I'm certain to get the death penalty." There was nothing they could tell me to convince me otherwise. As far as I was concerned I was finished. How could this happen to me? I had not even really lived and I thought I was about to die. It was a horrible feeling. For the rest of the ride I just sat silently, sinking into the morbidity of my own thoughts.

A Short Journey into the Long Night

What it all came down to is that I was just a man who had been involved in mistakenly and foolishly taking the life of another man. Remorse doesn't even begin to describe how I felt when it hit me in the gut. My self-esteem fell so low that I really didn't care whether I lived or not. Was I feeling suicidal? No. Just depressed and alienated from all that is worthy in a human being.

This may not make any sense to the reader but I couldn't remember exactly what I did that day. I remember it was cold and raining and I was running down an alley panic stricken. The torture and beatings from the police helped in filling in the blank spots in my memory; also, the blank spots were filled in by the guy who claimed he was my crime partner on that fateful day. I barely knew this guy and for the life of me I don't remember committing any crimes with him ever.

This just compounded my fear and self-loathing. This was the state of mind I was in when my lawyer, a public defender name Joseph Noskay, came to see me. Right away I said to him, "Look, let's get this over with. I want to plead guilty!" His response was not what I expected. He said, "No you don't want to plead guilty! If you do that now you will surely get the death penalty." I told him that I didn't care. Mr. Nosky told me that his job was to fight for my life and that if I didn't want him to do that then he would suggest that I get another lawyer. Then he told me that given the circumstances of the case he thought I should live and that he needed time to convince the judge.

I thought that this was some kind of trick that I couldn't quite figure out. Maybe Mr. Noskay was just trying to give me hope in what he knew was a hopeless situation, kind of like the priest giving you your last rites knowing damn well you ain't going to heaven. But Nosky did make me think that as long as I held the dice there was no chance of me throwing craps!

In the City Jail there were a lot of older guys who knew my father and most of them I also knew from the hood. They could see from my sullen mood and staying to myself that I didn't really want to be bothered but they reached out to me anyway. Judson, Big Newt, Pop Self, Peter "Rabbit", Baby Huey, Danny Boy, Isaac McIntosh, Hurst, Ivy, the twins Jerry and Perry, Nappy Cap and others encouraged me not to give up. Judson gave me law books to read and suggested that I participate in my own defense. Big Newt was a jazz musician bass player and he told me that when I get to the joint I would meet some fine musicians out of St. Louis and Kansas City who would gladly teach me music. Danny Boy wanted us to get down together in the books because he thought knowledge would be the key to getting out.

Out of all the people I met in that jail Danny and I truly became life-long friends. We will meet Danny Boy later on in my story. I took the advice of some of my comrades to heart and started getting into the books right away. The only problem was there was nothing to read out side of Readers Digest, Ebony magazine, Jet and the daily newspapers. Judson Holt saved the day. He showed me how to order books from the book of the month club. I only remember a couple of the five books I ordered: H.G. Wells' *The Outlines of History*. For some reason my mind found escape from my present problems by becoming submerged in the history of humankind and its problems.

I've always liked history, particularly ancient history. And I loved the way historians like H.G. Wells wrote history, the story of how humanity evolved from simple aquatic life forms to become creators and makers of their own history. Besides Outlines of History Wells' also wrote *The Time Machine* which was a creative confirmation of his belief that humanity would one day master the manipulation of time , space and matter. Now today astronomers talk about the reality of worm holes; and have machines here on earth that can assimilate or create conditions like those that exist in outer space, and these machines can also smash atoms. So Wells could be right. The human race, if it doesn't destroy itself, may in its own little corner of the universe become masters of manipulating time, space and matter.

For me, then and now, history explained everything. It explained how and why I existed as a part of evolution and not as a creation of some super human power. Wells had me thinking about matters I had never thought about before. It seemed as if humanity's only reason for existing was to create a better world here on earth. History was the story of how we evolved from the slime to the sublime; at least this is what I learned from H.G. Wells.

I also ordered *The Story of Philosophy* by Will Durant which I read about ten times. Then finally it dawned on me that Western philosophy had no pat answer to questions regarding the meaning of life. At this time I thought that one picked a philosophy that best fits his or her needs and wants. Facing the death penalty and held firmly in the grip of the cynicism that characterizes the life of outlaws my thirst for knowledge was motivated by the desire to find meaning in a poverty stricken life that seemed meaningless. I remember seeing Shakespeare's "*MacBeth*" on TV while in the City Jail and I immediately remembered the lines claiming that life is "...a tale told by an idiot full of sound and fury signifying nothing...."

Jail is really about a lost or deprivation of freedom in the most basic sense. Not only are you confined in a small space with other people, some of them being total strangers, you are also without privacy. Almost everything you do is in the presence of others. Such a situation is seemingly not conducive to anything but killing time and that involved such activities as shooting dice on bunk blankets, watching TV, telling jokes and war stories, having fights over the slightest disagreements and so on and so forth. The weekends went the slowest so this is where most of the horseplay and time-killing activities were concentrated. Monday through Friday from eight o'clock in the morning until six in the evening was when court was conducted and everybody took this very serious. People with similar cases tended to flock together and keep up with each other's cases.

This was our own little way of getting a reading on the judge and prosecutor. Judge and prosecutor, these were the two most important people in the process. In fact they were even more important than your lawyer because very few people went to trial. Plea bargaining and confessing guilt not trials and the presumption of innocence is what rules the criminal justice system, And the reason for this is quite simple: 90% of those who are defendants are poor and/or the racially and nationally oppressed. You are awaiting trial and hoping that they will offer you a deal you can run with so you don't go to trial. It was a no win, no win situation. Either you plead guilty or go to trial and get convicted by an all-white jury. So whenever someone came back from court the question was: What are they offering? Your very life is in the balance and like it or not we were all being legally hung, it was just a question of whether they were going to hang us high or low. Back then we were racially designated as Negroes and there were virtually no Negroes involved in deciding how justice would be dispensed in matters of crime and punishment.

I talked to a number of people who were opposed to the death penalty but they were all on a mission of mercy and offered no legal help. There was one exception, a man named Clark whom they called "The Hoodlum Priest". He came as a priest to see me at the City Jail. I remember when I first got the visit I thought: "Damn! They are so determined to kill me that they're sending the priest early." Father Clark was by no means your typical priest for he not only took the side of the underdog he acted like the underdog. Father Clark told me that he had seen a lot of young men executed and that such murder on the part of the state was reprehensible and must be opposed until it is stopped.

I agreed but I was sitting there thinking what in the hell could I do. And then, almost as if he were reading my thoughts, Father asked: "Do you want to live?" Without even thinking about it I said, "Yes! Yes I do want to live!" And that was all I needed to say to win the smile and support of this great man. Even had I said I didn't want to live Father Clark would have still fought for my life to be spared. I really don't know the details of what he and others opposed to the death penalty did on my behalf; however, I do know that their opposition to the death penalty was principled and uncompromising and that all of us who faced the death penalty back then who were not executed owe our very lives to the tireless efforts of people like Father Clark.

The other thing in my favor with respect to the death penalty is that the newspapers were focused on another capital punishment case. Lloyd Lee Anderson and I had been in reform school together and now we were in City Jail together on the same tier. Lloyd had been indicted for murder five times and all the alleged victims were white and one of them was a fourteen-year-old boy.

He was not very talkative and stayed mostly to himself but when he did speak he expressed the same bitterness and hatred for official society we all shared except he went much further in his hatred of racism. Our initial reaction to racism was to hate white people in general because one believed white people hated us. This can become a pathological fixation and justify all sorts of senseless, blind alley rebellion. Lloyd hated all white people because he believed that they were the ones responsible for all the social misery he experienced in life; as far as he was concerned he was like a captured soldier in a war and he expected no mercy from his enemy.

He went to trial before I did and was sentenced to death. I remember him being defiant to the end, which came about four or five years later, when he was executed. On the day he was executed the whole prison was locked down and the convicts, both Black and white were silent all that day. I guess deep down in our hearts we all knew that Lloyd's fate could have easily been ours. When the priest came to offer him his last rites he cussed the priest out as well as the warden and members of the press. He was defiant to the bitter end and we loved him for it.

All of the frenzy around Lloyd's trial took the attention off of me. He was found guilty and sentenced to die in the gas chamber. Execution then was mainly done by gas, the electric chair and hanging. I think Colorado used a firing squad. When Lloyd came back on the tier at city jail you could hear a pin drop. He looked around at all of us with a tragic smile on his face and went to his cell. It was quiet all night. After Lloyd got the death penalty the media quieted down somewhat.

COLD OCTOBER

In October of 1961 it was my turn to be tried for my alleged crimes. I will never forget that day. It was a cold October day and I was prepared for the worse. My lawyer had told me that if I wanted to live I would have to plead guilty and so I did even though the prosecutor refused to waive the death penalty. The judge accepted my guilty plea and ordered a pre-sentence investigation of my case and criminal history. In November 1961 I was sentenced to life and fifty years in prison and I was grateful, very grateful for the opportunity to live. In a letter to my mother I apologized to her for all the hardships I had caused her in my short life and I promised her that I would dedicate what was left of my life to the good of humanity by helping others as I had been helped by people like Father Clark; I told her that I had found a new religion and it was the search for the truth about myself and my fellow human beings. Why was one person's happiness seemingly based on another person's destruction? Why I had come up in a world where my poverty and deprivations had me looking on the possessions of others with covetous eyes? I hated my own station in life and the way I lived because I felt that I was entitled to the same life as the boasted rich.

Was I wrong? Yes! You can't lie, steal, rob and kill in order to be happy unless you are rich and morally bankrupt. But how does one justify one's own existence in a society where morality for the poor and Black says one thing and for the rich and white quite another? The Judges, prosecutors, police and indeed all official society were there to keep me from getting out of the impoverished hell they had put me and my people in. I saw no way out within the rules and regulation they had set up for me to follow. How can wanting money be evil if you're poor? Why would God punish those who are already being punished by society for being poor or born Black? The Judge told me that I was a threat to society, a depository of evil that needed to be banished for life. I felt remorse for what I had done that harmed other people but I felt no guilt or responsibility for the circumstances of life that brought me to that point of desperation. Such were the thoughts that occupied my mind as I prepared to go to prison to start my sentence of life and fifty years.

Long Day's Journey Out of the Night

"Those who enter here, leave all hope behind"

The train for prison always leaves early in the morning so they start rounding the prisoners up in the jail around 5:00 AM to chain us all together. Back then they were taking fifty people on the train every month. We went from the City Jail to Union Station (the train station) in buses and when we arrived we quickly boarded the train as if we were sneaking out of town. The train ride was about two and a half hours long and uneventful. As the train pulled up to the prison many of us took what we thought might be our last look at the "free world" (prisoners called outside the prison walls "the free world"). We entered prison by way of a huge iron gate and over the top of the gate carved in stone were the words: "Those Who Enter Here Leave All Hope Behind".

I learned that these were the words that hung over the "gates to hell" in Dante's *Inferno.* Just pass the gates we entered a building with a large room of lockers, showers, benches and tables. Our shackles were removed and then we were stripped naked and lined up in five rows of tens. Everyone was told to bend over for rectal inspection as the guards proceeded to shine flashlights on our rectums shouting, "Spread your cheeks". This humiliating experience took several minutes that seemed like hours. Afterwards we all took showers and got dressed into our prison clothes. As soon as we were dressed the guards led us to our cells.

All prisoners had to spend the first thirty days, isolated from the rest of the prison population, in the so-called "Reception and Diagnostic Center" or what the prisoners called "The Fish Tank". The name "fish tank" came from the days when the prisoners in reception eat with the rest of the prison population. As the new prisoners moved through the line everyone would be watching them like you watch fish in a tank.

From the point of view of the prison administration the whole point of reception was to get the prisoners orientated to the rules and regulations of the prison and to have the prisoners diagnosed for diseases and socio-pathological and psycho-pathological behaviors. We were given TB shots, psychological tests, and a thorough physical examination. The warden and his staff lectured us on how the prison was operated and finally the classification committee assigned you to a work detail.

There were basically two job categories: state and industry. State jobs were things like food service, porter jobs in the cell blocks and yard work and in the hospital. Industry jobs meant working in the soap factory, tag plant (making license plates), tailor shop, mattress factory, and furniture factory. State jobs paid ten to fifteen cents a day and industry jobs paid a dollar a day or about twenty dollars a month. The medium of exchange was cigarettes and they cost twenty-five cents a pack. This meant that if you had a state job you earned a little over a carton of cigarettes a month and if you worked in industry you earned about seven cartons a month. This huge income gap was deliberately perpetrated by the system. Before I finished my bit in the Diagnostic Center I asked the Classification Committee to send me to school; they refused and assigned me to the garbage detail in the kitchen.

My first day in population I remember standing in front of this huge medieval structure called A Hall. It looked like something out of a Gothic tale and was the only cellblock for Black people in the whole joint. Only the "fish tank" was an integrated cellblock. A Hall was where I would live for the next five years. It was cold in the winter and sweltering hot in the summer. We slept in cells of four and six men in double and triple deck bunks. There were seven hundred prisoners in A Hall, which made it also the most overcrowded cellblock. As far as being a prisoner these were without a doubt my most degrading and humiliating years of incarceration. Twice a week we were herded, one hundred and fifty at a time, into the showers like cattle. The showers were often scenes of homosexual aggression and sometimes homicide. Speaking of aggression there was more physical assaults and murders in A Hall then all six white halls together. The white halls had one and two men cells: so most of their rumbles and killing scrapes took place on the yard during the weekends. Racial segregation was literally killing Black prisoners and nobody cared accept their families and friends.

One thing about A Hall was very personal with me; it convinced me immediately that I needed to apply myself to the law books so I could find a way out of this medieval torture chamber. After attempting to read a few law books on statues and procedures I realized that I really needed to get back in school and start tightening up my formal education. Finally, after over a year of hounding the administration they allowed me to go to school full time. I went back to the eight grade (that was my tested level) but within a year I had my GED. I did so well in school that they offered me a teacher's job and I took it.

Little did I realize that in taking the teaching position I was joining a sort of elite within the prison system. Actually, there were two schools: one of higher learning and one of lower learning. The school of lower learning is what made us the elite because in that school you could be a part of the safe cracking class or the class on how to make counterfeit plates. In fact, there was a big scandal in the prison around 1964 because it was learned that the prison print shop was printing counterfeit money. The prisoner who snitched was given prosecutorial immunity and released. Besides the craftsmen we had in the school of lower learning we also had the prison paper hangers who were the jail house lawyers; they were generally located in two places: the school and the prison library. The prisoners who worked in the prison library were the guardians of the law books there and those of us who worked in the school were the legal researchers and writ writers. In those days, unlike now there were no court mandated Law Libraries in prison. We created our own "Law Library" with law books donated by "free world" libraries and the personal law libraries of prisoners upon their release from prison. The prisoners who worked in the library created on their own initiative a legal reference section that they watched with the greatest of care.

It was during the time that I was a teacher's assistant that I really began to develop a love for natural science and the history of science. My first fascination was the history of physics and mathematics; I read Einstein and Infield's *Evolution of Physics,* Eric T. Bell's *Development of Mathematics*, the biographies of Marie Sklodowska Curie and Pierre Curie, and Niels Bohr. I read Fiske's *Outlines of Cosmic Philosophy*, which was a fascinating work on the theory of cosmic evolution. I remembered that H.G. Wells had written that one day humanity would become the masters of time and space and so I saw the history of physics as the story of how humankind's study of matter in terms of its composition (atoms and elements), laws of motion (terrestrial and extra-terrestrial), various forms and levels of energy (electricity, moving bodies, etc.), the study of mechanics (laws of falling bodies, gravitation, etc.) and thermodynamics (heat as a form of kinetic energy at the molecular and sub-atomic levels transforming into nuclear energy at the macroscopic level) as a way toward mastering time and space. From Archimedes to Einstein physics is clearly the science that lays bare the fundamental laws of change governing the development of the material universe.

I was learning how nature worked naturally and how it worked with and through human beings. I came to see human beings as a force of nature governed by the same physical and chemical laws that govern the sun, moon and stars. If matter can be neither created nor destroyed then, in my mind, this meant that there was no creator. I became an atheist, and I naively thought that to be a scientist was to be an atheist. The little I learned about philosophy by reading Will Durant is that philosophical materialism was closely allied with science. At any rate I preferred positive knowledge to speculation and superstition.

The way I reinforced what I was learning in science was to teach it in school. I started going way beyond the textbooks on general science by giving the students lessons in elementary physics. Mr. Burger who was the "free world" teacher I worked under was at first opposed to going outside the regular study outlines and textbooks but little by little I convinced him and then he started to bring in films on science. We used the Bell Telephone "*Science Series*" and material from the United Nations Educational, Scientific and Cultural Organization (UNESCO). Mr. Burger was an African American who hailed from the state of Mississippi; he worked in the prison as a teacher while studying for his master's degree in education at Lincoln University. Like so many other students at Lincoln University in Jefferson City, Missouri Mr. Burger was supporting himself while going to graduate school by working in prison, which happened to also be in Jefferson City. The prison was founded and built in Jefferson City after the Civil War. Black soldiers founded Lincoln University after the Civil War. Historically there developed a relationship between these two institutions whereby Lincoln University provided social workers and school teachers, who were invariably people of color, and the town of Jefferson City provided the prison guards who were overwhelmingly white and of German ancestry. The Germans who settled this area in the late 1840s were abolitionists. So here was truly one of those remarkable anomalies of history peculiar to institutionalized racism; you had Black people who were former slaves and Germans who were former abolitionists working in a prison system that perpetrated the degradation of Black people. At any rate getting back to my story. Mr. Burger had definitely become an ally to me in my humble attempt to introduce the marvels of modern science to that segment of the prison population going for their GED. Had Mr. Burger and I stuck to the teaching of science we would have been able to pursue our enlightened curriculum indefinitely or at least until Burger's completion of his graduate studies.

In 1966 we brought Black history into the classroom and this created a controversy and a confrontation with the warden that led to our demise. Here's how it happened. We may have been in prison but we were civilly dead by law. In actuality we too were being profoundly affected by the Civil Rights movement and the resurgence of an appreciation for Black history; oddly enough my first serious exposure to Black history happened through the pages of *Ebony* magazine when the senior editor, Lerone Bennett, Jr. started a series of articles on Black history entitled "Before The Mayflower". Almost every literate prisoner in the joint was reading and discussing these articles.

The Muslims who were having meetings on the prison yard approached me about teaching them Black history. I told them I was not qualified because I only had a superficial knowledge of the subject. Their leader, a brother out of Kansas City who was a brilliant orator, told me that they respected my knowledge and knew of my activities in the prison school and he said, "We would be honored brother Chapman to have you teach us." I was embarrassed by his comments because I now realized that whereas I knew a great deal about western philosophy, history and science I had very little knowledge of Black history. So to prepare myself for the task I plunged into the study of Black history and culture. Mr. Burger would get books for me from the Lincoln University Library and the Library of Congress through the inter-library loan system. I started with W.E.B. DuBois and I was glad that I did for here was a man of unbelievable erudition who had in his pool of knowledge the great scientific achievements of the nineteenth and twentieth centuries, who saw two world wars, the rise and the beginning of the fall of colonialism, the birth of the first socialist country, the rise of African liberation and the struggles for national liberation in the colonies and the decisive defeat of Jim Crow, racist segregation. He was not only a commentator on these great historical events but a participator and a great agitator and propagandist for progressive social change throughout the world. DuBois stood proudly as a Negro in a western world whose science, literature, philosophy and religion relegated Black people to a subhuman status out of step with the progressive march of human civilization. Such a man, I thought was eminently qualified to teach me Black history.

I became a devoted disciple of DuBois reading such works as *Black Folks Then and Now: History and Sociology of the Negro, The Souls of Black Folks, Dusk of Dawn, Color and Democracy, The Philadelphia Negro, Black Reconstruction, The World and Africa and John Brown.* I tried to read these works in the chronological order in which they were written so I could follow the evolution of DuBois' thinking. At this time I was already familiar with the economic works of Karl Marx and I considered myself a Marxist. It was fascinating seeing how DuBois was moving toward Marxism and how he pioneered in laying a scientific basis for the study of the Negro problem in America and of racism in general. As far as DuBois' relationship to the social sciences in the United States I see him in the same light as Lenin saw Rosa Luxemburg in the Social Democratic Party of Germany, like her he was "...an eagle in a chicken coop..."

Now I was ready to study scholars like O.C. Cox who had written *"Caste, Class and Race"*, showing the relationship between capitalism as a system of economic exploitation and racism and class as sociological concepts and E. Franklin Frazier who in his *"Black Bourgeoisie"* did the first attempted class analysis of the African American community. I should also mention Eric Williams' *"Capitalism and Slavery"*. Although none of these scholars were Marxists they provided a wealth of information and historical facts demonstrating the unshakable truth of historical materialism.

Armed with this knowledge I proceeded to offer classes to the Muslim brothers. I went to their meetings on the yard and gave them the lessons of Black history from a DuBoisian and Marxist perspective. In a short time, there were nearly fifty prisoners gathering around for my presentations and this was causing quite a stir with the guards and white prisoners. In the eyes of the prison officials that many Black prisoners meeting had to be up to no good and it had to be stopped.

I tried to prevent a confrontation by going to the prison chaplain, who was a reasonable man. The chaplain was white, but he was also tolerant and personally he believed the Muslims were entitled to their own worship space; he also knew that I was an atheist and that I was teaching Black history but that didn't bother him in the least. The chaplain's name was Rev. Larsen and he was a man who loved to debate ideas so long as they were in "*The Great Books of the Western World*". He never ceased to be amazed that I, a Black man, was actually capable of discussing the philosophical ideas of Aristotle, Plato, Descartes, Spinoza, Bacon, Locke, Berkeley, Hume, Kant and so on. Before Chaplain Larsen was able to accommodate us the Warden ordered Major Poiry to have us disbanded and to bar me from the school for teaching communism.

This was 1965. Major Poiry, senior officer of the guards invaded the school with about five other guards known as the goon squad. I was about to go to the dining hall for lunch when I was ordered to go into the principal's office. As soon as I entered Major Poiry closed the door and locked it from the outside. I was surprised but I did know what was going on. This was the crackdown. They confiscated all my books and writings and sent me to the hole. I did ten days of solitary confinement and was sent to work in the prison soap factory. I was working on a book called "*Science and Africa: Essays on the Part Which People of Color Have Played in the Development of the Natural Sciences and Mathematics*" so I wrote the warden and requested that he return my manuscript. The warden responded in a letter saying that he had burned my manuscript. I was furious but there was nothing I could do. What the warden didn't know is that I had smuggled out a copy of the manuscript to John Henrik Clarke, an editor of "*Freedomways*" magazine, a quarterly founded by W.E.B. DuBois and Esther Jackson in 1961. (The manuscript *Science and Africa* is now to be found in the archives of John Henrik Clarke at the Schaumburg Public Library in New York City). What made me furious is the fact that he thought he was destroying my only copy.

The prisoners were also furious because they clearly understood the racist nature of the attack. Also, I knew some of the white prisoners like Roger Zinn, Tom Ashburn, Walter Nolan, and Grant Thompson (a Marxist) who also opposed this attack on me by the warden. Walter Nolan, who was the greatest legal mind of all the jailhouse lawyers, decided to help me fight the warden. Our strategy was to file a civil right suit pursuant to Title 42, Sections 1981-1985 of the United States Code. These were federal statutes passed right after the Civil War to protect the freed slaves from any sort of racial discrimination under the color of state law. In other words, these were the laws that took away states' rights in the South during the Radical Reconstruction era. They were still on the books and Nolan showed me how to use them.

What amazed me about Walter Nolan is that he was versed in all the Civil Rights cases such as NAACP vs. Button and the civil liberties cases like Scales vs. United States (a "communist conspiracy" case). Nolan was by no stretch of the imagination a Red or a partisan for racial equality, but he understood the relationship between civil rights, civil liberties and criminal justice. I remember him telling me that the Communists in the Scottsboro case (during the thirties) most vigorously championed the whole question of the right to counsel, which was beginning to reemerge in the sixties with the *Escobedo v. Illinois* case. With Nolan's help I was able to draft a serious civil rights complaint against the warden in which I not only raised the issue of First Amendment rights to pursue knowledge and an education by reading books and expressing your beliefs in writing without fear of reprisal but also the issue of racial discrimination and segregated facilities. I provided the court with a breakdown of all the skilled and unskilled jobs in prison showing that Blacks were disproportionately represented in unskilled jobs and grossly underrepresented in skilled jobs. We described the living conditions in A hall compared to the living conditions in the white cell blocks demonstrating that African Americans were forced to suffer over crowdedness and other conditions of confinement in violation of the Eight Amendment to the United States Constitution (forbidding cruel and unusual punishment). We filed our petition/complaint in the United States District Court for the Western District of Missouri and the Court allowed us to proceed *In Forma Pauperis* (i.e. waived filing fees) and issued an Order to the Warden to respond. The issues were joined and the legal battle was on.

A communist I met in prison known as Ulysses Grant Thompson introduced me to Marxism. He had been involved in the trade union movement, I think he was accused of blowing up a truck or something. Apparently, Ulysses approached me because he knew about my activities among the Black prisoners and respected the work I was doing in the prison school. He passed on to me some copies of "*Freedonways*" magazine and a "*Marxist Handbook*" by Emile Burns. In this magazine there was an article on Cuba by the Black historian, John Henrik Clarke. I remember seeing a note, scribbled in long hand, attached to the article and it read: "Read this and learn the truth, it won't cost you a dime! Ulysses." I read it and I had no problem believing that Castro was opposed to racism and that the new Cuba would be based on racial equality. I figured this was why the rich white Cubans hated him so much.

The "*Marxist Handbook*" was an introduction to the philosophical, political and economic writings of Marx, Engels, and Lenin. At the time I was a little deeper into philosophy. In fact, I had just finished an excellent book by Frederick Paulsen called "*Introduction to Philosophy*" which was a detailed exposition on the two basic trends in philosophy, namely, idealism and materialism from ancient to modern times. This literature on Marxism was like a breath of fresh air because I was definitely getting consumed in what Sir Francis Bacon called "the sublime fumes of metaphysical subtleties." Even before I picked up this book on Marxism I had already seen from the arguments of Diderot and D'Alembert (who gives an excellent history of British and French materialism in the introduction to his "*Encyclopedia*") and other materialists that idealism went contrary to natural science and was more or less in league with religion and superstition. Of course, in all the books I had read on the history of philosophy there was often a short acknowledgement and then a quick retort of Karl Marx. Even Bertrand Russell, in his comprehensive work on the "*History of Western Philosophy*", mentioned Marx only to dismiss him contemptuously. Consequently, when I read Emile Burns' i*ntroduction to the, "Handbook"* I became suddenly aware of the fact that Marx had been treated unjustly by his fellow philosophers and the academic establishment. I wanted to know why. What is it that was so sinister about his philosophy that even people who called themselves atheist and democratic socialist recoiled from it? My first reading of the "*Communist Manifesto*" let me know why the mouthpieces of official society were all opposed to Marx and his ideas. In clear and concise language Marx and Engels set out before me the true meaning of history and where I fitted in as an oppressed person and as a member of the working class. All my life I had felt the slings and arrows of oppression. I saw no way out that was not based on fantasy until now. I only saw misery in my misery. Marx showed me the revolutionary side of my misery. I was no longer helpless, now I could consciously be part of a revolutionary movement designed to empower the wretched of the earth.

In prison we organized a Marxist-Leninist study group around the *"Handbook"*. Out of this study group came what we called our "Collective" which took on certain practical tasks such as fighting to desegregate the prison facilities, to unite Black and white prisoners around issues of common concern, to get Marxist literature in the prison through legitimate channels and start PE (political education) classes among the prisoners, to fight for higher education programs for prisoners and establish strong links to the progressive movements on the outside.

With respect to the racist practices inside the prison we established contact with Black Assemblywoman Daverne Calloway and encouraged her to come into the prison facilities to see for herself what was really going on. When one of our comrades, Jerry Spragins, was released we gave him a letter to deliver to Hershel Walker, one of the leaders of the Communist Party in St. Louis, Mo. This was around 1966. Comrade Walker immediately established contact with our collective and that was the start of a relationship with the Party and the progressive movement that would last for years. These things were happening at a time of mass struggles for peace, racial equality and a progressive realignment of political forces that would put the USA on the road to socialism. It was a time of crisis, of widespread discontent among the masses. I was attracted to the Communists because they were consistent and effective organizers. If they said they were going to do something you could count on them to do it, and this was especially the case with Comrade Walker. The Party was truly impressed with our accomplishments inside the prison walls. Fortunately, comrade Walker became interested in my case and asked me to write a brief biographical sketch. About three years later a defense committee was formed in my behalf. (I wrote the bio-sketch in 1966 and my Defense Committee was formed in 1969). Without going into a lot of detail now let me just say that it was the mass movement to free Angela Davis that paved the way to free me and many other political prisoners. My defense committee predated Angela's but I firmly believe that had there not been a movement to Free Angela Davis many of us, like the late Nuh Washington (a member of the Black Panther Party), would have died in prison. Later I will give a more detailed account of how the mass movement to free Angela Davis generated a broader movement against racist and political repression that stayed the hand of execution of the ultra right (during the seventies and eighties) on a number of issues from the Ricco statues, to labor's right to organize, to the death penalty, police crimes and political prisoners.

It needs to be said that in the summer of 1966 I had excerpts from my manuscript "*Science and Africa*" published in "*Freedomways*" magazine also appearing in the same issue were poems by "Bumpy" Ellsworth Johnson and Tom Ashburn. I had no idea at the time that there would be a movement to free political prisoners or that prison reform would ever find its way to anyone's political platform. We will return to this topic later.

In addition to drawing the attention of the Assemblywoman Calloway to prison conditions we were writing Professors at Columbia University about bringing college courses into the prison as correspondence courses. I had developed correspondence with a Professor Robert Carter having opened a discussion with him on the question of plasma physics. To our pleasant surprise some of the professors at the University of Missouri in Columbia and Rolla Missouri were communicating with Mr. Strickland, the Director of Prison education, about actually doing college courses inside the walls. At first they brought in some pilot courses just to see how it would work. The courses were American History, World Literature and French Language. The warden allowed me to participate in this pilot program for two reasons, the principal one is that the professors, especially Professor John Dahm, requested that I be allowed to participate and two is he wanted it to be a success because it was happening doing his watch. Also since the university was funding this the state prison got good publicity on the issue of rehabilitation through education without paying a dime! At least for the time being everyone was happy.

About twenty Black and white prisoners participated in the college courses enthusiastically. In the first semester everyone made such good grades that courses on economics, sociology and psychology were added and our student population doubled. Professor John Dahm became such a staunch supporter that he started exploring the idea of getting a grant through vocational rehabilitation to start a regular junior college in the prison. Finally he applied for the grant and it was given on the condition that the Junior College would be set up at the Medium Security institution in Moberly, Missouri. This program was launched in 1969 and we were also allowed to keep the initial program going inside the walls.

Professor Dahm was definitely not a Marxist and did not have the slightest interest in becoming one. He was in fact a Republican but he respected my beliefs and he wanted me to work with him on the idea of promoting rehabilitation through education. Being that I was a prisoner he thought I could help him gain some important insights on how to approach the question of prison reform through education. As it turned out we worked together very well by sticking to the practical tasks at hand and steering clear of ideological confrontation. In fact Professor Dahm taught me the secret of how to write grants and get them granted. You follow all the guidelines and make the lowest bid. Like most simple formulations it has lots of practical complications, but it definitely works. Prisoners could now earn Associate of Arts Degrees while in prison.

Our dear Professor said why not go all the way, why not a BA degree while incarcerated. He went back to the Department of Corrections and said, "We can take the ROTC building on the Rolla campus and turn it into a minimum security honor camp for prisoners who want to go to college and earn their BA after getting their AA. There was room for seven prisoners. John Dahm wrote the grant got the bid and wanted to start the program in the fall of 1970 with the students who had at least a 3.4 grade average. He went to the warden and asked him if I could be sent to Moberly to get my AA so I could be a candidate for this program. He told me later that the warden almost shook his head off saying no. Meanwhile Professor Dahm and I continued to do our thing. I now had over thirty credits and was making straight A+'s

There is more to life in prison than studying and going to school. As we mentioned earlier our collective was also committed to fighting racial discrimination. We were already in the courts on the issue of discrimination in jobs and racial segregation in housing. The courts were moving slow and the racial tension was steady building. We have to go back to the first incident, which came shortly after we filed the suit. The warden came up with the idea that he would show the courts and the public that integration can't work. The warden said we are going to start integration by sending five Black prisoners at a time to G hall. G hall was an all white cellblock with about 190 prisoners so the plan was to send five Black prisoners until racial balance was achieved. We knew that this was a phony gesture designed to fail. So, we discouraged participation. Our position was if the warden is serious then he should send 95 Black prisoners at the same time so as to discourage violence.

Somehow the warden was actually able to find five Black prisoners to go on this suicide mission. We pleaded with them not go but they actually felt like they were being brave. And thus, it happened. First day after they moved over was uneventful. The second day white prisoners, who wore pillowcases over their heads like hooded KKK, murdered three out of the five Black prisoners with prisoner made shanks. Even before they unlocked the cells in A- hall Black prisoners were rioting. The warden had a machine gun mounted outside A-hall and basically closed the prison down. For weeks we were totally isolated from the white prisoners and then the warden announced that he had gotten the perpetrators and placed them in administrative segregation. And then out of the blue the warden put one of the alleged perpetrators back in the prison population. As soon as he hit the yard he was physically assaulted by Black prisoners and almost killed. No one was punished. After this incident there was a cooling off period that ended those particular racial tensions. The warden, in effect gave Black prisoners a way of venting their anger since he could not provide the state with enough evidence to prosecute. But this was by no means a solution, the prison remained segregated as ever and the warden was desperate for a way out.

Let us just add an important footnote that this is the prison that the assassin of Rev. Martin Luther King, Jr. escaped from and it was during the watch of this same Warden Harold Swenson, who never prosecuted the KKK murderers of three Black prisoners. A newly arrived Black prisoner in his sixties accidentally went to the white side of the dining room and had a seat. Apparently, he didn't realize what he was doing yet he was attacked by white prisoners and severely injured. Danny Boy, a fellow prisoner I had been in the City Jail with and a study partner of mine in mathematics came to me saying "How about you and I having lunch on the white side of the dining room today?" My response was "I think that's a wonderful idea!" Come lunchtime Danny and I sat on the white side of the dining room and everybody knew why we were doing it. One of the so-called white gangsters "Slick Stidum" said to me "You know this is wrong! Do you want a race riot?" I refused to talk to anybody in the dining room because I needed no distraction just in case we were attacked.

But later I did say to him that we didn't want a race riot. As far as I was concerned the warden wanted one and obviously some of the white prisoners shared the views of the warden. What we wanted was unity between the Black and white prisoners against the administration. Slick said, "There is one thing I will say about you and Danny Boy, you guys either got a lot of heart or you're fucking crazy." Fortunately, there was no race riot but it was only because the unity of the Black prisoners could not be broken. The organized portion of the white prisoners was divided between the racist, Nazi ideologues who swore by Hitler's *"Mein Kampf"* and the gangsters who swore by Machiavelli's *"Prince"*. There was tension in the air but we didn't let that stop us from challenging racism.

There were twin cellblocks known as B and C halls, F and G halls, and H and I halls. B and C halls had two men cells and the rest of the halls were one-man cells. The warden had hit upon a new ruse. He would fill up G hall and C hall with Black prisoners and turn A hall (which had been an all Black cellblock) into an integrated honor cell block with TVs, pool tables and unlocked cell doors. This scheme actually left about 90% of the prison population still racially segregated and whites still held the best and most skilled jobs. The most positive thing about this change is that it was definitely a dramatic improvement in the housing of Black prisoners. Overnight we went from living four and six men to a cell to two and one men cells. No one was mad about this change we just felt that it was a damn shame that Black prisoners had to die to bring this about. Well the Black Zulu Warriors, a faction that split off from our collective, was not pleased with any of this "reformist bullshit". Their leader was a brilliant and dedicated brother called Brother Dean and his Lt. was a very anger-driven prisoner out of Kinlock, Mo. known as "Gangster".

Their thing was that we had become too soft in our response to racist violence. Legal struggles were a waste of time. What we needed to do, according to the Zulus, was "fuck up" some white guards and let them feel the wrath of the people. Our position was that the only winnable struggle under prison conditions was a legal struggle. Prison riots always played into the hands of the oppressor and homicidal prisoners who just used a riot as an opportunity to murder whoever they didn't like. Also, we needed allies like Assemblywoman Calloway who were not going to back us up unless our struggle was legal. And most importantly legal struggles could help bring about reforms that could get prisoners out of prison like the study release program was in fact doing. The revolution was outside the prison walls so the whole point is to get people out of the prison system.

In spite of the super-militant rhetoric of the Zulus we continued to press forward with our agenda. We put together a petition to the court calling for the complete and unequivocal desegregation of the prison system. Over 300 African Americans and a handful of white prisoners signed the petition. The warden refused to send the petition out and was propositioning prisoners to take their names off the petition. He (the warden) even stooped to pressuring prisoners to say that we forced them with violent threats to sign the petition. Needless to say this created a lot of tension in the Black prison population. The Prison Guard Goon Squad became very aggressive and started attacking a lot of the young Black prisoners with Chemical Mace. Some of the Zulus were rounded up, taken to solitary confinement and brutally beaten. A brother called Sleeves was mysteriously hung in his cell and they said it was suicide. All these provocative actions naturally led to a violent confrontation.

It happened quite spontaneously when a white prison guard was 'roughing up' a Black prisoner in the G hall corridor. One of the prisoners allegedly threw acid stolen from the soap factory in the guard's face and in a flash we took over the cellblock. The comrades in our collective came to me and said this: "Brother Chat," that is the name I was known by, "our whole cellblock is in rebellion. We need to make a collective decision now as to how we will respond to this...We can't be neutral!" I told them that is correct for there is no such thing as neutrality doing a rebellion. We should take the helm and steer the rebellion toward non-violent resistance as soon as possible. Food strikes and work stoppages are the most frequently used forms of non-violent resistance in prisons. We called for a rally on the flag (i.e. the ground floor) of the cellblock. Speaking at the rally I said something to this effect:

"We did what we did (the violent act to the guard and taking over the cellblock) because we are tired of being treated less than human beings because we are Black. We are tired of being discriminated against, brutalized and murdered. But we can't change this by simply rioting. We must organize. Lets select or elect a committee to represent us so when the warden comes and ask what is to matter we can tell him all we want is our day in court so let the petition be mailed to the court."

This speech got us all on the same page and most of us realized we could not win in a violent confrontation. So, when the warden came and said who is your spokesperson we gave him the Committee of Five, which is what the brothers called us. The meeting actually took place in a room right outside the warden's office. First of all, the warden said he would listen to what we as individuals had to say but that he would definitely not now or ever recognize us as a group representing Black prisoners. The warden looked straight at me after his opening and I knew right then that I would be singled out for whatever punishment he had in mind. None of us were afraid to speak but since he was looking at me I spoke right up. I told him I realized what he had done by saying he was willing to speak to us as a group in front of the other prisoners. Now that we're behind closed doors the truth comes out: he only wanted to identify the so-called "ring leaders". I told him, "You can do what you will with us but unless the racism is dealt with you are still sitting on a powder keg. We truly regret the assault on the guard. But please understand that this thing was not planned, the Goon Squad and half measures in ending racial segregation in the prison provoked it."

The warden's response was cynical, sarcastic and demeaning. "Who do you Black pricks think you are", he yelled. "I'm sending all of you back to the cellblock to tell the rest of the prisoners to peacefully return to their cell or we will call in the National Guard if necessary and force them back into their cells." We all just sit there quietly and then the warden pressed on saying, "Well what's it going to be convicts?" I nodded yes and said, "Okay, we will deliver your message."

When we returned to the cellblock I told the prisoners that the warden had lied to us. Now the ball was back in our court. "What's the move?" shouted the prisoners. "We strike," I replied. I said that we would not return to our cells, nor would we eat or go to work until our petitions were released to the court. Later on, the state troopers were called in. They were armed with shotguns loaded with birdshot. They fired upon us several times and we were forced into our cells to keep from getting shot. Soon as we were locked down the Goon Squad came for me first, and they were armed with shackles and a riot gun. I was chained up and taken to administrative segregation. In fact, he put all five of us in administrative segregation. The rest of the prisoners who participated in the protest were kept on lock down unless they agreed to take their names off the petition.

My first week in segregation I filed supplemental pleadings with the court requesting a court order enjoining the actions of the warden. Our position was simple: by tampering with petitions and coercing prisoners to take their names off the petition the warden was ipso facto in contempt of court. The court's response was to issue a show cause order. The warden responded by alleging that we were using the petition process as a smokescreen for starting a riot. Once again, the issues were joined and this time the court appointed us lawyers. Eventually our petition was mailed to the federal court after the warden unconstitutionally altered it. Yet the warden refused to release us from administrative segregation. In fact, since we were complaining about racial segregation the warden decided he would have forced integration in administrative segregation. He took the most militant white racists of the prisoners in segregation, killers and escape artists and Black revolutionaries and nationalists all in the same section of the maximum-security unit so we could spin our wheels fighting each other.

It almost worked. For several months there was constant arguing between the Nazis and the Black nationalists about who was the superior race. Our comrades did not participate in these stupid, racially provocative debates. Instead we talked back and forth with our comrades in others cells along the cat walk about socialism and the need for working class unity, and when one of the white prisoners would engage us in a non-hostile way we would simply point out that with poor people it's about class and race both being used to divide us and keep us poor. To those white prisoners who were obviously not Nazis we said, "Look at how the narrow Black Nationalists and White Supremacists agree with one another on the issue of racial segregation. There is no difference between their thinking and the thinking of the warden. They're like slaves on the plantation who agree with the master but are never invited to the master's table."

Then something interesting happened. They brought in a white prisoner name Ray and put him in my cell. He was bleeding like a stuck pig from having been beaten by the guards. When they literally threw him in my cell, which was a one-man cell, he cried, "Oh, you beat my ass and then throw me in with a nigger!" "Ray," I said to him, "why do you think they put you in the cell with me? In this one-man cell with me?" "Oh I don't know Frank," Ray replied. "They probably want me to kill you or fuck you up!" This guy was so beat up that he could barely walk or stand up. I just looked at him and broke out laughing. "What can you do to me Ray, shit you can't hardly stand up. You better hope I don't fuck you up!" I said still laughing. Ray was lying on the floor next to the commode looking up at me with a smirk on his face. He proceeded to take off his shirt and stuff it in the commode; then he flushed it causing a flood in the cell. This was the way prisoners protested in administrative segregation when something went down they didn't like. "Okay Ray, so you want to protest do you?" I grabbed the bars to my cell door shaking the door back and forth yelling, "Alright y'all come and get this crazy motherfucker out of my cell!" One of the Zulus shouted at me, "Hey Brother Chat what happened to that Black and white unity shit you been preaching?"

The Zulu brother was right this was a test of unity and we couldn't afford to fail it. "Alright," I said, "we are protesting the way they're treating Ray, a fellow convict. Everybody flood their shitters and get in the gate", (i.e. shake your bar doors). And that is exactly how the rebellion in the maximum-security unit in 1969 began. We didn't eat or sleep for three days, we just raised hell. Naturally the goon squad showed up. The "troublemakers," starting with Ray and me were taken to a deep max cell which is sort of like a cell within a cell. About ten of us were crowded, naked into a cell built for four-six people.

Then they did something very cruel. They watered us down with a 90 pressure fire hose and sprayed Chemical Mace on us. And while we were gasping for air they cut off all ventilation for several hours. We thought we were going to die, and then the pain became so great that we wanted to die. Some people just passed out or went into a coma like state. It was a horrible experience but out of it we bonded like you wouldn't believe. There was no Black and white anymore, no Nationalists and Nazis; we were all just convicts against the warden.

When the warden came and tried to separate us into Black and white cells we refused. We said we'd rather die together as men than ever give in to his racist bullshit again. Those of us who stuck together had a new respect for each other that was beyond the comprehension of the guards and the warden. In fact it was even beyond the comprehension of some of our comrades. But it was a fact we were united and we inspired the whole prison population. To try to break our unity the warden made one last stand. He put all of us that he had fire-hosed in the death row cells and when the other prisoners in administrative segregation protested by flooding and noise-making he randomly picked out 10 of them (five whites and five Blacks) and asked each one "Do you support Chapman and those rebel bastards on death row?" When they replied yes he had them beaten down with riot guns and clubs, forced them to take off all their clothes and get on their knees at gunpoint. After he made them crawl around for a while proclaiming they were dogs he made them form a single line while still on their knees and place their noses in each other's rectums. In this posture the prisoners were forced to crawl out of the cellblock and onto the prison yard in the freezing October rain. Obedience to the warden's sadistic orders bought no relief to the compliant prisoners for they were still mercilessly beaten.

None of us who actually started the uprising on death row were approached by the Warden's goons or asked to crawl on our knees. Why? I don't really know why but I believe the Warden knew we would have refused and so he deliberately picked prisoners he knew would comply out of fear. He knew from experience that we did not fear him for he had already taken us to the point of death and not one of us begged for mercy. No kind of resistance (passive or aggressive) works if you are not willing to die for what you believe in and what you are fighting for. To rebel in prison is to risk being killed or violently assaulted by the authorities. Yet while we stood firm in our position of non-compliance with the Warden's assaults upon us we did not in any way belittle the prisoners who were beaten into compliance. It was the Warden not the prisoners who earned our disrespect.

After this outrage something very strange happened, which still boggles my mind to this day. They had moved me to the Death Row cells and not only was I the only African American on this cell block I was the only one who had a cellmate. These were generally single man cells. But they welded an extra bunk in the first cell on the row and then put me and a white prisoner name Billy Joe Tyler in the cell together. Billy Joe was a big, burly white guy who was supposed to be part of Bobby Burns' racist clique. Apparently, the warden was trying to set me up. In fact, one of the guards even said before they moved me on the row, "Hey Chapman we got an integrated cell just for you!"

I thought there was going to be a problem with Billy Joe for sure because he was not a part of our protest in Administrative Segregation. But to my surprise Billy Joe knew about our protests and he said, "I didn't ask to be in no cell with a nigger but I know why they put me in here. They want us to fight, but I ain't doing shit for the Warden, so if you don't fuck with me then I ain't going to fuck with you." I quickly replied, "Okay! I'll go for that." And for the next few days we just kept an eye on one another. The silence was finally broken with a question: "Why do you want to integrate with white people?"

This broke the ice. I told Billy Joe that prison was like slavery and that white prisoners were sort of like House Negroes. They were just better treated slaves. He could relate to this, so we finally got to the point of seeing that it was "us" against "them." Billy Joe refused to be the Warden's tool and for this they beat him with steel-tip clubs and moved him to another cell block. I saw white prisoners like Billy Joe and Jackie Lee Noble who had racist beliefs unite with us against the Warden. I can't explain it but I experienced it and it just made me believe that through struggle the impossible is possible, it just takes longer.

Jackie Lee deserves special mention here. He was a white prisoner who made the transition from a Nazi to a revolutionary and for this he was singled out by the guards because he was a leader among his fellow prisoners. Jackie Lee was savagely attacked by the goon squad while being called a "nigger loving scum-bag" his response was "It beats being a pig scum-bag like you!" He refused to crawl or beg and was beaten into a coma. He stayed hospitalized for weeks and then he was transferred to another prison and we never say him again.

Somehow word got out to our comrades on the streets and when they heard of these outrages they immediately sent lawyers in to see us. Even the ACLU, which rarely if ever defended prisoners publicly condemned the warden's actions and promised to take legal action. Assemblywoman Calloway came into the prison and called me Lionel Jones and several other prisoners out of our cells. She assured us that we were not alone. We insisted that the lawyers find out where Jackie Lee was and all they could tell us is that he had been sent to another prison, possibly Walla Walla prison in the state of Washington.

The warden was losing his battle to stay the hand of progress. Now we had a whole team of lawyers, all of them white but one and that one was Curtis Crawford, an African American and former prosecutor from St. Louis. They came to help us with our civil rights suits. Within weeks all of us except for me were released from administrative segregation and placed back into the prison population. I was put in a white suit and placed in a special newly created cellblock called inter-max. The prisoners called it "Chapman's cellblock" because I was the only prisoner in the block for the first couple of days. Every day I was marched to and from the mess hall in front of the whole prison population dressed in white coveralls. Other prisoners were not allowed to talk to me but they did. "Hang in there Brother Chat", they would shout.

While I was in inter-max they shot me with a drug called "polixin". It was supposed to make me sleep but in reality it was some kind of psychotropic drug that completely disoriented you. My mind was chaotic and I couldn't focus on anything. I couldn't even sit down and write a letter. My lawyer, Arley Woodrow, came to see me while I was under the influence of this drug and I had the most difficult time talking to him because my tongue was swollen. It took about two weeks for this drug to wear off. My lawyer threatened the prison Doctor with a law suit. If I hadn't had Arley to fight for me the prison authorities would have used this behavior modifying drug to mentally incapacitate me. Of this I am absolutely convinced because I've seen this happen to other prisoners like Herbert Richardson, who under the influence of this drug, went from being a prison intellectual to being in a stupor most of the time.

Coming Out of the Night Full of Hopes and Dreams

Getting out of administrative segregation and back into the prison population (without the white suit) I became just another prisoner and this gave me a sense of joyous relief. I was given a single man cell and allowed to go to the yard every day and mingle with other prisoners. I was very warmly greeted by all the prisoners. We were all very proud of the black and white unity we had achieved while in administrative segregation.

Even the most recalcitrant racist, white prisoners, who deemed themselves "Nazis," admired our defiance of the warden. Oddly enough some of the Muslims who were in the Nation of Islam were the only ones who remained openly frozen in their opposition to integration but some of them joined us. However, let me quickly add that most of the Muslim brothers followed Brother Malcolm X and they never sided with the Warden against us

Recreation consisted of going to the movies and the TV recreation room once a week and yard everyday. On the weekend we had yard from 8am to 8pm in the spring and summer, and from 8am to 6pm in the fall and winter. The warden was giving us these long periods out our cells to relieve tensions. Prisoners could only congregate in groups of fives unless they were participating in sports or musical groups. Consequently, we formed study groups that consisted of five persons.

Our basic text for the study groups was the three volumes by Maurice Cornforth on *Dialectical Materialism, Historical Materialism and Epistemology.* We were convinced that by studying these works we would have a solid foundation in the theory and science of Marxism-Leninism.

Now that I look back on it our approach to the study of Marxism I can see that it was very formalistic. We started with the three laws of dialectics which were simply stated as: 1) The unity and struggle of opposites. Meaning that everything is defined by its opposite. 2) The transformation of quantity into quality. Meaning that vis a vis incremental quantitative changes everything makes a qualitative leap into its opposite. And 3) the negation of the negation. Meaning that if the law of the unity and struggle of opposites discloses the source of development, and the law of the transition of quantitative changes into qualitative changes reveals the mechanism of development, then the law of the negation of the negation expresses the direction, form, and result of development. Things tend to develop in cycles that spiral upward.

If this sounds mystical it is because divorced from the controls of reality, it is metaphysical, i.e., dialectical idealism. According to this philosophical perspective everything moves like this: Thesis (position), Antithesis (opposition) and Synthesis (composition). Lenin, as far as we were concerned, provided us with the most concise, coherent and candid exposition of dialectics. Said he:

"In our times, the idea of development, of evolution, has almost completely penetrated social consciousness, only in other ways, and not through Hegelian philosophy. Still, this idea, as formulated by Marx and Engels on the basis of Hegel's' philosophy, is far more comprehensive and far richer in content than the current idea of evolution is. A development that repeats, as it were, stages that have already been passed, but repeats them in a different way, on a higher basis ("the negation of the negation"), a development, so to speak, that proceeds in spirals, not in a straight line; a development by leaps, catastrophes, and revolutions; 'breaks in continuity'; the transformation of quantity into quality; inner impulses towards development, imparted by the contradiction and conflict of the various forces and tendencies acting on a given body, or within a given phenomenon, or within a given society; the interdependence and the closest and indissoluble connection between all aspects of any phenomenon (history constantly revealing ever new aspects), a connection that provides a uniform, and universal process of motion, one that follows definite laws—these are some of the features of dialectics as a doctrine of development that is richer than the conventional one. (Cf. Marx's letter to Engels of January 8, 1868, in which he ridicules Stein's "wooden trichotomies," which it would be absurd to confuse with materialist dialectics.)." (See

Karl Marx: A Brief Biographical Sketch and Exposition, by V.I. Lenin).

Like Marx and Lenin we rejected dialectical idealism and embraced materialist dialectics as both a world outlook and as a way of confronting and changing the reality of our oppression.

Things tended to stabilize and fall into a routine. Our collective of about ten people met (in groups of five) on a regular basis. I was participating in the college program with Professor Dahm and pursuing my legal work on the civil rights suit and my release. My lawyer told me that I was wrongfully convicted because when I was about to be tried for murder I was in fact an escapee from a state hospital. Yet my lawyer, Joseph Noskay, or no one else for that matter ever informed the court on this. Arley said I may not have been competent to stand trial being that I had escaped from an institution for the mentally ill. We filed a post-conviction petition for relief. In the Summer of 1971 the Circuit Court of the City of St. Louis ordered me back to Court for an evidentiary hearing on my motion for post-conviction relief. We were scheduled for a hearing by Judge McFarland.

INTERLUDE
Songs For My Father, Hershel Walker, Arley R. Woodrow And Danny Boy Jackson

Before I continue my story I must take a moment to acknowledge four men who helped in shaping my life by showing me that the depths to which we fall is always overcome by the heights to which we rise.

Blues For Chatwail

I learned at a very young age about my father's reputation in the streets. They called him "Chatwail" because he was a good hustler and a musician. The old school hustlers, from pool sharks to con artists, use to say to me "Are you Chatwail's son for real?" And I would answer "Hell yea!" "Well," they would continue, "you need to know that your daddy is one of the gamest Negroes in this town." I would think to myself, "one day they're going to say the same thing about me."

I wanted to be like my father because I wanted people to like me like they liked him. My father was a disciple of Charlie Parker (the be-bop creator) and so I followed be-bop like it was a religion, learning about all the high priests and priestess such as Ethel, Lady Day, Ella, Dizzy, Miles, Monk, Coltrane, Cannonball, Philly Jo', Mingus, Sarah, Carmen, Dinah and Gloria. But I also wanted to be a part of my father's life and that wasn't happening. My father, Frank Chapman, Sr. and I never had a relationship that was wholesome or real until I went to prison.

Once in prison I met many of my father's friends there like Hank Taylor, a drug addict thief whose flamboyant behavior (cracking jokes with him laughing the loudest) always kept everyone in good humor. Then there was T.J. Ruffin, the serious gangster, who was an incorrigible drug dealer and cold blooded killer yet a man of high moral standards. According to T.J. you stayed true to the game no matter what and in a few words that meant no snitching, keeping your word and paying your debts.

When I came to prison guys like this knew me through my father for they were his friends not mine. Nonetheless by the code of conduct of the streets they felt obligated to look out for me, and besides they said my father had said to them "Look out for my son." "Looking out" meant that T.J. and Hank would let other prisoners know that they had my back. T.J and Hank told me that if I needed cigarettes or commissary to get it from them and under no circumstances was I to get this stuff from anyone else. In this way I wouldn't owe anybody anything. One way of forcing young, new prisoners into homosexual acts was to give them commissary in a friendly gesture and latter on insist that they pay it back or do sexual favors.

I had sense enough to stay clear of these snares but T.J. stepped in to make it quite clear that I was "Chatwail's son" and not to be disrespected, period. I must admit that it felt good to have the protective hand of my father over me while in jail. He became my hero again. I was always asking T.J. and Hank about my father but all they ever said was "Chatwail was a standup guy...a real thoroughbred, regular and a good hustler..." While this made me feel proud it really didn't tell me anything about my father that I didn't already know. I started writing my father with my questions and he answered my letters.

I learned from my father that he was a dedicated musician and that he wanted to be a professional musician more than anything else in the world. He loved Charlie Parker (the Yard bird) and be-bop. But being addicted to drugs short circuited his ambitions. He didn't make enough money playing music to support a drug habit that was costing at least $150 a day. Consequently, he became a professional thief, hustler and con artist.

I remember when I briefly stayed with my father seeing him sitting on the bed, holding his head crying and telling me "Son, don't ever do dope...this is the worst thing I've ever done..." Then he would go on to tell me how for a little temporary euphoria he lost most of the things in life he held dear. He said he loved my mother, and yet he wouldn't quit dope to keep her and his family. He told me that my being with him was no place for a kid to be; that I should be in school and doing the things that kids do with other kids. He made me promise him that I would never use drugs and then he told me he was sending me back home to my mother.

I remember how sad this made me because I couldn't help but feel rejected. In spite of him pressing me to promise that I wouldn't do drugs there was nothing I wanted to do except be like him. So his warnings meant nothing to me. You can't tell a child to do as I say and not as I do. The thing I wanted most in this world was to be slick, hip and cool just like my dad. Such is the human condition, we learn by and through social circumstances. I learned that my father was right because being hip, slick and cool landed me in the slammer (jail) with a life and fifty year sentence. Being in prison was the dose of reality I needed to take a realistic look at what my life had become as a result of trying to be a successful outlaw. My father warned me but the hard and true lessons came from the pain of experience.

While I was in prison my father made an earnest effort to quit drugs. He cleaned up his act and moved to Jamaica, Queens, New York. He wrote me about how good he was doing living the square life with his girl-friend Cleo, and being a working musician. During this period I was studying music myself with dreams of becoming a be-bop musician like my father. In my letters to him I wrote about music and how I was applying myself by studying music theory and harmony and doing my *Hannon Virtuoso Piano in Sixty Exercises.*

My father would write me back giving me instructions on how to construct and color chords with overtones and do chord progressions. He showed me how to do numerous chord progressions in 12-bar and 8-bar blues formats as well as rhythm changes. I learned from him how to explore and enrich the harmonic underpinnings of the Standards and Broadway show tunes.

It was great. For the first time ever my father and I were in a relationship that was spiritually and psychologically healthy. He was not giving me moral instructions and admonishments on how to live; he was showing me things, taking up time with me and communicating with me about things we held in common. Even though I was in jail and he was a thousand miles away I welcomed this opportunity to share my life with my father.

Then suddenly like lightning out of a clear blue-sky communication stopped. I heard nothing. I wrote letters pleading for some response but there was nothing, but this void of silence and it was ripping my heart out. In prison you feel emotional pain more sharply because you are so limited in what you can do. Most of the time the only contact you have with loved ones and the outside world is through letters. But the way you deal with emotional pain in prison is you don't. It kind of goes away or to paraphrase Langston Hughes, it becomes buried in your soul to sag like a heavy load, ticking like a time bomb waiting to explode. Just as the pain was subsiding and I began once again to emotionally separate from a loved one I was called up to the visiting cage for a visit.

As I entered what we called the visiting cage (a room where you were separated from the person visiting by bars and a thick see threw screen) I saw my father sitting there smiling. He was 47 and looked 67. He had lost most of his bottom teeth. His deep, reddish brown complexion had turned gray, giving him that sick off of dope fiend look.

I took a seat and stared at him through the wired screen and bars that separated us. I wanted to embrace him but couldn't. "I'm real sick son," he said in an out of breath voice. The words were clear but his voice was trembling. When I looked into his eyes I saw specs of blood, like little tiny, red dots. I was crying inside and trying, for reasons unknown, to hold back the tears. I was too emotionally choked up to speak.

"I'm dying," my father continued, "but I am so proud of you... please be the man that I failed to be...." There were other things said and regrets expressed but I don't remember the words. What I recall most vividly is the unspeakable pain I was in for I knew I would never see my father again. He died two weeks later. My father had went back to using drugs and that is what killed him.

I was hit so hard emotionally until I nearly fell into a state of utter depression but my prison comrades where there for me. Especially my friend Danny Boy was there for me. Danny said, "You have to fight for your right to survive. You can't give in or give up ever because that is the day they will destroy you!"

Taking Danny's suggestion I became even more determined to keep struggling. My father's words "be the man I failed to be" was a challenge to be sure but I refused to see myself as being or becoming better than him. The message I heard in my father's words was don't blow your life away doing drugs; that getting high is not the pursuit of happiness but the path to slavery and self- destruction. If I learn from my father then he died so I could live, his life was another bitter lesson for me. He showed me how you lose the blues in the search and struggle for the good life.

Danny Boy Comes Through

I met Danny Boy in the City Jail, and as I mentioned earlier he was there with me when I was facing trial. Danny was two years my senior and a well known Hustler and gambler from downtown St. Louis. I had heard of him but met him for the first time in life when he came to the City Jail in the spring of 1961. He was a very easy-going, intelligent person but he had a reputation for being very violent if you crossed him. Everyone respected him, the wolves and the lambs alike. He and I hit it off right away because we both loved jazz and he was all into Coltrane, Miles Davis, James Moody, Eddie Jefferson, Sarah Vaughn and the whole be-bop set.

But music was about the only subject we agreed on. We constantly argued about law, history and any other subject that came up in the course of a conversation. Actually these altercations with Danny helped me a great deal because I had a tendency to sometimes let my imagination get away from the narrow line of facts. He would always nail me down by saying, " You've got to prove that, show me the facts." And when I would find the correct information I would show it to him even if it proved me wrong.

I got to prison in Jefferson City just a few months ahead of Danny. But when he got there we immediately hooked up and started studying together. He saw that I was serious about studying mathematics so he asked me to partner up with him so we could study algebra. I agreed and we proceeded to meet up on the yard every Saturday and Sunday and holidays to study. Progress was consistent and quick for in no time at all Danny and I were doing quadratic equations. Once you get the procedure down in math there is nothing to argue about, the answer can always be proven. Not so in politics, philosophy or art.

When it came to politics and philosophy Danny and I hardly agreed on anything. He hated racism but denied that there was any connection between racism and capitalist exploitation. He told me I was wasting my time trying to teach prisoners about socialism because socialism was something that they neither understood nor wanted. He would say, "These greedy bastards want the same things the capitalist wants, money and power, and they will do anything to get it. I wouldn't trust them as far as I could throw them."

So, I was just a little surprised when Danny came to me that day (which I've already told you about) and asked me if I wanted to protest by sitting on the white side of the dining room. However, it was indeed a pleasant surprise and I was so glad he thought enough of me to ask me to do this with him. In spite of all our disagreements this joint act of defiance had us united and bonded like never before.

But the day soon arrived when Danny Boy had to go home. I was glad to see him go but I was also sad about the possibility of losing a friend. He said, "Frank, what can I do for you? I don't want to see you die up in here. So, tell me, how can I help?"

I told him that I had read about a man in St. Louis who was a Black man and the head of the Missouri Communist Party and I wanted him to get in touch with this man for me. Danny smiled and said, "Is that all you want?" "No," I continued, "I want you to convince him to help me get out of this rat hole..." His response was simply, "Okay. I can do that for you, my friend."

Danny was not about saying things he didn't mean. He backed his words up with action. When Danny went home he contacted Hershel Walker, conveyed my message and thus began my Defense Committee and the movement to free me from prison.

Herschel Walker

I learned about Herschel Walker, the Chairman of the Missouri Communist Party, in the pages of the St. Louis Argus newspaper. There was this article about a group of people trying to establish a W.E.B. Du Bois Clubs of America chapter right across the street from the Nation of Islam Mosque.

Herschel, I learned later, joined the Communist Party in 1930 which means he was around when they organized the Share Croppers Union, the International Labor Defense fighting for the Scottsboro Boys, hunger marches and the great union organizing drives during the Great Depression. When Danny contacted Herschel, and told him about what we were doing in prison I got an immediate response. It came in the form of a letter that was smuggled in. In his letter to me Hershel said that as a revolutionary he stood in complete solidarity with our struggle for justice within the prison system and that he and the Party would also use every legal option to gain my freedom. After this initial communication Danny Boy became the liaison between Hershel and I; and for several years Danny wrote under my sister's name and kept me informed about everything.

Hershel became my mentor even while I was in prison. The first thing I learned was revolutionary impatience and patience. One needed patience in the ebb tide of struggle not in the flow of the tidal wave of struggle. During those years in which we were slowly building a Frank Chapman Defense Committee, Herschel worked hard and with patience and dogged determination he kept the Committee going even when it was down to three or four people. He got my family involved, especially my mother, who yelled out in the courtroom the day the Judge sentenced me to life and fifty years that she would never stop praying and fighting for my freedom. My mother always called him Mr. Walker and when she described him to anyone she always said "He's the kindest and most caring man I've ever known."

At once a Frank Chapman Defense Committee was set up; three of the members had been my comrades in prison, that is, Danny Boy, Bill Cheeks and Dean Johnson. There was one well known sister from the community, Rita Gatewood and my newly found Red friend, Hershel Walker. Later on the Committee would broaden out to include more prestigious members of the community, like Dr. Betty Lee and Dr. Henry Campbell, but this was the righteous core that got us started. The first order of business was to secure Arley R. Woodrow as my defense attorney and get me a typewriter. During the next ten years Herschel became my political father. He was the first Communist I met and came to know up close, and he deepened my love and commitment to socialism by his deeds. Whatever he said he would do that is precisely what he did, and I never heard him make an excuse for stumbling or being wrong.

The Peoples Lawyer, Arley R. Woodrow

When I first met Arley R. Woodrow it was not in the visiting cage but in a special meeting room for visits from professional people like lawyers, politicians, psychologists, law enforcement officials and so on. The room was bright with light and only a table separated us.

Arley very patiently explained to me that he had been sent by Herschel Walker and he then asked me if I wanted legal assistance in getting out of prison. I couldn't say yes fast enough. There followed as I recall a long and detailed discussion about my life and how I ended up in prison. It was a very exhausting interview or Q and A. At the end of it all Arley told me that there was a serious legal flaw in my case and that in his opinion my conviction was unlawful. My immediate response was that I had already admitted to committing the crime. Arley's position was that I was incompetent to stand trial because I was an escapee from a state hospital for mentally-challenged patients.
I asked Arley if this meant that I was "crazy" and he said that the mere fact that I was a patient at a state hospital raised the question of my mental competence to stand trial and that this question should have been answered by the court prior my being prosecuted.

My reaction to all this was how could I have missed something as obvious as this. Part of the reason is that I didn't want anyone to know that I had been in a state hospital for the mentally challenged, so I never brought it up. Also, at the time I was facing these murder and robbery charges I was so full of guilt and shame that I just wanted to get my sentence and move on. Now, eight years later, having survived I was ready to challenge my conviction and sue for my freedom.

We begin by preparing a post-conviction relief motion. We reviewed all the records on my case and Arley was right, there was nothing in the Court record indicating that I was ever in a state hospital; and according to the same record my lawyer didn't bring it to the Court's attention. There was also nothing about me being beaten, tortured and placed in isolation cells until I confessed. After we had finished our post-conviction motion for relief and was getting ready to file it with the original trial Judge Arley suggested that he include me as co-counsel. I agreed and subsequently the motion was duly filed. As it turned out my original trial judge (Kornners) was dead and we ended up with Judge McFarland, a so-called liberal Judge.

It was mid-summer 1971; that's all I remember. I don't remember what day of the week it was or even the date that I was taken back to St. Louis. I do remember that it was a beautiful cloudless day when two prison guards shackled me up in chains, put me in a nice, spacious car and drove me to the city. Upon arrival at the City Jail I was processed and placed on a tier or cell block with other prisoners who were awaiting trial or waiting to go back to prison.

There were a number of prisoners that I knew. Most of them were guys that were two and three-time losers and this was their third or fourth time going back to prison. I also saw young 17 and 18 year old kids who were frightened and had no idea of the hell they were about to be inducted into. But in spite of all this it felt good to be back in the city with the possibility of winning my freedom. The next day I got a quick visit from my sisters Yvonne, Kathleen and Sharon. I hadn't seen them since my father died in 1967 yet it seemed as though they had changed. Hell what else do you do when you're in your twenties. They brought me clothes and cigarettes and stuff. They asked me in earnest, "Frank is there any chance that they will let you go, you know they said you killed a white man..." I didn't want to create any false hopes so I said

"I know it is very rare that they let Black people go free on legal technicalities but I have a good lawyer and I have to try…" They had come in smiling and full of joy but they left feeling a little sad and overwhelmed. Their visit just made me more determined, I was ready to have my day in Court.

The same day Arley and I stood before the bench of the Circuit Court in St. Louis with Judge McFarland presiding. It had been 10 years since I last appeared in this Court to receive a sentence of Life and Fifty years. Outside the courthouse it was a beautiful day and there was a picket line with people carrying signs saying "Free Angela Davis and All Political Prisoners" but there are no words for how I felt that day standing before the judge, eager to plead for my life yet frightened beyond belief that my freedom hung in the balance and depended solely on whether or not Arley and I could present a compelling case. At this time I was still ignorant as to the power of the movement even though there were people outside the jail chanting "Free Angela Davis!" "And All Political Prisoners!" I didn't know at the time that this was more powerful than any legal argument.

Arley presented the basic facts of the case saying that the State knew I had escaped from a State Mental Health Institution and that I had been placed there by a Circuit Order, and yet this was never brought to the Court's attention. The prosecutor responded that there was nothing in the record indicating that the state was aware of my escapee status and that my lawyer apparently was not aware of it either. Arley retorted by pointing out that the prosecutor had no proof of what my lawyer knew and that since my former lawyer was dead he could not be asked if he knew. However, Arley argued that there was a presentence investigation and that these records probably show that I was an escapee. The Judge then interrupted asking Arley was he able get these records. Arley said that all he had at this time was a copy of the Circuit Court order and that he had submitted that as evidence. And so it went back and forth for few minutes that seemed like an eternity.

In concluding, Arely asked if I might be able to address the Court. The Judge looked both puzzled and perturbed. What could I possibly say that would influence the decision of the Court. At this point my lawyer informed the Court that it was I who had researched and written the "Memorandum of Law…" supporting our motion for post- conviction relief. With a great degree of reluctance, the Judge allowed me to address the Court.

Now that I look back on it basically all I did in addressing the Court was to emphasize that the U.S. Supreme Court in Bishop vs. United States had already established the precedent ruling for my case and that is that if there was a question of mental competence then the Court should have refused to accept a guilty plea. The Judge seemed impressed favorably with our argument but all he said is that he would seriously take these matters into consideration and render a decision later.

Thereafter and while still in the Court room I was approached by Daniel P. Reardon, the former Circuit Attorney who had prosecuted me in 1961, I was about to be escorted by guards when Reardon, extending his hand, announced, "I am Dan Reardon and I just want to say that I was impressed by your argument...How did you become so versed in the law?" I just simply replied by saying "I studied it." I couldn't believe that the man who was trying to get me sentenced to death was now complimenting me and wishing me well. Yes, he actually said he thought I should get the relief I was seeking. He left me baffled. My lawyer, seeing that I was somewhat taken a back told me that Reardon no longer worked for the state but was in fact now a defense lawyer.

I was returned to the City Jail. All my jail house comrades thought that not being taken straight back to prison was a good gesture or at least a demonstration that the Judge was willing to give me every consideration required by law. I wanted to believe them for after all optimism was my only option. While in the City Jail there was no restriction as to who I could write so I wrote everybody. My lawyer wanted me to use the time I would be waiting for a decision wisely. He suggested that I do a biographical sketch focusing on my prison experience and I did. As it turned out it was a rather long essay outlining my activities, trial and ordeals as an African American prisoner. I called it "Pages From the Life of a Black Prisoner" and the whole thing was published in the Fall 1971 issue of *Freedomways* magazine. An open letter to my mother explaining to her why I had become a Marxist-Leninist and a revolutionary was also published by *The Daily World* (the Communist Party newspaper). I thought it was a great newspaper that fought for working class solidarity and against racial oppression, and so I was really honored when they published that letter I wrote to my mother defending and exposing socialism.

Being in the City Jail also afforded me the opportunity to correspond with a mathematics teacher in New York City who was writing a book on "African Mathematics". Her name was Claudia Zaslavsky and she had read the excerpts from my manuscript "*Science and Africa*" ["*Science and Africa*" was never published as a book but the manuscript is in the archives denominated "John Henrik Clarke Papers and Documents" in Harlem's famous Schomberg Library.] that were published in the 1966 Summer issue of *Freedomways*. Claudia wanted to cite some passages from it in her soon to be published book, *Africa Counts*.

For next five years we wrote to each other discussing mathematics, prison reform and some of the burning issues at that time confronting the Black Liberation Movement. To my pleasant surprise she shared several of these letters with her students and fellow mathematicians. For example, it was through Claudia that I learned about the Black mathematicians Lonnie X Cross (Nation of Islam), Sam Anderson (Black revolutionary) and Beatrice Lumpkin (Communist Party, math teacher and union activist). I was getting lots of mail from Claudia and her students, from Esther Jackson, the managing editor of *Freedomways*, and a host of others who were concerned about prisoners and the conditions in the prison system. I shared the letters with the prisoners on my tier because I wanted them to know that they were not alone and that people on the outside were beginning to see that prisons too were racist institutions that needed a radical overhauling.

Ironically while I was decrying prison conditions from the City Jail the Attica Uprising jumped off in New York. Our eyes were glued to the TV for we knew instinctively what these brothers were doing. We knew that they were putting their lives on the line, that they were willing to die to demonstrate to the public the unspeakable horrid conditions that existed in the prison system. We knew that Governor Rockefeller was going to send in state troopers and the militia to quell this uprising and that prisoners would be slaughtered en mass. We knew from experience that the authorities are always eager to give prison riots a blood bath and then afterwards accuse the prisoners of the blood letting. Rockefeller did send in the troops and they murdered 43 people.

The Attica prison uprising was much more than your usual prison riot sparked by brutality and wretched conditions. It was a well thought out rebellion that forced the powers that be, and the people, to take a look into the insensitive and cruel world we allowed to exist in our penal institutions. It was a revolt by penal slaves which dramatically demonstrated that prisons are as shameful a fixture of American life as slavery ever was. The Attica brothers were not demanding that prisons be abolished but that the inhuman treatment be done away with so that prisoners would be allowed to be educated and reformed in order that they could become productive members of society.

The 1300 prisoners who rose up in Attica sacrificed their very lives in order to give a voice to the struggles of prisoners everywhere who were fighting for their human rights that were habitually violated by the daily horrors of prison life. The Attica Brothers were basically non-violent and treated the hostages they had taken humanely. The negotiations allegedly broke down when the prisoners demanded amnesty and Governor Rockefeller refused to meet with the prisoners. On Monday morning, September 13, 1971 Governor Rockefeller sent in the state troopers and national guard to seize the prison. Forty-three people, including hostages, were killed. This massacre was perpetrated in the name of restoring order and sending a message to prisoners that said in effect that prisoners' demands to be treated with human decency would be ignored.

We, those of us who were engaged in struggles against inhuman prison conditions, will always remember the immortal words of the Attica brothers on the eve that Rockefeller ordered the slaughter. They made this declaration: "If we can't live like men, then we must die like men!!!" The day before the massacre I turned 29 years old; and about two weeks later Judge McFarland denied my motion for post-conviction relief. I was returned to the maximum-security prison in Jefferson City, Missouri.

Arely came to see me shortly before I went back to prison in Jefferson City. He was very sad and I could see the tears welling up in his eyes. He said, "I've failed you. We should have gotten a reversal!" I simply responded, "You have not failed me. We can appeal this. We must continue to fight, comrade..." I was deeply moved that here was a man who had only known me for a few moments in a lifetime and he showed as much concern about the outcome of this case as my own family. And he was not just a man but a man who was quite capable of putting the welfare of others above his own. Arely R. Woodrow was much more than the most dedicated lawyer I've ever known he was also one of the best comrades I've ever known or had.

Back To Prison And New Found Hope

I had come too close to freedom to give up now. Even though I was returning to prison I still had great hopes for winning my case and snatching victory from the jaws of defeat. There was also the hope and inspiration given to me by the Attica brothers, whom I believed made the ultimate sacrifice in order to bring to the attention of the world the despicable and inhuman treatment of prisoners in these United States of America. I had my day in court, now perhaps the prisoners who bled and died and sacrificed their mental and physical health would also have their day in court.

But the greatest source of my new found hope was the national/international campaign to Free Angela Davis and All Political Prisoners. I had read about the work of the Communist Party through the Civil Rights Congress and other mass forums fighting for the freedom of the Scottsboro Boys and Angelo Herndon but nothing I had read prepared me for what I saw the National United Committees to Free Angela Davis and All Political Prisoners do. Immediately after Angela's arrest there was a spontaneous movement of protest; across the nation, thousands of people organizing a liberation movement to Free Angela Davis. In New York City, black writers formed a committee called the Black People in Defense of Angela Davis. By February 1971 more than 200 local committees in the United States, and 67 in foreign countries worked to liberate Angela Davis from prison. My defense committee in St. Louis fused with Angela's committee. We shared the same people. This was mass struggle on a national and international level like we have never seen before or since. So rich and variegated was this movement until to this day no one has been able to capture its depth and breadth in films or books. The Black revolutionary thinkers and Communists who helped to engineer this movement were Charlene Mitchell, William L. Patterson, Henry Winston, Ted Basset, Grace Basset, Esther Jackson, Jim Jackson, Kendra Alexander, Franklin Alexander, Sylvia Woods, Josephine Wyatt, Ishael

Flory, Margaret Burnham, Louise Patterson, Mary Louise Patterson and of course Angela Y. Davis. I am sure I left out some people who played a key role in developing the strategy and tactics of this movement. I thought of them then and I see them now as being among the great revolutionary, movement builders of the twentieth century. But there was also those on the ground warriors like Deacon Alexander and Rose Chernin (in L.A.), Herschel Walker and Coraminita Mahr (in St. Louis), Mildred Williamson, Willie Williamson and Queenie and Ronelle Mustin (in Chicago), Damu Smith (in St. Louis and Washington, D.C.), Anne and Carl Braden and Mattie Jones (in Kentucky), Anne Mitchell (everywhere), Michael Myerson, Claudia Loftis and a whole battalion of folks in New York— and these are just the people I knew. Before the campaign to free Angela and all political prisoners my defense committee was never no more than a half dozen people. In 1971 it grew tenfold to include workers, school teachers, artists and intellectuals.

My first day back in the joint I was greeted by my prison comrades with good news; they said the Communist Party newspaper, *Daily World*, featured an open letter I had written to my mother while in City Jail. As I have already stated above the letter was explaining to my mother why I had become a Black Marxist-Leninist. This was remarkable because the very fact that a revolutionary newspaper was being mailed to prisoners was a result of the Federal Court issuing an order forbidding the warden to hold our mail because of political censorship. The flood gates were open now; we were getting all sorts of radical books donated. My lawyer sent me a lot of back issues of the *Black Panther Party Black Community News Service* papers . We were getting in books like "*Negroes With Guns*" by Robert Williams and "*Right to Revolution*" by Truman Nelson; and "*Soul on Ice*" by Eldridge Cleaver and "*Soledad Brother Letters*" by George Jackson. International Publishers made sure that we got plenty of literature on Marxism-Leninism and critical works by Black Communists like William L. Patterson, Claude Lightfoot, Ben Davis, Henry Winston and Angela Davis. I can't even began to describe the impact this sudden flood of revolutionary literature had on our morale and eagerness to get free so we could join the struggle on the streets.

But while we were being jubilant about our gains the warden was plotting our demise. Judge Oliver, a federal judge from the Western District of Missouri had informed the Missouri Attorney

General that he was writing a court order to desegregate the Missouri Department of Corrections. The Attorney General said Missouri would not appeal. The Warden had run out of options, for there was nothing he could do now but yield to the order of the court. At the time I had no idea that these developments had taken place. The Court first notified the Attorney General in the name of a peaceful transition, for after all we were prisoners who just might get defiant when we find out that we won at least a legal victory in our efforts to have the prison desegregated and the constitutional and civil rights of prisoners respected. But before we discuss the warden's response to our legal challenges we need to talk briefly about how things were developing among us prisoners.

While I was litigating my case in St. Louis our prison collective, under the leadership of Larry Thomas, had continued to meet. Also, we had an important new addition to our ranks and that was Leon Dent, from the Black Liberators, a St. Louis based defense organization. Like the Black Panther Party, the Black Liberators believed in the right to bear arms and defend themselves and the movement against armed attacks perpetrated by the oppressor and the police.

The Black Liberators seized the time and the headlines when Adam Clayton Powell, the African American Congressman from Harlem, came to St. Louis in 1968. The Black Liberators, armed with shotguns, pistols and carbines were at the airport when Congressman Powell arrived. The police confronted them as to why they were there armed. Their response was that "we are tired of our leaders being violently attacked and murdered so we are here to protect our leader, brother Adam Clayton Powell."
The police ordered the Black Liberators to put down their weapons and they refused, saying that if the police tried to disarm them then some people would die and it wouldn't just be black people dying. The police backed down and the Black Liberators proceeded to provide Congressman Powell with an armed public escort while he was in St. Louis. Of course, all this created quite an uproar with the establishment white media making all sorts of wild claims about black militants advocating violent revolution.

Catching Leon Dent and Rev. Charles Coen (the leader of the Black Liberators) at a later date while they were unarmed, the police took Coen and Dent into custody and brutally beat them so bad that they had to be hospitalized. Dent was beaten into a coma and even though he came out of the coma he had epileptic seizures for the rest of his life due to his being beaten and tortured by members of the St. Louis Police Department. Brother Leon was definitely a freedom fighter. He was a fearless and very capable soldier.

Leon Dent came to prison in 1971 to begin serving time on a five year sentence stemming from some kind of weapons charge. As soon as he was released to the prison population Leon joined our collective. He had the heart of a lion but he had no discipline. Our methods of operation, which was sustained by iron clad discipline, were not to Leon's liking; he stood with us 100% in our legal struggle to desegregate the prison system but he was not in favor of studying revolution as a science and he believed that the Christian doctrine had all the answers to all human problems. When we would be studying and having discussions Leon would be somewhere confronting other prisoners about their wicked ways and out of these confrontations developed fights that often led to violence. Almost every week Leon was having fist fights with prisoners who disagreed with him. It was crazy. We were spending a lot of time trying to keep these squabbles from becoming killing scrapes. In prison the criticism of the knuckles can't supplant the criticism of knives. What really saved the day for the antagonized is that the prison authorities put Leon in the hole (solitary confinement).

After Leon was sent to the "hole" we were able to cool down "the wild bunch" (a group of young prison thugs) and the (Nation of Islam) Muslims. In point of fact they were so glad to see Leon gone until they really didn't need to be "cooled down" at all. One of the Muslim brothers said to me, in a signifying but gleeful manner: "Well, they finally put your man Dent in the hole."

I did not share Muhammad's attitude about Leon going to the hole for in the hole he would be vulnerable and possibly subjected to violence. I knew that given Leon's defiance, and the racist attitudes of the warden and his prison guards, he could be killed. So, what could we do? How could we help?

We were allowed to have so-called "privileged" communication with our lawyers; that is, we could write and seal a letter and the prison authorities were not allowed to censor it. I immediately sent a letter to my lawyer asking that he contact State Assemblywoman Davern Calloway and let her know that she needed to come into the prison right away and visit Leon because his life was in danger.

About a week later Representative Calloway did come in and visit with Leon and made inquiries to the warden regarding his treatment. This was enough to hold the warden's goon squad in check for the moment. Whatever Leon's issues may have been with other prisoners he was in fact a political prisoner who was regarded dangerous and deadly by the prison authorities. Because he was in prison for allegedly assaulting law enforcement personnel he was a marked man. Given the gravity of the situation I spoke to Leon repeatedly about the need for him to kind of lay back and avoid at all cost confrontations with the guards and other prisoners. Sometimes he would agree with me and say, "I know brother, I have to be cool. I'm in captivity." But in a day or two he'd be right back having confrontations. He would confront the prison thugs about their taking advantage of weaker prisoners; and he confronted the guards about their brutalizing behavior toward Black prisoners.

Just as things were beginning to stabilize with Leon we got word that two members of the Black Panther Party were coming to us from the City Jail in St. Louis with a boat-load of time. We had read about Thomas McCreary, Henry Shasha Brown, Ron Carter and a sister Panther having a shootout with the St. Louis police. Ron Carter was killed, and the police alleged that the sister got away, after having thrown a hand grenade at the cops. Thomas and Henry were captured, tortured and brutally beaten.
As soon as these brothers came into the prison population they sought me out. They said that they didn't want to meet with our entire collective, which consisted of about ten of us. They wanted to meet with me because they heard from other prisoners that I headed up the collective and was well versed in Marxism-Leninism and the law.

I agreed to meet with Thomas and Shasha and so we met one weekend on the upper-yard in the recreation room. The rec-room was where prisoners played ping-pong, chess and checkers, card games, did exercises and watched TV. Usually there was only two or three guards watching over us. We found us a bench near some prisoners playing chess in order not to appear to be having a meeting. Thomas and I pretended to be playing with Shasha sitting there as a spectator.

Thomas opened the discussion by telling me about their ordeal with the police and their subsequent trial and conviction of armed assault on the police. Then Shasha said they considered that they were targeted by the police because of their involvement in the movement and being members of the Black Panther Party. They had lawyers and outside support from a network of movement people and their focus would be on getting out of prison.

I listened very carefully and I had a thousand questions to ask them about the movement and how they came to be a part of it. I wanted to know what the response of the masses were to the Black Panther Party program. I wanted to know about the split between the cultural Black Nationalists and the revolutionary Black Nationalists. Why was the East Coast and West Coast sections of the Party feuding? Was George Jackson really a field marshal in the Black Panther Party? And so on and so forth.

Thomas and Shasha answered all my questions in detail and I could see that they really liked my inquisitiveness by the way they carefully and thoroughly answered each question. Prisoners love hearing stories about what's going on outside the prison. And I was no different for I wanted to know how the revolutionary movement was developing as well as the movement to Free Angela Davis and all political prisoners. I had read George Jackson's *Soledad Brother*, but nothing prepared me for these brothers, for here was all-the-way live revolutionaries who were quite willing to die for their beliefs. I was willing to die too but I didn't want to die in prison unless it was absolutely necessary. Huey P. Newton was talking about "die for the revolution" or "revolutionary suicide". My thoughts were to live for the revolution and die if needs be. But at any rate I knew that these were ideas that had not taken hold of the masses and I believed that the demands of the moment required revolutionaries to address the immediate needs of the people through political campaigns for systemic changes. The civil rights movement, in spite of all the repression it had been subjected to, provided lots of lessons on how to organize the masses from where they are at politically, socially and economically. In fact, the civil rights movement kicked the door open for social change so effectively that everybody thought their time had come. All we had to do was seize the time. The reason why we were in prison having this discussion with movement people was because the ruling class had also seized the time and brought about a regime of repression.

After much discussion these brothers decided that they would take a low profile and not join our collective. They said they would, from time to time, have private discussions with me and stay focused on their legal case. I had to respect their wishes, but they had no idea about what prison life was like in here. They were in fact marked as militants and trouble-makers when they walked in. We went about our usual affairs of studying and having small discussion groups of 4 or 5 people meeting on the yard. But just when the prison authorities were acting as if they had developed a tolerance for us, other prison groups started developing plans for confrontation. There were the Zulus, the Nation of Islam Muslims and another group called the "Wild Bunch". The Zulus were loose canons who tried to mix Marxism-Leninism with cultural nationalism. They were very subjective in their organizing approach in that they suffered from macho-mania. But they were also some really stout hearted brothers who hungered for justice. And I never gave up on them.

The Nation of Islam Muslims were straight forward Black Nationalists who wanted a separate country, a Black Nation within the United States that would have its own sovereignty and be self-determined. They were non-confrontational when it came to challenging the prison authorities but very confrontational when it came to challenging us, their fellow prisoners. The warden gave them a place of worship but insisted that they have nothing to do with the struggle to desegregate the prison. In fact, some of the Muslim brothers went a step further and started to try and pressure us into dropping our desegregation suit. However, it must be said that most of the Muslims were friendly and respectful toward us.

The Warden, Harold Swenson, and his deputy Donald Wyrick exploited these differences in such a way as to justify isolating us from the rest of the prisoners. Here's how it went down:

A rumor to the effect that we were planning on taking guards hostage got mysteriously started. So, on this one evening when we were having evening yard I was approached by a couple of guards who said, "Chapman, the Warden wants to see you in Control Center." I knew that this meant trouble but there was nothing I could do but comply. Control Center was a barred-in cubicle in the administrative unit of the prison that controlled the movement of prisoners to and from the cell block to every other part of the prison.

When we arrived at the control center I was taken to a room enclosed by a large, see-through glass. In the middle of the room was a long metal table surrounded by about a dozen chairs. The room was empty. The two guards escorted me in and politely said, in a contrived friendly voice: "Have a seat Chapman, the warden will see you shortly." Then they left me there alone. After a few minutes passed I saw the Deputy Warden, Donald Wyrick approaching the door by way of the small hall way I could see through the glass. He was smiling and shaking his head as if to say I got you just where I want you.

Wyrick entered the room with about four other guards stepping up quickly behind him. I remember him saying something stupid like "Have you been waiting long?" I knew then that the Warden was not coming and that who I would be seeing would be the goon squad. The Deputy Warden went off into a long tirade about how me and my little band of militants were planning on taken him and his guards hostage and have us another Attica. I responded by saying that our only plans were to seek our legal remedies in court, nothing more. Before I could finish my statement he pulled a slap-jack from his back pocket and struck me across the forehead. As soon as I hit the floor the four goons jumped me, held me down and hand-cuffed me. My hands were cuffed in front instead of behind and I was thinking that this was good because I could at least use my hands and arms to shield my head. Now at least a half a dozen or more guards were in the room.

I acted more hurt then I actually was but that got me no mercy. The guards who rushed into the room as if I was resisting were armed with steel-tip billy clubs and as they started wielding on me the Deputy Warden yelled let's take him to C-basement (that's what administrative segregation was called) and make him beg and crawl in front of his black brothers. And that is what they did. They took me to C-basement, tore all my clothes off so I was forced to stand naked in front of the other prisoners and then they beat me bloody until I fell to the floor unconscious with a concussion, three broken ribs and a broken wrist. But I did not crawl or beg. I did not utter a word or cry out in any manner except to say just once: "I am a human being and I do not deserve this!" They called me a black communist bastard, they said "That whore Angela Davis can't help

The trip to Eddyville with Captain Deerduff was four hours long and full of boring sights of flat corn and wheat fields and miles and miles of trees. Deerduff tried several times to start up a conversation. I really wanted to ask him a lot of questions about where we were going but I didn't want to show any signs of fear so I just sat quietly in pain, thinking that perhaps this was my end.

My most vivid memory of this painful and boring trip, stuffed with anxiety, is the last mile of narrow, winding road leading up to the prison. The prison suddenly appeared, a massive, gray-colored stone structure sitting on the shore of Lake Barkley and the Cumberland River. This prison is also known in Kentucky folklore as the "The Castle on the Cumberland".

Compared to the prison I came from this was a small maximum security joint that first opened its gruesome gates in 1889 and was opening them for me around December 11, 1971. It had a population of about 800 whereas the prison I came from in Jefferson City, Missouri had a population of about 3400. Pursuant to a U.S. Supreme Court decision Eddyville Prison had just closed its death row where prisoners once awaited execution and the prison itself was founded by former Confederate General Hylan Benton Lyons in 1884. Also according to folklore Italian stonemasons erected this grotesque, medieval-castle-like structure with massive granite blocks quarried from down the Cumberland river. The day I arrived at this place was a cloudy one with a very slight drizzle of rain; and suffice it to say that I was in incredible physical and emotional pain.

Upon entering the prison I was unshackled and taken straight to the Warden's office. The Warden was a former football player named Henry Cowan. He was a big, burly man who took pride in being an arrogant racist. I remember that when I was escorted in to his office by Captain Deerduff he greeted me with an insult. "So you're the militant nigger from the Missouri Pen!" He shouted.

This is the prison in Eddyville, Kentucky

The meeting with Warden Henry Cowan was basically about orientation, the communication was simple and straightforward. He said he would not have any of that civil rights nonsense in his prison, period . Cowan then proceeded to tell me that there was a prisoner by the name of Darryl Blakemore who was a member of the Black Panther Party in Louisville, Kentucky and that he wanted me to know that I shouldn't be trying to buddy up with Darryll or any of the Black militant troublemakers. Making sure that I understood that he (the Warden) was giving me no quarter it was further pointed out that if I was seen congregating with other militant prisoners I would be thrown into administrative segregation immediately. At this point Warden Cowan asked Captain Deerduff to turn over my files and transfer papers. After a quick check of the documents he ordered Captain Deerduff to unshackle me. Shortly thereafter I was told that I was being placed in Administrative Segregation for two weeks before being released into the general prison population.

Administrative Segregation is different than the hole (solitary confinement) because you were allowed to have a mattress, toiletries and you were served three meals a day. But when in the hole you were stripped down to nothing but a pair of shorts and forced to sleep on a concrete floor and served only one meal a day. In the hole they were limited by law to confining you for no more than ten days. In Administrative Segregation they could keep you there indefinitely.

While in Administrative Segregation, a number of remarkable things happened. The prisoners found out I had come there from another institution for being engaged in some sort of militant activities; their response to me was very friendly and they wanted to help out in any way they could. They also heard I had been beat up pretty bad. There were prisoners who cleaned up the floors outside our cells (called cat walks) and they would carry messages either verbally or written. These prisoners told me when to get on sick call so I could get x rays, which would provide evidence of my injuries. The prison hospitals are administered by prisoners. Once they got me to the hospital they gave me x-rays, and bandaged 3 broken ribs on my left side to restrict their movement. They were very helpful in my recovery. This went on for two weeks. I received my first visit the second week I was there, before I ever left Administrative Segregation.

My visitor was Professor John Dahm. He was the architect of the study release program at the Missouri facility. He was also responsible for the community college that had been started in Moberly Missouri where prisoners could get associate degrees. He came to visit me and tell me that he and a number of other professors were asking the warden about transferring me to Moberly to be involved in the college program and I could get my AA degree rather than being held prisoner in Kentucky. Contrary to the intent of the statute I was there under, Kentucky did not offer any rehabilitative programs. If they were really interested in rehabilitation, they would have sent me to Moberly instead of Kentucky. Of course, the warden ignored these demands on the grounds that I was plotting to start a riot. Professor Dahm refused to believe this and he asked the Warden was there any evidence other than the word of another prisoner. Of course, the Warden couldn't provide any evidence of me doing anything illegal. To be sure I was being punished for successfully leading a legal struggle to desegregate the Missouri State Penitentiary.

We had a long visit and he left me some money for the commissary. He assured me he was working as hard as he could within the constraints of the department of corrections and his position there. My second visit was from my family; my sister, Sharon and a comrade of mine who had just got out of prison, Robert Jameson. Oddly enough Kentucky had much more liberal visitation regulations than Missouri. Anyone who came from out of state could get a one day visit. This allowed me to be more hopeful as I was not isolated and I could resume my struggle in the courts. The first thing on my agenda was to file a motion for a Writ of Habeas Corpus in the federal court in Paducah, Kentucky. The basis of the motion was that they violated my constitutional rights by transferring me to a prison in a state where I had committed no crimes. The only thing that gave them legal authority that they could cite was the interstate compact law. But that law did not apply to me because the purpose of that law was for rehabilitative purposes and I was moved for punitive reasons.

I immediately filed the motion in Federal court, and by the third week the federal court acknowledged receipt of it. Usually the federal court requires that one exhaust all of their state remedies before they act. However, I did not have any state remedies. Because this was such a unique case the court sat on it for a while. I did not hear from them for quite a while.

During this time my life in prison was uneventful. I reestablished contact with my Lawyer, Arely who asked me to try and focus on helping him prepare my appeal brief to the Missouri Supreme Court. Also, I was given a job in the kitchen peeling potatoes I limited my association with the other prisoners because I knew the warden was looking for any excuse to throw me into Administrative Segregation. However, I did communicate with the other prisoners. For instance, at the basketball games the ones that wanted to talk to me would sit next to me at the games. They wanted to know what was going on and what books to read. I put them in touch with radical and progressive publishers who provided free books for prisoners. Darrel Blakemore and I spoke mostly in the dining hall since the rule was we couldn't walk the yard together. He told me we were not the only political prisoners in Kentucky. There was also the Tinsley brothers who had been tried and convicted in a racially charged environment for killing a white man. They were sentenced to death. Their sentenced had been commuted to life because the Supreme Court had overturned the death penalty, ruling that it was unconstitutional and discriminatory. Thousands got off of death row as a result of Furman v. Georgia; and Angela Davis was able to make bail. Furman v. Georgia was a United States Supreme Court decision that ruled on the requirement for a degree of consistency in the application of the death penalty. The case led to a de facto moratorium on capital punishment throughout the United States, which came to an end when Gregg v. Georgia was decided in 1976.

The Tinsley brothers represented a popular case in Kentucky where a number of civil rights organizations like the Southern Organizing Committee and the NAACP and others in Louisville became active in this case to get justice. Through my discussions with the Tinsley brothers and Darryll Blakemore, I found out about Ann Braden. According to these guys Carl Braden (Anne's husband) had been sent to the Eddyville penitentiary for plotting to overthrow the government of Kentucky. It seems that he and Anne Braden were guilty of having sold their home in Louisville to a Black couple. The home was in a white section of Louisville. As a result the segregationists in Louisville carried out a smear campaign against the Bradens by calling them communists and accusing them of subverting the government. The Bradens were a part of the Civil Rights movement from day one.

The Tinsley brothers got word to Anne Braden letting her know that I was there in the Eddyville prison and I had been sent from Missouri due to my efforts to integrate the Missouri State Pen. While I was in the Eddyville prison, Ann Braden visited with me; it was shortly after Angela Davis had been aquitted. She told me they were in the process of forming an organization in Chicago called the National Alliance and that the people who were doing this were the National United Committees to free Angela Davis and all political prisoners. She also told me that the Kentucky people were working with this committee as well as the Black Panthers and they would be forming a new organization called the National Alliance Against Racist and Political Repression. This group would take up cases in prison where people were political prisoners and they included in their definition of political prisoners also persons who had started advocating for civil rights once they got to prison. Prisoners advocating for civil rights increased the possibility of being kept in prison longer. This definition included me as a political prisoner.

I was pleased to get these great tidings from Anne, but I still couldn't see how that mass movement that freed Angela would also free me. These are the things that were going on. There were a few incidents that occurred that almost sent me over the edge. One was the murder of a prisoner on the yard. We were standing in front of the commissary on the yard and a prisoner got into the commissary and took a hostage.This was a mentally challenged prisoner. He brought the hostage out into the yard area holding him with a knife at his throat. You could tell the prisoner was mentally deranged by his behavior. He was walking around in the open. One of the prison guards in the guard tower shot him in the neck and killed him. This almost led to a prison uprising. They locked us down and they came to my cell and got me and took me to an administrative segregation cell, next to Blackmore. They came around and interrogated both of us asking us if we had anything to do with the prisoner taking the guard hostage? We kept denying it and explained the prisoner had mental issues. But they insisted that we were there and then Warden Cowan said, "We know we can't prove it but we will be watching you and if we can get anyone to say that you had anything to do with this we will try you guys for murder." I believe this was an attempt to intimidate us. We didn't even know the prisoner and the Warden knew that. I told them that this was ridiculous. After this they increased the number of guards in the yard. Also, if there were more than 3 prisoners gathering together in the yard they were broken up or threatened with going to the hole. The whole prison was tense and this went on for months.

Meanwhile, I finally heard from the courts. They asked the Warden for a response to my claims of being illegally held. I could not wait for their response. By this time I had been down there for 11 months. One day while in the yard my name was called "Chapman, 03719 report to the yard shack." They sent me to the administrative building where I was told I would be seeing the Warden. I was really anticipating something ridiculous. Maybe someone told them I had something to do with the hostage situation and they were going to act on it. All kinds of wild thoughts were going through my head. While outside his office I saw Donald P. Wyrick who was the associate warden who previously made the attack on me. He was heading towards me in the corridor, he went into Henry Cowan's office and they came out together. Cowan told me I was going back to Missouri. I asked if I could get my belongings and he told me that guards were getting my books & legal documents. They shackled me down and took me out of there.

When I got to the car, Wyrick and another guard we called "Mace Man" (because he was always spraying Mace in prisoners faces) put me in the back seat. That was unusual because usually one guard would be in the back while the prisoner sat in front. They told me I was the luckiest man in the world because they were taking me back to Missouri. "You will meet with the parole board," said Wyrick. "Then," he continued, "we will send you to the medium security facility and you can enroll in the Moberly community college program."

I was speechless; primarily because I absolutely did not believe them. I thought this was a ruse. Along the way, we stopped for lunch and they offered to take took my cuffs off in the restaurant, but I insisted that they leave them on because I was afraid they were going to do something. They told me I had to start learning to trust them. They asked me if I wanted anything to eat and I told them I would wait until I got to the prison. We went into the restaurant and I watched them eat. I was very suspicious about this whole thing. I could not believe they were taking me back to Missouri only to release me to the Moberly Community college facility inside the prison.

I got back to the Missouri state penitentiary and they released me right into the population. They gave me a cell in the H Block which was now integrated but at the time I was sent to Eddyville it was not. I went into the yard and the prisoners who were in my collective were glad to see me. Several prisoners rushed up to me and said they thought I was dead. I was only allowed in the yard for that one day. But I was able to talk to all of the people I had worked with to bring about the changes. For example, when the federal desegregation order came down, they did it immediately. They even hired black guards, some of whom had been prisoners before. This was dramatic change from 11 months before. I remember that I felt that this was a very surreal experience and also happy because we had won the fight against racial segregation in the prison. I stepped back into a desegregated prison for one day.

The very next day I was taken before the parole board and they gave me a contract. If I went to Moberly and got my AA degree they said they would release me. As soon as I would get my AA degree that is how soon I would get released into the study release program at the University of Missouri in Rolla, Missouri. If I completed the coursework there for my BA, they would then parole me.

This was in late November, 1972. I already had about half my credit hours needed to graduate from the Junior College. I thought

I could do this in about a year. This was far more than anything I had hoped for or dreamed of during my stay in Eddyville. I had stepped out of a nightmare and was about to embark upon the road to freedom.

This is how this part of my life is going: I am in a desegregated medium security prison-community, getting my education after 11 months in Kentucky. I had no idea of what lay before me. I knew it was a medium security facility and I knew I would have a room, not a cell. No stone walls, only fences. It was a very relaxed environment compared to the maximum-security facilities I had been in. There were no restrictions on the mail. I could write to anyone and anyone could write to me. I had a key to my room. It was like a transitional place where I could take on more responsibilities toward taking on independent living in preparation for living outside of prison.

I started writing articles for magazines, like *Proud Magazine* in St. Louis Missouri. I had some articles published in *Freedomways* in New York. All the people I had to sneak to write before I could openly write to now. The visitation was very relaxed. I could have contact visits where I could touch others, and have hugs and kisses. There were playing areas for the kids. It was a totally different world. Moberly was more humane; and more accommodating to the rehabilitative process. I had no idea how it was going to work out but I was just glad to be coming out from behind the Wall. I could almost smell my freedom. I knew now I was going to get out. All I had to do was to stay the course and not do anything stupid. This was a turning point in my life in prison. There was light at the end of the tunnel and it wasn't a train.

On the Road to Freedom

After 11 years or more of being incarcerated in a maximum-security prison and then to be suddenly out of it is a very challenging experience. In a maximum security prison, you are very restricted in your movements. You can spend up to 16 hours in your cell every day and as little time as 5 hours a week on the yard. This is what it was like my first five years in prison

You have no control over your mail. I was allowed to write and receive letters only from people they approved. You are under a high level of political scrutiny and if they believe your mail or contact was associated with the civil rights movement, for instance, then they would not allow you to have it. We had to develop a system of smuggling mail. We also had to go to court to fight to get mail from people who were not our immediate family.

It was a segregated facility with blacks receiving the worst treatment. We were 4 to 6 men in a cell while the whites were in one and two men cells. Black prisoners were concentrated in the unskilled and dangerous jobs. For example, the embosser machine that impacted the license plates with numbers was notorious for cutting off fingers. A disproportionate number of Black prisoners worked the embosser. If someone lost a finger, they were given a $15 a month payment for the duration of their sentence.

We started challenging these things legally around the mid 60s so by 1969 we had made a lot of headway as a result of litigating civil rights suits. The federal courts ordered some of the censorship taken away. We finally had court orders where we could write anyone and receive letters from anyone outside the prison. The courts ruled that all legal mail could be sealed so it could not be censored. These were all Federal Court orders based on civil rights statutes passed in the wake of the Civil War and the abolition of slavery. And it must be said that it was the jail-house lawyer prisoners who initiated and led these legal battles for prisoners' rights. We recognize the enormous contributions of the National Lawyers Guild, the Center for Constitutional Rights and the National Prison Project of the American Civil Liberties Union but they all came behind the spear-head forged by the prisoners themselves.

When I was transferred to Moberly I was leaving all of this behind – the good, the bad and the ugly. I was going into a situation I did not know anything about but I was glad to be going. I had heard that the conditions there were much more livable and it was not segregated. Blacks worked in the print shop and participated fully in the Junior College program. They were entirely differently situated. We understood that the conditions were better because of the legal struggles and battles we won in maximum-security prisons. This opened the doors for prisoners to be re-socialized and rehabilitated.

So, my first month in Moberly was my orientation I met with deputy warden Schultz who was as far as prisons go, a fairly liberal guy. He said he believed in giving prisoners a chance and in being fair. He believed that good behavior should be rewarded just as bad behavior should be corrected. Myself and two other prison inmates, Ron Jones and Albert Bradford approached deputy warden Schultz about us having a chapter of the NAACP in the prison. The JC's had a chapter; the Muslims had a place to worship, the alcoholics had AA, narcotic addicts group had their group. We were asking to have another group which would be a civil rights group – the National Association for the Advancement of Colored People (NAACP), a reputable black civil rights organization which had been a pioneer in the struggle against racial discrimination.

The Deputy Warden said he didn't mind us having an NAACP as long as we didn't use it to militantly organize prisoners against the guards and prison authorities. We assured him we wouldn't do that. We wanted to increase the consciousness of the prisoners as to their rights. We wanted to advocate for prisoners that all human beings have recognized rights under the Constitution and the United Nation's Human Rights Charter. We could not make a deal that if the prison authorities went against us that we would remain quiet. With that Deputy Warden Schultz laughed and said that he would not think we would ever be quiet. But he could not tolerate strikes, work stoppages or any other acts interrupting prison discipline. He told him us that the other organizations were also advised that they could exist only so long as they didn't disrupt the orderly flow of the institution. We agreed to do that and we pledged that we would use the channels legally available to us to advise prisoners of their rights and advocate prison reform. With these modifications he agreed that it was a reasonable request.

Afterwards we got in touch with Ida Boone who headed the NAACP regionally out of St. Louis, Missouri. We asked her what the process would be to charter a chapter in the prisons. She said the NAACP had never set up a chapter in a state prison, therefore, she would take it to the national board of the NAACP and get back to us. They approved and after about 3 months we got our charter and we were the first one ever NAACP branch chartered in a state prison. Now they exist in other prisons throughout the country.

We started a NAACP newsletter just like all the other branches. We named it "*Rare Earth*" – after a popular white music group that was radical and basically peaceniks. We put a picture on the cover of the newsletter of a black man being lynched (hung from a tree) and the blood was dripping down onto the earth. So rare earth was written on the cover in blood. The warden had a fit. He called it provocative and started clamping down on us.

We had a long debate over this. The debate consisted of this: the warden felt it was stirring up the black prisoners. Our position was that they didn't cut the televisions off in the prisons and jails when Dr. king was assassinated or when civil right workers were being attacked by dogs or when there were riots. None of the TVs were cut off and the prisoners weren't put in their cells. Nothing happened and this newsletter, we said, was not as provocative as any of those actions. We were not trying to provoke anyone, we just wanted to raise the consciousness of the prisoners about the positive progress of the civil rights movement.

All of us had benefitted from these gains and we are a better society because of it. The Deputy Warden said he wasn't trying to tell us how to run our newsletter but he wanted us to show something positive on the cover. We agreed to showing the NAACP marching for civil rights on the back of the front cover so that people could see where the struggle started and after many years of peaceful struggle how many things such as racial segregation were outlawed.

That was our first encounter with repression in the Moberly facility and we were satisfied with the results. We could see that this Warden was open. Later we asked if we could have an NAACP banquet where different outside groups would come in and share their experiences. We would have food provided by the NAACP but he insisted that the prison would provide the food. I think what might have contributed to his attitude was the fact that our NAACP meetings were flooded with both black and white prisoners. We had to get bigger space because we had so many people. It wasn't just because they wanted to get out of their cells because they weren't in cells. They were in rooms and had a lot of freedom. They were coming because they were genuinely interested in learning about the NAACP. Most of their information about the NAACP was from the Nation of Islam Muslims or authorities who had negative feelings about the organization. At our meetings they started learning about Black scholars and writers like W.E.B. Dubois, and more and more the prisoners wanted to read more literature. Over time many became enlightened and overall it was a very good experience.

This wasn't all we did. I had to go to classes and do my own course work. I became deeply involved in the study of History and made it my major. The part of history I was interested in was intellectual history, and the history of working people. And my fantasy was how to combine these two. I felt I had a perfect case of it with the teachings and writings of Karl Marx and how he revolutionized the teaching of history in Europe. I started studying the socialist movement anew and started reading Sydney and Beatrice Webb who wrote a history of trade unionism in England. They were Socialist and wrote brilliantly about the rise of the Chartist Movement and the spontaneous and conscious development of class struggle in England. I started looking at the ideas of Socialism that had developed from Babeuf to Marx and Engels to Lenin from the standpoint of intellectual history. I found there was much more to it than was found in standard text books. Socialist theory and practice were developed by a whole host of people such as Rosa Luxembourg, August Bebel, Karl Liebknecht, Frantz Mehring and Clara Zetkin in Germany. Then I found out about Karl Marx's

daughter who married a French socialist and how they contributed to the socialist movement. I discovered that Pierre and Marie
Currie and Albert Einstein were socialists. I found out that Albert
Einstein even wrote a piece for *Monthly Review* magazine explaining why he was a socialist. He was also a friend and defender of
Paul Roberson which was very brave considering Roberson was
under attack by the House Un-American Activities Committee.

I also learned about how socialism affected the working class in
St. Louis. I learned about Joseph Weydemeyer who was a Prussian
general, a devout friend and follower of Karl Marx, a colonel in the
Union Army during the Civil War and a founder of the communist
movement in the United States. Weydemeyer fought in the 1848
revolution on the side of the liberals. He was also a member and
founder, along with Marx, of the Communist League. When he
came to the US he started the German periodical called *Die Revolution*. Finally, Weydemeyer settled in St. Louis. At that time St.
Louis was the home of the railroads so there was a strong middle
class and proletariat being developed there. I read somewhere
that it was Frederick Engels who suggested that German revolutionaries settle in Missouri. During the Civil War President Abra-
ham Lincoln appointed Weydemeyer the military commander of
St. Louis. St. Louis was a military district headed by this communist, Joseph Weydemeyer. He was considered one of the heroes of
the Civil War and later the founder of one of the first communist
clubs in the U.S.

I also read that Marx was a racist or at least that he made racist comments about Ferdinand LaSalle. The evidence of this was culled from
some personal correspondence between Marx and Engels. When I
read about this I had also previously read Karl Marx's *Capital,* more
than once, where clearly he shows the relationship between the en-
slavement of African people and the rise of capitalism; I had also
read his letters on the Civil War and I did not find nothing, not a
single sentence in these writings that smacked of racism. However,
I would not argue from this that Marx or anyone else is incapable of
expressing racist attitudes. But I did and do argue that racism as an
ideology and an institutionalized practice was created by the capitalist ruling class and is perpetrated by capitalism and that the doctrine
of socialism founded by Marx and Engels advocates overthrowing
the bourgeoisie through working class solidarity and is the antithesis of racism, sexism and national chauvinism.

This is where trying to connect the ideas of history and the workers' struggles took me. I even did papers on this issue. One of my papers was titled "Vide Poche" which meant empty pockets, a nickname then for St. Louis because of the rapidly growing numbers of working class poor in that city. In my paper I traced the history of the communist clubs in St. Louis and the workers association up to the 1877 workers strike. This "great strike", as it was called, had to do with the railroad workers fighting for unions and decent wages and working conditions.

The interesting thing about the year 1877 was that all the major rail road junctions from St. Louis to Philadelphia went on strike at the same time. The strikers were called communards which was the equivalent of communists in those days. The striking rail road workers in their actions were compared to the communards who participated in the Paris Commune uprising. The Paris Commune was a revolutionary socialist government that ruled briefly from March 18 to May 28, 1871. The rail road workers who went on strike in 1877 were being accused of causing the same havoc as the Paris Commune rebels caused. The other interesting thing about this is that Rutherford B. Hayes, then President of the United States, took the Union troops from the South and moved them to suppress the railroad strikers. I linked up the workers rebellion of 1877 with the overthrow of Radical Reconstruction in the South and the disenfranchisement of the African American people. To my surprise I got an A. That convinced me that I might have skills in this area. I decided that history would definitely be my major.

I acquired a girlfriend while I was in Moberly. They let us go to the women's prison in Tipton, Missouri. To this day I can't figure out why they did this. But they were very casual visits. We met in open yards and were allowed contact within limits. There were women and men guards on either side. But they didn't use a heavy hand and they let us socialize, flirt around and dance. They said this was part of our re-socialization for us and the women. Here I met this beautiful woman – Brenda Jenkins from Kansas City. She was so beautiful with her big Angela Davis like 'fro and she didn't look like she belonged in anybody's prison. She was also very arrogant and snubbed any of us that tried to talk to her. But I kept trying. She finally told me to quit wasting my time and to leave her alone because she didn't want to get involved with any felons. I backed off but I left a little sad. When I got back to Moberly I wrote her many romantic love letters. I went rambling through the classics such as Shakespeare's Sonnets, Victor Hugo, Oscar Wilde, etc. in search of appropriate romantic expressions that might capture her feelings and mine. I went to great lengths to woo her with words and make her feel the passions she had unleashed in me. I used lines from the German poet Frederick Schiller, who wrote *Don Carlos*. I used passages from Khalil Gibran's *The Prophet*:

When love beckons to you follow him,
  Though his ways are hard and steep.
And when his wings enfold you yield to him,
  Though the sword hidden among his pinions may wound you.
And when he speaks to you believe in him,
  Though his voice may shatter your dreams as the north wind lays waste the garden.

I quoted lines from songs like 'Love Walked In' "and took my troubles away." I pulled out all stops. I wrote her for weeks but never received anything back. But I never gave up hope or for one minute caved in to disappointment. Then one day I received a thick envelope with pictures in it and the sweetest letter. The pictures were of her and the letter was thanking me for brightening up her days. She was hesitant in writing because she thought initially the letters were not real. But after a time she enjoyed them and really appreciated them because she could tell I put in a lot of work. So, I thought, that I had at least succeeded in making her feel what I felt.

She said that she understood that we were coming back to Tipton in two weeks, which surprised me because I didn't know if we would ever go back. This time I got a very warm reception from her. She grabbed my hand and we sat at the picnic benches and she gave me a nice juicy kiss and we talked and fell madly in love. This made the rest of my stay at Moberly very enjoyable. Now she was writing me 2-3 letters a week. I found out things about her and she tried to discourage me by telling me she was going with a man in his 60's before prison and she was in her 30's. She told me she had 4 children by this man. But I didn't' care. My mission as I saw it was to make her believe that only I could make her happy because the love I felt for her was greater than anything I had ever known or imagined. If she wanted to go back to him after prison I still would love her, and wanted her to be in my life even if just as a friend. My grades suffered a little bit until the teachers commented on why I was slipping. I did open up to one of the professors who said that happened all the time. I started getting more disciplined but it was very hard. I never knew I could think about someone so much and have someone occupy my brain that much.

Music, Philosophy, Writing and The Movement: Up Close And Personal

Before continuing to the next chronological phase of my life's journey there are four things I want to talk about that will never get into the story chronologically because they are like butter spreading throughout my life. Music, Philosophy, Writing and The Movement

Music

I became interested in and grew up with the music in the streets of St. Louis in the 1950s and my interest developed under the guiding hand of my father. My musical development began quite young and became a core piece of my life. My father aspired to be a musician, he played guitar and with him it was almost like a religion; he was a devoted follower of one of the greatest innovators of modern music – Charlie Parker, a legend who came out of the big swing bands in Kansas City, Missouri. All bands then, that is in the 1930's and 40's, were dance hall bands. They went around in the chittlin' circuit and played dance halls. Every black community had at least one if not more dance halls. Some of the famous ones were like the Savoy in Harlem. So "Stomping at the Savoy" with Count Basie and others was popular from New York to California even in the fifties.. Stomping was another word for dancing.

My father played Charlie Parker's music – I remember hearing him play it continuously since I was the age of 7. They played what they called 78 records – 78 revolutions on the record-turn-table per minute. We were always listening to these records. I remember humming Charlie Parker's song "Chi-Chi" and from then on my nick name was "chi-chi". So I grew up on bee bop. Most of the kids my age were listening to rhythm and blues – Bo Didley, Chuck Berry, The Drifters, The Clovers or Fats Domino. But I was listening to Charlie parker, Fats Navarro, Dizzy Gillespie, Lester Young, Coleman Hawkins, Duke Ellington, Dexter Gordon and Waddell Gray – that was the music my dad played. One time I had Lewis Jordon on the radio and the "Chattanooga Shoe Shine Boy" was on and I heard the boogie rhythm and I got caught by it for a minute and my father said get that corn field music off my radio. If it wasn't jazz or bee bop he didn't want to hear it.

My father listened to classical or long hair music like Beethoven and Bach sometimes but never the popular music the kids were listening to. He always had something negative to say about it. I grew up with a negative attitude about rhythm and blues and rock and roll and I became one track minded like him. I just listened to jazz but I could not ignore the world in which I lived. I lived with young people and went to school with them. When I became a teenager I had to learn the current dances so I could take out the girls I was interested in. We did the scat and the bop and they were dancing to rhythm and blues tunes like "Money Honey" by the Drifters, "Blueberry Hill" by Fats Domino or "Please, Please Don't Go" by James Brown; and so I developed this schizophrenia where in my social life I was listening and dancing to rock and roll but in my most solitude moments when I was home alone or with my jazz buddies I was listening to be bop.

I also became a student of bebop and learned about all of the musicians who played. There was a group of guys in my neighborhood – we were young, but we considered ourselves culturally superior to those who liked rock and roll and pop music. We turned an outdoor coal shed into a club house where we would bring our records and steal electricity from neighbors to play them. We sat around for hours and listened to jazz and quizzing each other on who was playing each of the instruments. We kept each other abreast of jazz groups and musicians and their back grounds and lifestyles. It was like a fan club and that was how I spent a lot of my time with my jazz peers.

By the time I was 16 or 17 years old I was like a young jazz on the streets scholar – I knew all of the musicians and their histories and who played with whom – I would read books like the *Essence and Evolution of Jazz* by the French jazz historian, Andre Hodeir. I remember I read that and another book by Marshall Stearns. I started reading about the early groups from the turn of the century – the originators of jazz like Jelly Roll Martin, Scott Joplin, Louis Armstrong, King Oliver and others. I learned about all of these legends and the different eras of jazz – the rag-time era – the swing era and the modern or progressive jazz era in the 1940s. I really got interested in it. Our fan club group would talk about the history of jazz and all of the musicians and we were fascinated by this.

I remember that in 1959 there was a serious jazz joint in St. Louis called the Mello Cellar that all the local musicians came too after their gigs. It was a place where legends like John Mixon (bass), Joe Charles (drums), John (Albino Red) Chapman (piano), Peanuts Wailer (tenor), Eddie Fisher (guitar), Kenny Gouche (drums), Caroll Crout (bass), Freddie Washington (tenor), Tommy Strolls (piano), Gene Easton (alto), Clarke Terry (trumpet). I was in this club everytime the doors opened.

I carried on like this until about the age of 17 when I came to Chicago. My father had already been here for a few years but I stayed with friends of mine. I didn't stay with my dad because I left home w/o my mother's permission. My dad encouraged me to find my own way and not stay with him but get a job. I was okay with it because I felt like a man. The fascinating part of Chicago was that everything I dreamed about was here. I stayed at the Irving Apartment hotel on 43rd and Drexel. On 47th & Drexel was the famous Sutherland Hotel and it was like the Jazz mecca of the Midwest. They had a lounge with a stage built into it behind the bar. All the greats played there like John Coltrane, Cannonball Adderley, Gene Ammon, and Sonny Stitt. Those were names you commonly saw on the marquees and this joint was right down the street from where I lived; I thought I had died and gone to heaven. There were record shops on 47th Street with loud speakers blasting tunes by Miles Davis, Jimmy Smith and other jazz great's right onto the street. Jazz was very popular and unlike today where you have to search with a searchlight for a jazz radio station. Back then it was a big part of the culture and I am so grateful that I lived in those times

In terms of my musical development being in Chicago was very important. I ran into guys on 47th Street some of whom were musicians who loved the music and they had clubs like we had in St. Louis where we had record jazz sessions – we also smoked reefer and that enhanced the music. During that time I was also introduced to Beatnik culture. I got a book called *The Holy Barbarian* – it was about Beatnik culture in New York. It was about Zen Buddhists who were devout followers of jazz – they had their own cool language – they had expressions such as "like crazy man," "like that's groovy man," etc. They wore sunglasses at night, like Miles Davis. They were just real cool people. Nothing excited them & they had this philosophy that it was all about peace and arriving at a state of mind where you wouldn't be disturbed about anything in the world like, injustice, poverty, nuclear war – nothing would blow their cool.

This movement had its own poetry, music, politics and life-style and at its core was the bebop music and culture created by Charlie Parker, Dizzy Gillespie, Thelonius Monk, Charlie Mingus and others. They also used the word "hip" which meant that you had this inner knowledge of what was going on and what was going on with the music and the cats who played. This is brilliantly expressed in a novel simply called The Horn by John Clellon Holmes. If you were not into jazz and you didn't know who and in style between the different musicians the differences was then you were a square. They knew that Miles Davis was the greatest trumpet player ever and that John Coltrane was an upcoming genius of hard bop – the hip set was grooving and moving from bebop to hard-bop.

During this period when I was learning the most about music and my father tried to enroll me in a music school in Chicago in the South Loop – there were a number of music schools at the time. It wasn't very expensive - $5 per lesson. I learned the basics of the guitar and how to play a few simple tunes but I couldn't get up any enthusiasm for the guitar. While I was practicing on the guitar I wanted to play the piano. My teacher would not let me play the piano because my dad was paying for guitar lessons. I rebelled and quit taking lessons because I couldn't play the piano. My musical growth was stunted until I was arrested and imprisoned.

When I was arrested in 1961 and housed in the City Jail I met these musicians which I referred to earlier in our story. I met Big Newt who was a bass player and his name was actually Newton. Big Newt was a professional bass player who knew all of the musicians who were in prison. He told me who they were and told me that when I got to Jefferson City to check out Buddy Drew. He was a saxophone player who supposedly went to the same high school as Charlie Parker and who also played with him. I didn't put any stock in this story, but when I got to Jefferson City I discovered that during recreation the musicians would perform in the gymnasium. The prison provided the instruments. I heard them playing and I thought I was back in Chicago on Cottage Grove and 63rd street. I said who is that guy on the alto sax and someone said it was Buddy Drew.

So I decided at that point I was going to learn the piano – at the time I am only 19. I have had some exposure to music and I could read the lines and spaces of sheet music but I couldn't' really play an instrument. I started from scratch. I started practicing on the piano and asked some of the musicians for help. A guy by the name of Jimmy Harris played piano and I asked him if he would show me how to play. He said he didn't have time, but he could show me how I could teach myself like learning the scales – all 12 of them – and he took me down the piano and showed me sharps and flats and the natural keys. All total that is 12 keys and you need to learn how to play your scales in all of those 12 keys. He asked me if I could read and I told him a little and he said that all I would need is a book called *Hannon's Virtuoso Piano In 60 Exercises*. I thought he was kidding me. How can you become a virtuoso piano player in 60 exercises? But I bought it and it was incredible. It moved through the scales in a melodic way that made the playing interesting and also built up the fingers with speed, velocity and muscles. I practiced out of that book for years. Through Hannon's book I basically learned how to play my scales and my chords and that was all there was to learning the basics.

One of the musicians from Kansas City, Clifford Jenkins, who played tenor sax heard me playing the exercises and said – "you are playing Hannon", and even though I was struggling he said I could play with the band. Clifford said, "If you can play out of Hannon you can do it with us." Right then he wrote some notes on some music manuscript paper and told me to play it. I stumbled and barely made it through, and made a thousand mistakes but he assured me that I was ready for the band. He then gave me chords to play and I played those so easy that I was surprising myself. He called over Sonny Little , who played the bass; Sonny started playing a blues walk and I was playing with him and I couldn't believe it. Clifford explained that was what practicing does. From that day on he told me to practice with others and not just myself, which I did from that day on. I saw it was not as hard as I thought because I was firmly rooted in the scales and chords and picked up everything pretty easy. Clifford also turned me on to a book called *Jazz Improvisations for Piano in 5 volumes* by John Mehegen. It was an incredible book that showed you how to apply the techniques that jazz musicians had developed over the years in playing the standards. I worked the exercises in the book and learned how to transpose a song like a George Gershwin tune into all 12 keys. If I had stuck to that pattern I would have become a better musician but I got stuck in playing my favorite keys. I developed to the point where I could play music, I could read music and I could write my own music.

I wrote songs of all types and one for Angela Davis called "Serenade for Angela", which I was able to play for her when I got out of prison. When they had the riots in Harlem over the murder of Martin Luther King I wrote a song called "Harlem is Marching Now. "When John Coltrane died I wrote "A Tribute to Trane." I also did a piece I called "Soul Sisters Strut" and I continued to write on and off even when I got out of prison. Most of my stuff was written in prison. I was following those musicians who were following the movement like John Handy who did a piece when James Meredith was trying to integrate Old Miss – the all-white college in Mississippi. The White students rioted because they didn't want this black man coming to their college. In honor of James Meredith John Handy wrote a tune entitled "Tears of Ole Miss." Less McCann and Eddie Harris did a tune called "Compared to What," which was a protest song against the Vietnam War and every damn thing else. John Coltrane did a tribute to Dr. Martin Luther King and Ornette Coleman did a very tearful anti-war jam called "Fox Hole" . Such were the times in which we lived. I decided that I wanted to make a musical contribution to the struggle, to our Black freedom movement.

I developed my musical foundation while I was in prison and I continued to use it until this day. When I came home from prison I played with professional musicians from time to time and became involved with different groups. I became involved with a number of St. Louis and Harlem musicians, but the movement always took priority. I played with the drummer the late Kenny Gouche and developed friendships with the late John Hicks (a great and talented pianist), my brother-in-law Rasul Siddik (a great trumpet player), Mickey Bass (one time bassist for the Jazz Messengers and a phenomenal composer), Harlem saxophonists Bill Saxton and Charles Davis, drummer Greg Bandy, bassist Andy McCloud, guitarist Marvin Horne and a flood of others. I also became friends with Roy Ayers, a famous African American musician and probably one of the most financially successful jazz musicians other than Miles Davis. I had the honor and privilege of being around him and doing some journalistic writing for him. As you can see the music didn't take me away from the movement but it brought me to it in a different way and I always put the movement first. Nothing was more important to me than the struggle for African American freedom. I saw people put their lives on the line. Also when Malcom X was killed I did a piece for him – with words and music:

Goodbye precious memories
Unwanted agonies
Deep in my heart.
At last I'm free to be
 what I have longed to be
Deep in my heart.

It was a very sad piece and evidence of the fact that I was starting to feel through music or learning how to express my feelings through the music. When my father died I did the same thing. The guys in the joint with whom I was playing loved my music because of the depth of the emotions I was able to express. Even though I was imprisoned I was able to express through music my feelings and dreams. Art is about feelings and living and reflecting the human condition . Music is spiritually very intimate and I would even go so far as to say more than any of the other arts. Everyone does music unlike painting –or sculpting or writing, music is more communal – it's a broader collective enterprise in that everyone engages in music – even those without talent, it is the most engaging art there is. There are a lot of feelings and emotions that come out of daily life that is expressed in music and dancing and music relates to everything about human life, from sexual-mating to war; you name a human situation and music is in it.

An interesting phenomenon took place in the history of jazz – during the civil war African Americans played in the military bands.

They were playing march music and so jazz was heavily influenced by that because jazz is done in the same meter as military music. Also march music is played in weddings, funerals, parades – everywhere. Music played a major role in my spiritual development because I was a person who did not want to feel so music gave me an opportunity to feel without making myself vulnerable to other human beings. I could play music and feel safe. It became a coping mechanism for me.

Philosophy for the Oppressed

I want to talk about this because it happened in two phases of my life and is very much related to my music. Before I went to prison I was exposed to the beat movement and through them I learned about and became interested in Zen Buddhism and it became my philosophical pathway to atheism. Because I saw that Buddhists didn't believe in God yet they were spiritual. They believed in peace, in love and all these other great human qualities that go into the making of decent human beings. As a result of my exposure to them I came to the conclusion that it was possible to have a religion without having a personal or anthropomorphic God. It didn't occur to me to ask Buddhists if they considered themselves religious. When I got to prison I was self-loathing over the fact that I was 19 years old and sentenced to life and 50 years and with no idea of how I was going to get out of this. When I came in through the main prison gate I could see over the gate the quote from Dante's *Inferno*: "All who enter here leave all hope behind."

I wasn't going to follow that suggestion. I could not leave all hope behind. My music kept hope alive in me. I got a lot of spiritual or intellectual guidance and solace from music. I would listen to songs like "Don't Get Scared" by King Pleasure:

When you see danger facing you
Little boy don't get scared
When you see danger facing you
Little boy don't you dare scare
When you see danger facing you
Little fella let me tellya what I want you to do.

I want you to go right along
Go on give a little, take a little

'til you get that break
Don't be a knuckle-head and make the same mistake.

Now I know you never read
But remember what is said
Rather than live your life out in broken-hearted sorrow
You'd be better off dead........

I was singing this in my jail cell to encourage myself to fight and in a way I felt like that little scared boy in the song. However, when I started reading I started discovering things about people that showed me that I was not all that unique in my suffering and experience but that I was a part of the human suffering that affected millions of people. The first great book I read was the novel written by Victor Hugo – *Les Miserables* – 800 pages and it wasn't big writing. I couldn't put it down.

There was a prisoner who referred me to that book. It had an immediate and dramatic impact on my perspective on life. The main character, Jean Val Jean gets 20 years in prison for breaking into a bakery to steal bread to feed a hungry child. For this desperate criminal act he was sentenced to be a galley slave, meaning he had to work in the galley of a ship chained to his seat while under the lash using the oars with other galley slaves to drive the ship. The book was so vividly written that it kicked up my emotions, resonating in me feelings I had when I first entered into prison – automatically I was identifying with him – with that very low life– a wretched man living a wretched life driven by fear and desperation and totally devoid of shame and morality.

He met a priest who gives him a break like I did when I met Father Clarke in City Jail. He committed a criminal act with the priest – he stole silver candlestick holders from the priest driven by hunger from poverty. When the police take him back to the priest, the priest says he didn't steal the candlestick holders but that he gave them to Jean Val Jean and then the priest said he really meant to give him the gold candlestick holders. Here was a decent man who gave this wretched man a chance and then told him he would have to continue these kind, decent acts and pass them on. That changed Jean's life and he helped other wretched, poor people – prisoners of starvation like himself to get out of their misery. I wanted to be like Jean Val Jean – I saw a way out of my pain – to help other people – who were also in pain. I didn't have far to look – looking at my cell mates – so I started asking myself how I could help – what could I do? I didn't have any answers but after I read the book I made a pledge to myself that I would find a way. I started reading other books. In *Les Miserables* Hugo talked about Philiosophes –they were the people of the French Enlightenment – the great writers and thinkers of the French Enlightenment – so I started reading these people. I was very fortunate to find some of these writers in the prison library. I would pay the guys with cigarettes to get certain books for me. I started building my own library with the works of Diderot, Voltaire, Rousseau and others. From the French I started reading the English, mainly Sir Francis Bacon, John Locke, and John Hobbs. I gravitated towards the materialists and empiricists – then I read an excellent book by Frederick Paulsen – *Introduction to Philosophy* – as I have previously stated, in my opinion this was one of the best books. Germans had a way about them that was different from the French and English. They were determined to reconcile the basic contradiction of materialism and idealism, religion and science. Hence, Paulsen talked about all of the various branches and trends of philosophy in a way that made it easy for a lay person to understand. It gave you a history of idealism and materialism which were the two basic streams and everything else were just offshoots. Through Paulsen I met Hegel - who took all of the philosophical systems that ever were and (in his opinion) could be and put them into a dialectical system and summed it up by declaring that all that is real is rational and all that is rational is real. He ended the dichotomy between mind and matter – the spirit and the world. I didn't quite understand him because I was reading him through Paulsen but I really liked Hegel. So here I was wandering around this philosophical and metaphysical landscape in search of a pathway to freedom from ignorance and superstition and the futility of philosophical speculation. I was in search of a real positive science capable of dealing with the human struggle to end man's inhumanity to man.

I went back to Jean Jacques Rousseau's *Discourse on the Origin and Basis of Inequality Among Men*, whose opening statement is: "Men are born free but are everywhere in chains...." Starting with the philosophical fiction of the "noble savage", that is, man in his natural state unencumbered by the restraints of his fellows "Man" is a self-loving and compassionate creature. Driven by self-preservation first and foremost humanity's key to survival lies in self-love and pity acting together. If the natural condition of humanity was equality then how did inequality come about?" Rousseau explains:

The first man who, having fenced in a piece of land, said "This is mine," and found people naïve enough to believe him, that man was the true founder of civil society. From how many crimes, wars, and murders, from how many horrors and misfortunes might not any one have saved mankind, by pulling up the stakes, or filling up the ditch, and crying to his fellows: Beware of listening to this impostor; you are undone if you once forget that the fruits of the earth belong to us all, and the earth itself to nobody. I chose to believe that Rousseau was calling for revolution and overthrowing the powers that be but unlike Diderot, who was saying until the last priest and last king are dead man will never be free, he cringed before the ruling class. Francois Babeuf was another one I liked – he was probably the first communist that came out of the French Revolution. He was beheaded during the reign of the right wing, Thermidorian terror and he was said to have been a disciple of Sylvan Marechal who wrote *The Manifesto of Equals* which declared:

EQUALITY! The first wish of nature, the first need of man, the first knot of all legitimate association! People of France! You were not more blessed than the other nations that vegetate on this unfortunate globe! Everywhere and at all times the poor human race, handed over to more or less deft cannibals, served as an object for all ambitions, as feed for all tyrannies. Everywhere and at all times men were lulled with beautiful words; at no time and in no place was the thing itself ever obtained through the word. From time immemorial they hypocritically repeat; all men are equal,; and from time immemorial the most degrading and monstrous inequality insolently weighs upon the human race. As long as there have been human societies the most beautiful of humanity's rights is recognized without contradiction, but was only able to be put in practice one time: equality was nothing but a beautiful and sterile legal fiction. And now that it is called for with an even stronger voice we are answered: be quiet, you wretches! Real equality is nothing but a chimera; be satisfied with conditional equality; you're all equal before the law. What more do

*you want, filthy rabble? Legislators, you who hold power, rich
landowners, it is now your turn to listen.*

*PEOPLE OF FRANCE; By what sign will you now recognize the
excellence of a constitution? ...That which rests in its entirety
on real equality is the only one that can suit you and fulfill all
your wishes. The aristocratic charters of 1791 and 1795 tightened your chains instead of breaking them. That of 1793 was
a great step towards true equality, and we had never before
approached it so closely. But it did not yet touch the goal, nor
reach common happiness, which it nevertheless solemnly conse-
crated as its great principle.*

*PEOPLE OF FRANCE, Open your eyes and your hearts to the full-
ness of happiness: recognize and proclaim with us the REPUBLIC
OF EQUALS.*

Babeuf and Marechal were saying – we are all equal are we not?
The only thing that kept people unequal was government. If there
was going to be a social contract between the government and
the people then the people had the right to overthrow the existing
government and create a new government based the consent of
the people. Babeuf and Marechal were agreeing with Rousseau regarding the source of inequality but they went further to the left,
declaring that the people had the right to overthrow the government and the rich landowners. They even went to the left of the
American Revolution of 1776, which was basically a revolution of
rich landowners and slave-holders in the thirteen colonies.

I started seeing the relationship between government and politics. The French were teaching me that there are different classes
in society and that one class' political and property rights was often based on depriving another class of their rights, that is, class
oppression. The French saw this very clearly. I think Hegel did too,
but in his political philosophy he didn't really come out against
oppression – he certainly describes it in discussing the relationship between the bondsman and the nobleman in his book Phe-
nomenology of Mind. The relationship between the nobleman and
the bond-slave is such that the nobleman never experiences the
raw untamed aspect of reality. The nobleman experiences only
the tamed aspects of reality (such as silk sheets, clothes, elegant
furniture, castle, etc.) . All the sweat and blood that went into

creating his tame comforts – was at the expense of the blood, sweat and tears of another. Hegel understood the relationship between the oppressor and the oppressed but he didn't see the oppressed rising up and overthrowing their oppressors it was the French who saw that. Hegel was a great thinker and in many ways a benefactor of the French Enlightenment but he was tied to the German ruling class, Prussian absolutism, so all he did was pay lip service to the revolution.

It was during this period of my development that I met a guy in prison named Ulysses Grant Thompson. As I have previously stated, he told me he was a communist and he was a Teamster. The first person I met in prison who declared himself a communist was Wilson Jones, but he was not connected to any movement. Grant was different. He was in prison for allegedly trying to blow up a truck during a strike. Grant said to me that I am going to give you some stuff to read – one of them called *A Handbook on Marxism* edited by Emile Burns – now life was making sense to me – a combination of politics and philosophy that was about the liberation of oppressed people –this is what I had been looking for.

One of the first pieces in this book is the *Manifesto of the Communist Party* which says that the history of all hitherto existing societies is the history of class struggles, sometimes hidden – sometimes open – but always there between oppressor and the oppressed. And it is this struggle that leads to revolution which in turn leads to a reconstruction of society. That is where philosophy took me – like music it took me right back into the struggle. Now I was no longer caught up in studying about how the human brain processes human knowledge – the meaning of meaning and worshiping the God of Reason. Now I wanted to focus on the knowledge of science and how it can be used to liberate people – to create a better world and I thought that Marx and Engles had the right idea – the only way it could be brought about was through revolution and I couldn't see this as anything different than what Thomas Jefferson espoused. It was a question of revolution for whom and for what. For Jefferson it was for landlords, merchants, and slave-holders

Writing for the Struggle

All this time I was reading – I was writing – notes, essays, putting my thoughts on paper. I started sending this writing outside the prison. I started writing a book on Science and Africa where I could devastate the white supremacists by showing that people of color especially in Africa, made tremendous contributions to science and mathematics. I was looking at all of the different branches of science, chemistry, physics, astronomy, the social sciences in search of historical evidence that would prove that science was not the invention of the white man – it was going on in China, Asia and Africa for thousands of years and if the human race began in Africa it only made sense that human thinking began there as well. It was intellectual, white chauvinism on the part of some Europeans to believe that science and philosophy was something they alone created. The Greeks didn't say they founded mathematics – it was during the colonial era of European expansion that these Eurocentric ideas were pushed. The Greeks acknowledged their debt to Asia, to the Egyptians, Babylonians and Phoenicians. Those people of color had civilizations long before the Greeks came on the scene.

Benjamin Farrington was a Marxist historian from Ireland. Farrington wrote a book entitled *Science and Politics in the Ancient World* where he showed it was European chauvinism at its worst that attributed the origin of western civilization to the Greeks and put forth the notion that all advanced ideas came from Europe. This is what Farrington demonstrated through his research. But there were other British scholars doing great work in this area. For example, there was Joseph Needham's *Science and Civilization in China*, Lancelot Hogben's *Mathematics for the Millions* and J.D. Bernal's *Science in History*. These books encouraged me to write a history of science in Africa.

I began to see where I could make a contribution in these areas and I had my first article published in *Freedomways Magazine* in the summer of 1966 and the article is entitled 'Science and Africa." *Freedomways* was the quarterly magazine of the Negro Freedom Movement. Jack O'Dell and John Henrik Clarke wrote short introductions to my article. The article was also referenced in several publications, including The Journal Of Negro Education and the book *Africa Counts* by Claudia Zaslavsky Once again I am back in the movement. As I have previously stated earlier *Freedomways* gave the first national exposure of my case and was the first to call for my freedom. Through all of my wanderings I found my way to the key that would get me out of prison which was the Negro Freedom Movement which later would develop into the Black Liberation movement. Since my first publication in 1966, 48 years ago I have been writing for the struggle through numerous left, labor and progressive periodical publications.

Road To Freedom Continued

I was getting my associates degree in Mobley and the parole board said they would automatically parole me to the University of Missouri in Rolla Missouri to become a candidate for my degree. But it would be a very conditional parole – a study release – only for me to be on that campus and only for me to study. I could get furloughs for the week ends from Friday night to Sunday.

The Parole Board called me up for a review and what they said was that within the next month or so I would be getting my associates degree. I was due to graduate in May of 1973. The Board said that they would keep their part of the contract and put me in the study release program at Rolla but they said there was a problem with the funding. I would have to put up some of my tuition and living expenses because the block grant did not come through sufficiently to cover the seven people they normally send. They had to cut back some of the funding. They could help me with the stipend but I was on my own with respect to my tuition until the vocational rehab block grant came through. I had a choice of waiting until the grant came through, possibly the following year. Or, I could start in the fall and raise my own tuition money from my friends on the outside. In short they would release me in the Fall to go to school in Rolla if I could raise money to pay my tuition for the Fall semester.

Of course, I wanted to leave there as soon as I could. I asked them if I could get back to the board within a week or so with an answer and they agreed but told me to hurry up. I reached out to Hershell Walker and My lawyer Arley R. Woodrow and explained the situation. They said they could easily raise the money for me if the prison officials would release me on a furlough for the weekend so I could attend a fund raising event. Furloughs were permitted only as part of a pre-release plan.

Hershell told me that a white couple, Virginia and Russell Brodine, were on my defense committee now. Russell was a violinist in the

St. Louis symphony and his wife Virginia was an environmentalist and writer who worked with Barry Commoner at Washington University. Commoner was an icon in the environmentalist movement but I came to find out later that Virginia was the brains that kept him moving and writing several famous books on the subject. She was also a communist and a tireless supporter of the Black Liberation Movement.

I went back to the parole board knowing that they would say no because there was no way in hell they would give me a furlough. I told them exactly what my lawyer and Hershel told me about the Brodines, except I never mentioned that they were Reds. Someone with the Board checked the Brodines out and then they asked me for a phone number which I did not have. But the Board found that they were listed and apparently spoke to them. The Brodines in turn gave the Parole Board several other names of supporters at Washington University, including the Dean, who were interested in my case and in helping me to get out. They (the Brodines) said they could raise money and get people involved if the Parole Board would let me out on a furlough. The Parole Board agreed. I was totally and utterly shocked. How could this happen when a year ago these people were treating me like an animal?

The pace of my journey was increasing at a speed I was not expecting. In 1971 I went back to court seeking review of my case and a post-conviction remedy. In 1971 I was also brutalized and sent to Eddyville Prison in Kentucky and stayed there until 1972. In 1972 I came back to Missouri and ended up at Mobley and in 1973 they are talking about furloughing me. That was a head twister. But in addition to all this Hershel was telling me that a new organization was founded in the Spring of 1973 calling itself the National Alliance Against Racist and Political Repression. Hershel said this organization was headed up by Angela Davis and Charlene Mitchell and that he had raised my case with them and they had vowed to get me out. I was excited because freedom seemed eminent but at the same time incredulous that things were happening so fast.

I contacted Herschel and told him that they were willing to give me a furlough and they even suggested a date of a week end in May, about a month before I would graduate. Herschel told me "I will be there to pick you up that Friday morning and by the time we return you on Sunday, we will have your college tuition."

Mobley is about a 2 ½ hour drive to St. Louis. Herschell was there that Friday at 9 am on the dot. They had me sitting in the control center upon his arrival and from the time he arrived they took me to the front gate and let me out with my furlough papers. It had been 12 years since I had been on the outside.

I cannot even describe how I felt. This wasn't even freedom, it was just a taste. But the fact that they let me out of that gate with a guy who was a Communist and a leader of a radical political movement to free Angela Davis was mind boggling. I was, without very much success, still trying to process all of this mentally. I just told Herschel "I am glad to see you". He responded,"We are going to get you home". This was the first time I ever met him in the flesh. He was a very average looking elder with salt and pepper gray hair and glasses – kind of reminded me of a Black preacher. He had a distinguished look about him, yet humble. When he spoke he was even more humble. I had never heard Herschel speak as I had been dealing with him only through our letters. He led me to the car and said "come on we have lots to talk about." And boy did we have lots to talk about.

This man was very organized. He had a list of things to do. First thing was to go to my mother's house and spend a few hours with her. Everything he told me to do, I did. After that he told me I would have appointments with the media. There was a black woman who had recently gotten a job as a reporter for channel 5 – Robin Smith. We have an appointment with her. He told me that I was making history and people knew it. He said I was the first person in the history of the Missouri prison system who had ever received a furlough to go out and raise money to go to college. This is truly remarkable and he said don't think about it being just a great break for me but a door opener for hundreds of other prisoners who might be able to get out as well. This might be a whole new way to rehabilitate and re socialize prisoners in the future so a lot was depending on me.

We talked for hours about political stuff. I was very curious about how Angela Davis was doing with her new found freedom. He told me I would have an opportunity to meet her. I just listened to all of the amazing things he was saying. Now believing him, now realizing this wasn't just a fantasy. In short measure we ended up in front of my mother's house. Herschel got out and my mother was on the front porch. He said, "Mrs. Chapman I just brought your son home". My mother and sisters ran out and embraced me crying out, "Praise the Lord." They prepared one hell of a meal for me, which is how my family shows their love. We had a nice 2 hours to talk while they cooked for an army. I ate to my heart's content. We talked with my baby brother Darryll and my baby sister Fontina who were born while I was in prison. They all came to see me, sisters, brothers, cousins, aunts and uncles. This was truly a tremendous moment. Everyone was very happy. There was crying but they were tears of joy. After a few hours Herschel stepped in and told my mom that he had to take me because I had some important people to meet and things to do. My mother thanked Mr. Walker. I have never seen my mother as happy as she was that day.

We went to downtown St. Louis and I had an interview with Robin Smith in the park across the street from Channel 5 news building. The interview dealt with questions about the type of furlough I was on and the program allowing prisoners to go to college. In short I explained that I was in a study release program that only had been in existence for a few years. The idea was to use block grant funds to constructively re-educate and re-socialize prisoners to become productive members of society again. I was very honored and grateful to be chosen for this program even though they could not pay my tuition. She told me my case was one of the most serious cases being considered for study release because I had been convicted of a capital crime. She asked me if this held out hope for other prisoners who had been convicted of capital crimes and who were trying to rehabilitate and get back into society. I told her I thought it was and we had formed a group inside the prison called Lifers Inc. The purpose of the group would be to encourage prisoners to get involved with whatever rehabilitative programs were offered – taking the pathway to change which would be the only way they could get out. On that note we ended the interview.

Next we went to several radio stations. One of them was the disc jockey Ty Wansley. He had a very popular show in St. Louis and he was very popular. The interview with him was similar to the one with Robin Smith. What kind of program was study release? Was it designed to rehabilitate so that the prisoners could enter society as productive citizens? We went to about 5 or 6 radio shows which finally ended at 5pm. Then Herschel recommended that I take a nap at a friend's house , Jim Burns' home. He told me that he wanted me to rest up for the big fund raiser at 7pm at the Brodine house. So I did.

The Brodine's house was a small two-story mansion with many rooms located in Westminster Place, which was an interesting area in the middle of the ghetto. It was interesting because there were middle class professionals, artists, musicians, doctors, teachers, lawyers who lived in Westminster Place and the houses were gorgeous and had been built around the turn of the 20th century. Some were small mansions while some were full blown mansions. When we arrived, there were only 2 or 3 people and it looked like a wine and cheese party gone bad. After about 30 minutes the house was packed. There was a very interesting mixture of people in this small ballroom type room with chandeliers.

There were people from the black press, *The Crusader*, the *St. Louis American* and *The Argus* newspapers. All had reporters there. In fact the publisher and CEO of the *Crusader* was there. I think his name was Rogers. The Brodines hosted the affair. The people there were environmentalists, trade unionists, Black Nationalists, academics and intellectuals, movement lawyers, Socialists and Communists. Also most importantly the physicist Dan Kohl and his wife (a brilliant anthropologist) Mina Kohl were there. Dan Kohl had talked to the Dean of Washington University about getting me a Dean's scholarship for graduate school.

They were already thinking about my academic future way ahead of me. The Dean said yes but he wanted to announce it only after I earned my BA degree. He said the Dean scholarship would only cover the cost of graduate school after I would get my BA from the University of Missouri but I would have to raise other money needed for my undergraduate studies and other things I would need. I didn't need housing because the Department of Corrections was providing housing in an old ROTC building on campus that they had leased or purchased. But I did need money for books. I also needed money for insurance for the following semester in case the Dean decided not to extend my scholarship. Because Dan Kohl was a well-respected tenured professor at the college he was able to find others who would help raise money for me. My role was to speak to them and convince them that I was worthy of their support – at least that is what I thought my role was. I could not get out of prison without it. So I started out on that track telling them why it was important to help me go to school and how it was directly related to my getting out of prison. Without them I could not get out.

There was a black civil rights activist there named Percy Green who interrupted me. He was a very militant activist and he got up and said "Frank, you don't have to convince us that you are worthy of our support – we know that! What you need to tell us is how we can help you. What do you need? How much money do we need to raise?" I looked at Hershel and said I don't know I haven't figured that out. Hershel suggested $5,000. We felt if I could go back to the Parole Board with the promise of a Dean Scholarship and $5,000 that would do it to get me out. Hershel looked around the room and said, "Okay, now we know what we have to do so let's start writing checks. A few hours later when I left that room we had nearly $10,000. So, this all happened on Friday, my first day out.

Hershel took me to my mother's house that night and I crashed. By 10 am Saturday morning Hershel was back in front of my mother's house and telling her to send me out to his car. He told me we had a lot of work to do. I asked him if it would be as much as yesterday and he said it would be worse. We met many people all day long. We met with a group of local writers for *Proud Magazine*, a black magazine promoting civil rights. We met with several civil rights groups that I spoke briefly before. We met the National Conference of Black Lawyers group. I spoke to them about prisoner reform. I met with the American Friends Service Committee which is a Quaker based organization involved in civil rights, prison reform and the abolition of the death penalty. They were interested in my case. I met with some local youth groups who were trying to organize on the campuses. I met with the some Black youth organizations – they wanted to know what messages I had for the youth in terms of staying out of prison. I told them that what helped me while I was in prison was being involved in the struggle for Black Liberation and socialism and that was what I suggested that they do, get involved in the movement in a constructive way. The best way to deal with prison was not to get in it.

So Saturday was about meeting with political and religious leaders and other organizations that were involved in our struggle for justice and getting me free. I thanked them all for their support.

I met with Deverne Calloway, the assemblywoman who supported us in our civil rights movement inside the prison. I met with her and her husband, Ernest Calloway, who had been an African American labor leader with the United Mine Workers Union and also had been an educational director with the Teamsters. He was teaching urban studies at St Louis University. In fact, he created that department. That topped off my day. After I met them it was back to my mother's house again for another long sleep. Hershcel told me that I could sleep my head off since Sunday would be a day of rest as we did not have to be back at the prison until 9 pm. So I spent a lovely day with my family looking at their photo albums and being updated. Also family from all over St. Louis came over to welcome me home and tell me how proud they were that I had finally done something with my life.

At the end of the day Herschel came back around 6:30 in the evening and I said my goodbyes to my family and we headed back to Moberly Missouri. We returned to Moberly at 8:30 or 8:45pm. My furlough was officially over and I was returned to my cell/room. All I could think about that night was that I was going to get out of prison. I could not believe I was going to get out. It had been a long 12 year journey. But I knew I was not going to get completely out. I was going into a study release program that was highly conditional. If I messed up in any way, like my grades falling or I got a traffic ticket, I would be returned to prison. There would not be any due process, I would just be brought in, even if they just thought I had violated a rule. I was willing to take the risk because I thought once I got past those gates and was released into society, I would never return. I was determined to get free. Those were my thoughts that night and for the following months leading up to my graduation. I just applied myself and was on my best behavior. After I graduated in late June, all I did from that point until late August was to prepare myself for getting released to the University campus in Rollo, Missouri. But nothing could prepare me for that day when I would be released.

Sometime in August the person who was in charge of the ROTC people came up to get me. He was a young white man. He asked me if I had everything and I told him I did. He said I was traveling mighty light. I told him I didn't have much and all I wanted were the few books I didn't give away. When we arrived at Rolla I saw my friend Pat Glover, a brother named John Young and Jessie Curry, Pat Snyder, Bill Dykus, and Jimmy Michaels. We were a motley lot. African Americans, Italian, Greek, Anglo Saxons – about half white and half black. Those guys in that environment and out of prison were like different men. It is amazing what a more wholesome environment and humane treatment can do to make changes that people deep in their hearts want to make. Most people in prisons aren't there because they want to be but they are there because they are living in forced destitution and poverty. They welcome changes because it is a viscous cycle which continues until they die or the system burns them out. So these guys saw themselves as breaking the cycle. We didn't sit around talking about it, it was just a latent fact of life. We knew that others in prison were counting on us to break the cycle and carry the torch to do good for us and the brothers we left behind in prison. I must say that most of those guys carried the torch well. I only saw a few instances of anyone being returned to prison. Most of them graduated from school and never returned to prison. This program worked until reactionary politicians abolished it. This was a huge turning point in my life. Life would soon take on new meaning and I was being given the opportunity to prove myself and that I could cut the mustard. And I was very happy about that. This was how I entered the University of Missouri in the fall of 1973.

Block in the Road to Freedom

So here I was at the famous school of mines in Rolla, Missouri. Missouri University in Rolla was known as the school of mines because it turned out a large core of engineers who specialized in mining and geology. My first semester was surprisingly not very trying. I don't remember the courses I took but I remember taking a full 18 hours. Since I realized that the quicker I finished school the sooner I was going to get a parole. I did not come to mess around. I jumped right into my studies and to my surprise it was not difficult. All those years of reading while I was in prison paid off. I thought this was going to be more difficult than Moberly because I was in my junior year now. But actually it seemed easier because it was mainly about studying and writing a lot of term papers. I had developed some writing skills so once I mastered the format for the writing of term papers it was easy. Also, the fact that I was into my favorite subject, history, helped.

The most challenging thing that happened while I was studying at UM occurred in the second semester. I took some mandatory courses in Medieval history which proved to be quite challenging as I didn't know much about this, so I had to start from the beginning. I had written off the Middle Ages as the Dark Ages where heretics were burned at the stake or confined to torture chambers. I was surprised to learn that there was really a rather complex political structure replete with institutions of higher learning (universities and monasteries) based on a social and economic order of serfs, craftsmen, lords, noblemen, clergy and philosophers. Also in this period of history there was a flourishing Islamic civilization which through trade, commerce and conquest interacted with Europe and held firm control of the Mediterranean basin for nearly 700 years. It was new information that I had to digest.

There was another challenging course I took from a Professor Erwin Epstein. This was a study about the changing relationship between teacher and student in colonized countries. The course was centered around a book written by Paulo Friere, a Brazilian teacher/philosopher. The name of the book was *Pedagogy of the Oppressed* and it was first published in 1968 and translated into English in 1970. Professor Epstein was one of many professors who considered Friere a revolutionary and thought his work was firmly rooted in a Marxist analysis of colonial society.

I ran into a very serious problem in this course because Epstein was claiming that this was a revolutionary book that was like the handbook for liberation in Latin America. I strongly disagreed with that because this author while a potent intellectual, was not really talking to the oppressed but to the intellectual community which he was a part of. Although the book was in large measure based on his experience teaching Brazilian adults to read and write, Friere used very scholarly language steeped in philosophical abstraction. It was difficult reading. Not because it was profound like Hegel or Marx but more like someone who reads lots of philosophical works and valiantly attempts to present an amalgam of divergent philosophies. But he was not synthesizing it in any dialectical sense. His work, in my opinion, was nothing but eclectic, philosophical patchwork with a focus on education.

We exchanged our views sometimes over dinner at the Professor's house. Due mainly to my own intellectual arrogance exchanges were often vigorous but due to Dr. Epstein's amiable demeanor they were never hostile.

Epstein strongly disagreed with my views on the subject so he asked me to do a critique of *Pedagogy of the Oppressed*. I accepted his offer and proceeded to write a critique. I took the position that Freire was claiming to be a Marxist but that in fact he was just another philosopher believing that a new paradigm would lead to a change in the objective social relations between oppressor and oppressed thus bringing about a new world order. This was not Marxism, for Marxism starts from the premise that objective social relations determine subjective evaluation.

Confronted with such profound ignorance of Marxism in academic circles I was really starting to wonder if this was characteristic of higher education in the United States. Outside of Communist scholars like Herbert Aptheker and anti-communist scholars like Daniel Bell it seemed as though no one was seriously studying Marxism. Of course, these perceptions were based on my own inexperience at the time and many of them were corrected in the course of me doing this critique. For example, in my research I learned about "*Science and Society*", a Marxist quarterly magazine and "*Political Affairs*", the theoretical journal of the Communist Party. Through these publications I began to learn that there were Marxist scholars in various universities who were dedicated to advancing correct ideas about Marxism. But even so many of the professors and intellectuals at the universities had a very superficial acquaintance with Marxism and it came out in their writings.

So I was disturbingly surprised that Freire was passing himself off as a Marxist and that was what I focused on in my critique of *Pedagogy for the Oppressed.* I criticized him from the standpoint of historical materialism. I did this long piece showing that Marxism is not merely an interpretation of history but that Marx sought to put history on a scientific basis by not writing history based on ideas alone or the development of human consciousness but by writing history based on the production of material life (i.e. food, shelter, tools, etc.). Here let's let Marx speak for himself, said he: "The mode of production of material life condi-

tions the social, political and intellectual life process in general. It is not the consciousness of men that determines their being, but on the contrary, their social being that determines their consciousness."
"

In other words what made social existence possible was production—exchange and distribution—consumption. Without the means to make food and shelter, etc., no form of social existence could be sustained. This is what constituted the material basis of society, the foundation of culture, traditions and all the institutions that make up society. In other words ideas and philosophical beliefs developed on a material basis and that basis was the way in which people made their living – the economy. Marx was basically saying that the economic structure of society determines how that society functions in all other ways and that the political structure of society, with its institutional arrangements, develops to reinforce and to rationalize existing social conditions. Marx's doctrine, which sets forth the principles of historical materialism, is the only scientific sociology that lays bare the general active relation of the ideological products with each other and the economic conditions of concrete living.

Paulo Freire was going in the opposite direction. He was saying that it was peoples' ideas that could determine how they lived, that we could think our way out of oppression and into correct practice. Marx laid to rest this democratic superstition when he pointed out that people do not choose the circumstances into which they are born but they can change them.

I turned the paper in to Epstein and he said it was very good. Yet he had me re-write it several times. Then he said he was going to submit it for publication and I told him I did not have a problem with that. He submitted it to some periodical publication on history, and I don't remember which one. He showed me an edited copy of it and he was the sole author. He wanted to publish my paper under his name. I was shocked. When I confronted him about this he said he gave me an A+ and he literally helped me rewrite the article and had a lot to do with the finished product so he had no qualms taking the by-line. He said that was the only way it could get published because I didn't have any credibility or recognition in the academic world. He said I should see it as a sign of encouragement. But I was too angry to see how this was something I should be grateful for because my ego was involved. He wasn't even a Marxist and I could not understand how he could publish something from a Marxist perspective. I was also disappointed because he was a professor and I had had such high respect for professors based on my experience while in prison that I could not picture any of them doing something like this. It was a total lack of scruples – it really lowered my esteem for professors.

I became anti-academic. I started seeing universities as big intellectual farces where people were just trying to get prestige – to hell with the truth. From this point on I became a nuisance in the classrooms by trying to expose the professors by showing that there were other interpretations that they should be including and exposing the students to. Surprisingly enough this opposition did not interfere with my ability to get good grades. Going into my second year I quit taking school seriously. I saw it as an intellectual way of propping up the status quo. Again, this is the real world I was in. While in prison I had seen professors as credible intellectuals, but I was not meeting these kinds of people outside in the university. They just wanted to keep the status quo and to be politically correct. They were not about being critical of society. I got involved with some students there who were also of like mind who also felt they were being intellectually cheated and were pushing for more radical or leftist teaching.

The Black students were pushing for Black studies to be included in the curriculum. American history was presented from a white ruling class perspective. It was not a people's history but one showing and glorifying how the money barons got rich by exploiting workers, enslaving Africans and cheating and killing Native Americans. Around this time, I also joined the Mid-West Marxist Scholars Conference which was founded by the late physicist Erwin Marquit and other members of the Communist Party who were also professors. And I regularly corresponded with the American Institute for Marxist Studies (AIMS) founded by Herbert Aptheker.

We started putting out our own newsletter on campus. We started agitating for minority studies program. They did set up a program for black engineering students because many of them were unprepared in mathematics. These students, mainly from ill-equipped schools in the ghetto, did not have the proper background or foundation in mathematics needed for engineering studies. Therefore, they had a special program for them. They asked me if I would be willing to be a tutor in the minority engineering program. I didn't understand how I could teach this when I was a history major. But they reminded me that I knew basic math (algebra, geometry, trigonometry, and calculus). I agreed to a trial run to see if I could help.

I was thinking we finally got the administration to hear us. These students were housed in separate housing in what seemed like preferential treatment, but it wasn't; it was really segregation. The white students had been in separate housing all the time. The University claimed they were helping the minority students with this so-called preferential treatment. They gave them separate housing and classrooms. I got involved because I too thought they were helping the students. We completed one semester and grades went up. I became personally involved with some of the students like, Simeon, Margaret and Sharon. I became friends with them because I was the only black teacher they had. All of the professors were white on campus. These students really wanted to learn and excel and they studied hard. Most of them started making good grades and saw there was nothing mysterious about math and that all they had to do was apply themselves.

However, even after the students caught up they were still in separate classes. This made no sense to me so I began to ask the professor who was in charge of this. I found out when he held his classes and asked him why they didn't have classes with white and black students. He told me it was so the black students could catch up. I told him I did not understand since this was an integrated campus why whites and blacks were still separated like in segregation but he insisted it was not segregation but affirmative action.

At the time this was going on there was a big controversy about affirmative action in the society at large. People were saying Blacks people usually scored lower in academic tests because they came from oppressed social conditions or were just naturally inferior. There was the Moynihan Report (*The Negro Family: The Case for National Action*, 1965) and a whole train of scholars who were saying black people were unable to compete in college with whites because they came from an inferior culture. In fact, these were old arguments grounded in the racist sociology set forth by Abram Kardiner and Lionel Ovesey in a book entitled *Mark of Oppression* – their thesis was based on the theory that African Americans had been oppressed for so long they were mentally incapable of competing with white people.

To me this just seemed to be another justification for segregation. With that I quit the tutoring and we started organizing black students to press the administration to have the black and white engineering students in the same classroom. The response of the correctional officer, who was over us, to all this was not good. Remember that I am still in the department of corrections in a study release program. The corrections officer was the only prison authority at the ROTC building, which is where we were housed. He was like a prison guard. We had to report our activities to him and he said I was not to get involved with the black student groups and stated that I was doing the same stuff I was doing in prison. "We didn't send you down here to start trouble", he shouted. I told him he was giving me too much credit and that it was the black students who were agitating. But I didn't see how I was violating the contract since I was still a student and just participating in student activities. He told me it was not a student activity that was approved by the administration, so I would have to quit or be returned to prison.

This presented a problem. I spoke with the students about this so we had to figure out a way do get around this. We would not hold meetings on campus and any meetings with the administration would not include me. I didn't want to do this but I did. Eventually the ROTC corrections officer found out that I was attending the meetings off campus and told me he was going to have to send me back. I denied participating in these activities. He asked around campus at student affairs and professors and they all said that the group was not involved on campus and had not been picketing or protesting. They felt that what we did off campus was nothing they could control.

The students however felt they should protest and present their demands on campus. The professor for whom I did the tutoring came and asked me if I would be part of the negotiations with regard to the black engineering students being a part of the regular engineering classes. I told him no. I knew it was a trap. I knew if I did that, the next day I would be back in prison. I told him I would only be a part of the tutoring if they were returning the black students after they were tutored into regular classes. I would not be a part of the negotiations. The next semester they kept the tutoring program and black students were being given the full curriculum same as the white students. We even saw one student go into physics as his major. That was the most controversial thing that happened to me while in Rolla.

I did have a multi-dimensional life. I was going home every week end to St. Louis. I was participating in community activities, such as the W.E. B. Dubois club. We had a study group on Marxism and also discussed community issues. The big thing the community was struggling with was budget cuts affecting education and CETA (Comprehensive Employment Training Act) programs that had been helpings black youth develop basic skills. They were talking about eliminating summer programs – summer youth work programs. Some comrades I had met (like Jay Ozier and James Robnett) were working to create an organization called Community Youth United for Jobs to press for these issues. James Robnett was also a leader of the Young Workers Liberation League.

I also worked on prison reform. We had a death penalty in Missouri that was racially discriminatory – proportionately more blacks were executed than whites. But blacks were only about 10% of the population in Missouri yet consisted of 50-60% of the people who were executed. Some of the people on death row were suspect in that they gave confessions that were obtained in violation of due process. We got involved with some people called the Missouri Coalition against the Death Penalty which consisted of Margaret Phillips, the late Rev. Milt Stoh, some civil rights groups and the Lutheran Mission Association, the American Friends Service Committee as well as some Catholics like Father Zimmerman. I worked with them and went to their meetings when I could. They wanted me to do some public speaking for them, but I could not because I was still in the Dept. of Corrections. I promised to work with them upon my release. I was very limited at this time in what I could do. I tried to be involved in some kind of activity so I could get a true sense of what was going on the outside.

I should mention here that I did speak on prison reform at a Forum On Education held by the Institute of Black Studies at Washington University, St. Louis. The speech I gave was subsequently published in *Freedomways*. At this forum I had the honor of meeting the late Harlem educator, Preston Wilcox, and Sam Anderson also a great educator and community organizer from Harlem.

Brenda and I continued to write each other. They let her make phone calls and I talked to her a few times a week and kept our fire burning. She was about ready to come home and boy was I glad. She did finally come home. Before she went to Kansas City she came to Rolla, Missouri. I could not believe it, she just showed up one day. She wanted to see me before returning home to Kansas City. A friend of mine had a trailer at a trailer court so we spent some time there together. But I was really encouraging her to go home. She had 4 kids and I was still locked up. But she wanted to stay and get to know me so she could make up her mind as to if she wanted to stay with me or go back to Howard. I was all for this. We spent several nice days together and I finally took her to the Greyhound station and sent her back.

The good thing about staying active in the movement it really kept me from getting absorbed in myself. I was doing things for others and they were helping me. That helped me a lot because when Brenda was there I became self-absorbed and it was all about my feelings and the struggle took a back seat. Then she left and the struggle was back in the front seat. To tell you the truth I was happy. I knew I had to graduate or else I would never get out of prison.

Brenda asked me to come to Kansas City for some of my furloughs to meet her kids and really wanted to make a life. So I did. I hooked up with a friend of mine in St. Louis who drove me to Kansas City and Brenda and I met in a house. I came to find out, Howard, her partner before she went to prison, was a pimp who had several women. She claimed he was not her pimp but she knew where the money was coming from. But she didn't want a future with him she wanted one with me. I didn't think I could handle her life. I wanted to but I couldn't. Then she told me she was pregnant but said don't worry "I will have an abortion" because it was clear to her that my mind wasn't made up. She then wanted to know if I wanted to come to Kansas City and become a part of her life. I had to admit I had not really thought about it. I was involved in a very romantic picture of our relationship and not the practical reality of what I was really stepping into. I was heartbroken because

I knew I couldn't do this. Here I was not even out of prison yet and knew I would have to find a job, etc. I could not at this point see myself taking on marriage and her kids after I had been locked up 12 years. No, I could not fathom that. It slam dunked me.

I went back to Rolla broken hearted and sulked on it for a few days. A few days later I sent her back her pictures and wrote her a good bye letter. It was the saddest letter I had ever written. I told her I really did love her but it was a fantasy type love that had no practical end to it. I had to become re-socialized and I had no experience being in a family setting. Also I told her I planned to go to graduate school after I got out of prison. I did not have time to parent four kids between 6 and 12 and have a relationship with her. It was too overwhelming and I didn't have any answers. The only thing I knew for sure was I had to get out of prison. I had to finish school and go on to graduate and I could not do that and be a father and a husband. If I could do that, I didn't know how. It was goodbye. She wrote me back a short letter. She said she didn't read my letter because I had a way with words and when she saw the pictures she didn't have to read the letter to know it was goodbye. It was not what she wanted but she understood I had to live my life. She told me she was still open to my being her friend. But I never answered her letter. I couldn't. She was like a magnet and I knew if I were to enter her force field I would not be able to get away. I stayed away. I started to make women friends in the movement but none like Brenda.

It took a year before I became involved with another woman. There was a woman on campus named Conchita Agustus who danced and I played piano for her. She was in her late twenties and an older student like me. She was taking night classes. She had her own trailer off campus and I use to visit her. No sex was involved and we just became good friends. I played piano and she danced. We even put on some entertainment for the school.

She was a mixture of Indian, Spanish and African. She was beautiful too, including her spirit. She knew how to handle herself around men. But I never hit on her. I respected her. She had a male partner who was a captain in the army and the three of us would go out together. Of course, I had a curfew and very rarely I would stay in town on the week-ends but if I did I would stay with her. She filled up the hole Brenda left in my heart.

It's getting close to graduation now. Conchita is saying that we should do something special at my graduation on campus. The Black student organization wanted to give me a party. I graduated. I had a black gown on, a red shirt and a green tie – the colors of the black liberation movement. My mother came down with my sister Sharon. Some of the students I tutored were there also. My colleagues from the ROTC building who were my fellow students in the study release program were there also. I finished ahead of them because I took so many classes – I graduated a semester early.

In December of 1975 I graduated. The ceremony was beautiful. What I remember was that the dull part was sitting on the stage listening to the speeches and then getting my BA degree. I graduated cum laude. I didn't really hear the speeches and was glad when they were over. I was too involved with watching my family and the emotions were over coming me. I knew liberation could not be far away.

After graduation I had dinner with my family. I went to an appreciation with the black students and then I went to the ROTC building because it was almost 9pm. When I got there I saw, to my great surprise, Donald P. Wyrick, the deputy warden. He was there along with Sergeant Bogart, a prison guard. I knew something wasn't right. Why were they here. I had seen others graduate and they didn't come to their graduation. And, they had chains and handcuffs with them. I thought they were ready to take somebody back in. I didn't know it was me.

They said Chapman we have to take you back. I said, for what? They said because you are not in the study release program anymore. You still have to meet with the parole board. You have to go through the procedures, you can't just leave. I asked if I could say goodbye to some people. They gave me an hour and a half otherwise "we will consider you AWOL and call in state troopers," said Wyrick.

I went to the trailer court and told Conchita. I went with John Young who went with me for support, and I told her they were going to take me back to prison. I told her I didn't know what it was all about and that they told me it was procedure. She fell apart crying and I did not realize how deep her feelings ran for me. I told her it wasn't that bad, even though I knew it was bad. She told me I was like a brother to her and she loved me and told me she would be there wherever they take me. I told her to just wait and see this through and that I just wanted to say good bye and assured her I would continue to keep in touch and write her. I told her not to change the course of her life because of me. She said that it was too late and she would be there – the course of her life had already been changed.

I made it back in time. They chained me and took me, and Jimmy Michaels back and I felt very betrayed. I was afraid they were going to lock me up for good. I tried to talk to them on the drive back but they were very tight lipped. I was sure they were going to let me taste freedom and then lock me back up. But I was wrong. When we got back they didn't take me inside the walls, but took me to Church Farm. Church Farm was a prison where they grew things – cabbage, vegetables and raised pigs, etc. It fed the prisons and it was like a slave camp. It was another ray of hope. Maybe they weren't going to keep me because Church farm was like minimum security. There weren't any walls or guard towers. I thought maybe they are planning to let me out. Then they told me that both Jimmy Michaels and I would both be going before the parole board in a few weeks.

Visiting was every Saturday and Sunday. Your visitors could bring food and sit at picnic tables. And I would be damned – Conchita came the first Saturday. She brought food and we had a lovely picnic. She told me she had been praying for me and in her heart she knew I would be getting out. She said that no matter what happened I should stay in touch and if I needed anything, she was prepared to do anything.

At this point, my family didn't know I was back in prison. I am anticipating that I am going to get a good decision from the parole board but I am not certain. I am hopeful but still filled with anxiety. I didn't think they would have put me in Church Farm if I was staying and they didn't give Conchita a hard time especially since she wasn't family. They let me have the visit and that helped my paranoia. At this point it was strictly wait and see. Conchita and I parted with a kiss. Jimmy Michaels and I spent the days walking the yard and talking about whether or not we were going to get out.

Parole: A Giant Step on the Road to Freedom

It's very difficult to conceptualize or describe how I felt on the day that I got a letter from the parole board. First there was fear and trepidation. I knew the letter was from the parole board. I took a deep breath and tried to relax myself because I was very tense. I opened it up very cautiously started reading the opening lines. Right away the letter announced that I had been paroled on the life sentence and on the 50 year sentence. Then it said I would be released immediately. Sure, enough as I was finishing the letter my name was called over the loud-speaker and I looked around for Jimmy Michaels. I was going to share the good news with him. I saw him on the yard as I was going to the control center. I yelled out to him that I had been paroled. He gave me a great big smile and said "me too". We embraced each other and laughed and danced and then he said, don't forget me, Frank. I told him I would not.

Jimmy Michael was in prison because of some work he had done with the mob. He was known as someone who was with the mob but that was not how he conducted himself with me. As long as I knew him he was always involved in the educational system and he was always trying to improve himself. When you talked to Jimmy, he didn't boast about what an outstanding criminal he was. He never even talked about his crime life at all. He told me about his family, his wife and his daughter whom he loved very much. Even though he was convicted of racketeering, he came off as a decent guy. I came to find out he was heavily involved with some craft union. When we had our final words that day, he told me to be sure that I contacted him when I got out. He didn't want our friendship to come to an end just because we were out of prison. I told him he could contact me too and I left him a number and we exchanged information. My name came over the loudspeaker again. I went with a quickness to Control Center. They took us into the tailor shop and fitted us with clothes and told us we would be released the next day.

We had free access to the phones to call someone to pick us up. I called Herschel Walker and he knew about my release. He told me I was more valuable to the prison system on the outside than on the inside. We were an example of what the prison system was able to accomplish so, in a way, we took some of the heat off them in terms of prison reform. They could claim me as a success story. I didn't try to analyze what he said and took it at face value. I asked him when he was coming to pick me up and he told me Joe Scoggins was coming to pick me up. Joe was a Black militant social worker who worked with different organizations that were mainly Black led like the Black Social Workers Association, Action and the All African Peoples Revolutionary Party. But he was also an educator and a teacher. He got his masters in social work. He was teaching in one of the community colleges in St. Louis.

That night there was no sleep. We lived in a dormitory like place where we could visit each other's bunks until around 11pm; any time after that you were considered illegal and you could be disciplined. I remember that night I went to Jimmy Michaels' bunk and I was there way past the curfew. The guard saw us and said he knew we were going home and asked us to just keep it down. "If no one complains, I won't do anything", he said. He continued with, "Any complaints, you will go to the hole. If you go there, you know you won't be going home." That shut us up. We would have been foolish to continue even though he gave us tacit approval. We cut our visiting short. I stayed in my bunk until morning. I did not even doze off. My mind was all over the map and I was living in the future. I was already in the streets, going to my mother's house. I was already talking to Herschel. I was already contacting Conchita. My mind was in the future and I was trying to picture what it would be like going to St Louis and living my life as a free person. All I had to do was report to a parole officer periodically so I figured that I would pretty much be free to do as I please.

Finally dawn arrived and we had breakfast even though I wasn't very hungry. I was too excited for an appetite. Breakfast was over by 8 am and Joe was supposed to be there by 9 am. I took my stuff to the waiting area and waited. It seemed like time just crept by. Finally, shortly after 9am, Joe arrived and they told me I was free to go and gave me my parole papers. They told me the first thing I should do, even before seeing my mother, was to contact my parole officer. The parole office would be open until 5pm. I took my papers and we got in the car and started down the highway. I kept looking back over my shoulder and in the rear-view mirror. Joe asked me why and I told him I was looking for state troopers. I couldn't believe they were letting me go. Joe told me to relax, that

I was free and there wouldn't be any troopers. I needed someone to tell me that. It relaxed me. A burden had been lifted. I smiled and slipped off into a deep, dreamless sleep.

When we got to St. Louis Joe woke me up. We were in front of the parole officer's office. I went in with my papers and I asked to see my parole officer. It turned out the officer was a female, a young white woman with a stern look. She appeared to be very efficient. She was in her late 30s or early 40s and she told me: "Here are your scheduled times to meet with me. I am not a difficult person. If you report as you are supposed to there will be no problems. You are in school and we will treat that like a job. If for any reason you should leave school, you must let me know why. Other than that," she concluded, "we just want you to obey the laws and re-join society." To my surprise she also said, in effect, that from all indications my record, which filled an entire file cabinet drawer, showed that I was not the same person that I was when I went to prison. She encouraged me by saying, "So keep it like that. Go by the rules and everything will be okay." That ended my first en-counter with my parole officer. She gave me a scheduled calendar, her phone number, and everything I needed. I was free to go.

I went home. Home was not with my mother. Home was with a Jewish family that Dan and Nina Cole had referred me to. Nina and Dan worked with Herschel and my Defense Committee. Dan was the one who got the Dean to give me a scholarship. This family was friends of theirs. This family was called the Fichtenbaums, Leo and Myrna Fichtenbaum. Leo was a health specialist who worked in a community health center. He was very well educated and had some kind of a degree in health administration. Myrna was still going to school and working as a nurse at one of the university owned hospitals known as Barnes. They had a daughter named Heidi and two sons, Rudy who was studying economics and the other one was Carl who was studying medicine. They were very kind to me. They took me into their home as if I was a member of their family. They were also communists. Dan Cole who referred me to them was not. There were political differences between Dan and Leo but they were tolerant of their political differences. Leo and Myrna were Communists, but they didn't lay down any spe-cial conditions for me to be in the household. I wasn't required to join the Communist Party or study communism. They told me they were just supportive of whatever I wanted to do and hoped

I would continue my education and I told them I would. This was January 15, 1976.

The next day, I was at the university enrolling. I don't remember all the details, but I remember taking a full load in graduate school. My major was anthropology in a master doctorate program. If I wanted to I could opt out after I got my masters or continue for my PhD. I was there on a Dean's scholarship for one semester in which they paid for my tuition and books. The rest was up to me. They gave me a stipend at the end of the month of about $200 and that was for clothing and food which isn't a lot of money but I had a place to stay and I was eating there and they weren't charging me. Still I needed more money to live on and more was provided by the Marian Davis Scholarship Fund. This fund was created by some left-wingers during the McCarthy era to help progressive people and civil rights activists get through college. I used the modest funds granted mostly for clothing and other incidental expenses.

My first semester I believe I took courses with Alvin Gouldner, author of *The Coming Crisis in Western Sociology*, Gouldner was a very controversial sociologist – decidedly to the left. I had read Gouldner's work while I was in prison and what I appreciated about him was that he demonstrated with all the candor and candid brilliance of a great intellectual that value free sociology was a myth. He was, I thought, the most critical thinker at Washington University. I also took courses with Paul Piconne, another critical theorist and brilliant Italian-American philosopher and intellectual historian who was mainly to the left and a founder of the philosophical periodical known as *Telos*. There was an anthropologist I took a course from who was also my adviser. I also took history courses on South Africa. The majority of my courses were anthropology and philosophy.

The philosophy courses were good because you knew where the professor stood – he was an open Marxist and he invited discussions. We took traditional approaches as to how we broke the subjects up. Such as ontology, logic, and epistemology or the theory of knowledge; that was how philosophy as a discipline was studied going back to Aristotle. We had many a hairy discussion about the meaning of meaning. Different philosophical trends and schools of thought were critically examined. We studied a lot of Hegel and his off-spring such as George Lukacs, Sartre and Kierkegaard. As best I can recall the Philosophy Dept. was caught up in a dialectical dance between praxis and existentialism. In anthropology we mainly focused on cultural anthropology. I took physical anthropology but didn't like it because it smacked of racism. I could not understand how you could look at bones and derive from them all of the racial characteristics of a human being. Based on the bones they said they could tell whether or not the person was Caucasian, Mongolian or Negro. They were still using these terms like negroid and mongoloid to describe different races of humanity.

I remember this one professor who was teaching who had a bucket of bones and who showed how the bones had racial characteristics. I questioned the validity of all this; for how could one infer from bones what kind of hair texture a specimen had, or whether or not it had blonde hair and blue eyes? I felt like we were dealing with human beings and their development as a species. I couldn't see why it was necessary, from a scientific standpoint, to go into such detail and talk about people's eye color and hair texture, etc. I started reading more broadly and reading Franz Boaz, Melville Herskovits (*The Myth of the Negro Past*), and Ashley Montague. Montague did an excellent essay on being human. I saw these scholars as rejecting the notion of race and I agreed with them that race was more of a sociological concept .

I didn't see any biological foundation for the notion of races, on the contrary it seemed quite arbitrary to me. People had been intermingling for centuries and did not see each other as different races. The concept of race came up during the African slave trade. Ancient history doesn't talk about race – they talk about Egyptians, Romans, Greeks and Ethiopians but not about yellow people, white people, or black people. The concept of race derives from slavery and capitalism. I read Oliver C. Cox who wrote "*Caste, Class and Race*". Basically Cox said the same things that the anthropologists I was following said, namely, that there was no scientific basis for the concept of race – it was primarily a sociological construct. It makes artificial distinctions between people and turns them into hard and fast lines of demarcation.

I started writing terms papers during this period where I was really attacking the concept of race. And also I started looking at anthropology from the standpoint of it pushing the political agenda of European colonialism. More and more it appeared to me that anthropology was saying that some cultures were inferior to others and that western culture was the most advanced and more developed. The spread of civilization went from the more advanced cultures to the more primitive cultures. Western Colonialism justified the colonization of Africa, the Americas and Asia based on the premise that they were bringing the indigenous people a better way of living. Bringing them from savagery to modern civilized living. What was really going on was that they were exploiting the labor of indigenous peoples and extracting resources from their lands. In Africa it was economic exploitation of labor based on slavery.

I did one piece called "Fascist Excursions into Anthropology." This was a critique of writers like Robert Audrey who had written the book *African Genesis.* Audrey was an anthropologist who was advocating that a branch of ape like humanoid creatures in Africa eventually developed into blood thirsty violent human beings. He was trying to argue that war and conquest and slavery had its origins in human nature – it was the ineradicable nature of human beings to do these things. This was totally contrary to what classical anthropology had established as a principle, namely, that people do not live by instincts but that they live by social customs and traditions. We are not beavers, we don't build a dam because of an inborn pattern of behavior – we build them as a consequence of institutionalized learning, because we go to engineering school.

This had very serious political connotations. If people were warlike by nature, then we could never eliminate war. It means that there could never be peace. So, it was kind of like trying to establish the status quo as having a basis in nature. Social conventions, like war and prisons and slavery are no longer human made institutions but are biological necessities. We are this way because these things are biologically determined. When we really take a critical look at these arguments and the ideology they prop up, they're not different from Nazism. That is why I called my essay Fascist Excursion into Anthropology. That paper was not well received. I got a B. However, my paper was well received by the Midwest Marxist Scholars Conference in 1978.

I also got involved with the black student movement. They were strongly influenced by the Socialist Workers Party and other leftist groups such as the Progressive Labor Party and they were very sectarian. I didn't really become that active – I just went to a few of the meetings – I didn't really like their politics.

I worked with community groups – one of them was the St. Louis Alliance Against Racist and Repression. Actually it was called the National Alliance Against Racist and Political Repression – the St. Louis branch. I got involved in the struggles to free the Wilmington 10. The Wilmington 10 was a group of civil rights activists who were imprisoned in Wilmington, North Carolina as the result of fighting back against the KKK. We will tell their story in greater detail later. We organized letter writing campaigns, raised money for attorneys, and also publicized the case. We had our second national demonstration in 1977 in Raleigh, North Carolina, the Capital. I was still in grad school but I got really involved with mobilizing and organizing for this and getting people to participate. We carried three bus loads of people with 40 people to a bus to Raleigh. The national office was so impressed with us because we got more people than some of the other, larger cities, like Chicago.

When we got to North Carolina we were recognized. Angela Davis as a leader of the National Alliance Against Racist and Political Repression had worked on my case while I was in prison from 1973 to 1976 – they had done a massive amount of work. They used me as an example – if they could get me free – they could get the Wilmington 10 free. To be sure, while Rev. Ben Chavis was out on bond he spoke at a rally in St. Louis where he said I was a political prisoner and he supported the struggle for my freedom. But we must never forget that it was the truly mass campaign to free Angela Davis and All Political Prisoners that created the moral and political climate that made our struggles possible and victorious. I owed a debt of gratitude to Angela, Rev. Chavis and the entire movement so I had no problem working with them to help free others still imprisoned.

I got married for the first time in May, 1960 and it was over in May 1961. Maybe we were actually together about 7 months out of that year. It was short lived. Then there was the imprisonment and Brenda. I really wasn't able to get into that relationship. It never really developed because of the circumstances I have already discussed.

Now here I am in Washington University. I had already been there for a few weeks before I started talking to Coraminita. I met her before because she was in the movement. She was part of the National Alliance against Racist and Political Repression (NAARPR) and she was a very good student at St. Louis University. She was one of Ernest Calloway's brightest students. He was the guru of urban studies in St. Louis. He was a man of the people who became a professor. He started out in the coal miner's union. Professor Calloway was African American. He was well educated, hailing from Fiske University, before he became involved in the Teamsters. He made a very profound study of wealth in our country. He studied international and multinational corporations and he tried to link them up to local politics. In the courses he gave at St. Louis University he got the students involved in studying groups like Civic Progress.

I learned from Coraminita about his course because when she and I met and started talking politics, she showed me a flow chart Calloway had done which linked multi-national corporations to local politics. Civic progress was a civic/political organization composed of several corporations like Monsanto Chemical, Ralston Purina, Emerson Electric, McDonald Douglas and Budweiser. Also related to Civic Progress were other corporations like General Motors, Chrysler and basic, smoke-stack industries like US Steel and Peabody Coal. He showed the interconnection between these groups and how by their combined efforts they were able to control many cities in the country. He showed how all of the major geographic areas, Baltimore, Washington, D.C., and New York had their own Civic Progress like organization. Calloway considered himself a Socialist – he was not a friend of Capitalism. He was also the husband of Daverne Calloway who was the state representative who helped us in our fight to desegregate the Missouri State Penitentiary.

When I met Coraminita we had a lot in common and a lot to talk about. We were involved in the same organizations. When she graduated from St. Louis University I was a month away from coming out of prison. Lo and behold, the first job she got was at Washington University working for Barry Commoner (the then famous Ecologist). He worked with Virginia Brodine, a brilliant Marxist environmentalist. They were the main people who organized and developed the environmentalist group on campus that was studying how industrial greed was polluting our air and rivers. They were conducting scientific experiments as to what was happening and sounding an alarm that our ecological system was being severely harmed by industrial pollution. Barry Commoner had a laboratory where he and Virginia Bodine did their scientific research to measure and demonstrate through measurements the extent to which our air and water was being polluted by industry. Coraminita got a job in the lab. That is how she and I really got to know each other. We worked in the community together and saw each other on campus all of the time.

We started dating. She was a beautiful woman both physically and in spirit. She had a 5 year old girl from a previous relationship named Corlita. They (Coraminita and her daughter) were very close. Corlita's father and Coraminita were no longer together; he lived in St. Louis but was not a part of her life in any way. And she let me know that.

When we first started dating it was a little awkward because Corlita would come on the dates. I was dating two people. I think she was hesitant about getting into a relationship because she had just been in one and it didn't work out well. She wasn't that enthused about getting intimate with another man. Of course, I was pursuing her because I was very enthused about getting into a relationship with her and I let her know that. I let her know I didn't want to just be a friend or a comrade but I wanted to be closer. I started showering her with flowers and writing poetry and putting them in her mailbox; calling her on the phone and talking with her as long as she would allow me to. So little by little she started making concessions.

The first major concession was to go on a date without Corlita, it was just the two of us. We were able to get a little more intimate because the child wasn't there. However, we were both very busy at the time so there were limits on our time together. Even though we weren't seeing each other day in and day out in having this romantic relationship, we still started getting real fond of each other. What put the seal on it was I told her I had to go to New York to thank a number of people who had been involved in my defense committee and played a large part in me winning my freedom. The two main people I was talking about were Esther and Jim Jackson. Esther was the managing editor of *Freedomways* and Jim was an editor of *The Daily World*, and they were the first ones to publish my prison writings and they provided me with much moral support. While Jim was editor he also made sure some of my writings were published. He and I developed a relationship and that paper supported me in my struggle for freedom. Also John Henrik Clarke, who was also a contributing editor of *Freedomways* was someone whom I felt I had to see; without a doubt he was my mentor when it came to African history and he too played an important role in publicizing my case and supporting me as a writer. I asked Coraminita if she wanted to go with me and her answer was yes so long as I brought her daughter too.

I hooked up with an Libyan student friend mine named Mahmud Zawe who had a car and we set out on the 18 hour drive to New York, with very few stops. That was 18 hours we had to talk and explore each other mentally and I think that helped her make up her mind that she wanted the relationship too. We decided we would be intimate friends, go together and what not. It was not an engagement but a deeper relationship based on our common interests and common concerns and our sexual attraction.

This must have been around April or May of 1976. By June of 1976 we ended up down at the marriage license bureau getting a marriage license. I proposed to her on the return ride from New York but she kind of brushed it off. After the trip, she started spending more time at my place. I was uncomfortable because I was staying at someone else's house and we were not married. I decided to get my own place. She said, "Why don't I help you? If we are going to stay in each other's lives we should live together." I told her if we were going to live together we should just get married. She said there was a commitment involved and asked me if I wanted to make that commitment and I said absolutely.

We ended up at City Hall getting a license and a few days later found ourselves in the courtyard of a Lutheran church getting married by a pastor in the movement. The minister, Rev. Sterling Belcher, was also a close friend of Hershel Walker. Even though neither of us believed in God, we still had the ceremony. Because the pastor was a Black militant Lutheran preacher and heavily involved in the civil rights movement, we felt he was the most appropriate person to marry us.

After we got married we just continued to live as we had been. She quit working for Barry Commoner and spent a brief period working for the Black Leadership Training Program and then returned to grad school for her masters. We made a deal that I would work with her to get her masters degree and she would work with me to get mine and we would take turns taking care of Corlita. We each had days where we had Coralita. We also worked out an arrangement if neither of us could take care of her we would leave her with her grandparents. So that was the family arrangement. Every political campaign I was involved in, she was involved with me; whether it was the Free Mandela, or Free Ben Chavis and the Wilmington 10 or Save Homer G. Phillips hospital.

I was scheduled to graduate in May of 1978 but instead of getting my M.A. degree I got a blank sheet of paper because I owed the University 3-credit-hours. Immediately after I "graduated" I started working with the American Friends Service Committee, a Quaker based organization. (The American Friends Service Committee is a pacifist organization that is dedicated to ending social injustices, such as racism, poverty and all other barriers to human beings living in peace. I mainly worked on the Committee against Apartheid to get a following within the faith community with the focus being on isolating South Africa and not buying the Krugerrand and asking the churches to lead the way in the divestiture movement. To take any money they had out of banks that were investing in or doing business with South Africa.

I was also asked to do work with the Lutheran Mission Association around the issue of jails and the criminal justice system. Basically they wanted to hire me as an ombudsman to represent the prisoners in their grievances. That brought in some extra money – an unexpected bonanza. All of a sudden I had a lot of money in my pocket and so we decided that when Coraminita had a summer break from her studies we would go to Tan Tara for our honeymoon, in Branson Missouri. We talked to her parents about keeping Coralita for a week while we went to Tan Tara. I rented a car and we took off. That was probably the best experience ever. I had no idea what I was getting into. I had no idea I was going to a little paradise – one of the most beautiful places on earth. That part of the mountain range known as the Ozarks was a playground for the Native American Indians. I could see why. You didn't have to do anything, just be there. It was a perfect work of nature. There were lakes, waterfalls, wooded areas that had wildlife, you could rent a boat and go on the lake. We went out on the lake once and the lake was covered on different sides by beautiful forests. You go through these forests like on a water highway. It was amazing. I have very vivid memories of being there. I felt like, "wow, what a place."

We were both awestruck while we were there. In the evening there was dancing and festivities and we saw a Woody Allen play which was a hilarious spoof on Humphrey Bogart. There were ballroom dances in the evening; cocktails early in the morning. Unfortunately I was doing a lot of drinking there. I don't remember a lot about my last two or three days there because I think I was drunk. Coraminita said we got into arguments but I didn't remember. I had a few blackout drunks while I was there which was a harbinger of things to come. At the time I didn't realize it. I thought I was just being a bit excessive.

Things did calm down and for the most part we really enjoyed ourselves and we grew closer and went back to St. Louis. When we got back to St. Louis, something came up. Herschel Walker told me Charlene Mitchell, the executive director of the Alliance wanted to know if I wanted to go to Cuba. I couldn't because I was on parole. The parole officer was only authorized to give me travel permits throughout the United States. Since there wasn't good relations between the US and Cuba there was no way I could go. I suggested my wife and Hershel couldn't see any reason why she couldn't go. I called Charlene and pleaded with her to let my wife go so we wouldn't miss this opportunity of a lifetime. She said yes and we had to get all of the documents and my wife got a Visa to go to Mexico and from there went to Cuba. It was a 2 week trip.

When she returned from Cuba she was really so grateful that I had allowed her to go. She said she would never forget this experience and would always be grateful for my lack of selfishness in letting her go. Then she told me all about her trip and how she went into neighborhoods where the revolution took place and she spoke with the peasants in the cane fields and the cultural and women's organizations who were in solidarity with the colonized peoples' struggles around the world and in South Africa. She also had an opportunity to meet with Fidel Castro. I believe she said it was a short meeting at a formal dinner and each person there was allowed to speak about the struggle they were dealing with in their country. She told them about the struggles in St. Louis and about our struggles to free Mandela. She also told me how handsome, how attractive Cuban men were and how they were all over her. I wasn't too thrilled about that part of the trip but the rest of it made me feel good.

Corlita was going to school now regularly – it was an idyllic life. I was a happily married man and I had a wife who shared in my ideas and dreams and that was as good as it could get. I felt I had arrived. It was a very good beginning. I loved Coraminita and I still love her. We still talk once and a while. But during those ten years we were partners in the movement. She is a large part of my story.

During the Homer G. Phillips struggle, our relationship hit a wall. I was drinking more in those days. She asked me to stop drinking because when I came home sometimes and she was waiting in the bedroom, she knew I had arrived because she could smell the liquor all the way to the back of the house. That amazed me but I guess I was pretty pickled when I got home because she didn't like the smell of the liquor. This caused tensions in our relationship. She started drinking but she couldn't drink like me and my buddies. She would often leave us to go to bed after a few drinks while the guys and I would continue drinking until 2 am or so. My drinking increased in frequency and Coraminita was trying to point this out to me in her own way. She never denied me any closeness because of this. We continued to grow close all the way up to the time we finally broke up. She was a very understanding woman. She had seen a better side of me and saw it slipping away and she tried to stop that from happening. But at that time she believed I just had some out of control moments and that I would get it back together.

Alice Windom and My Life as an Organizer

I am out of prison and participating. My mind is all over the place but my practice is mainly going in two directions. I'm going to graduate school to get a degree in anthropology and also I feel obligated to the movement because the movement was responsible for my freedom. I had no choice – I had to give back because the movement had done for me more than I could do for myself; it had in effect saved my life.

Of course, the movement was also helping me stay in college through The Marion Davis Scholarship Fund. The Fund was founded in 1961 as a memorial to a teacher and political activist who died of breast cancer in 1960. Marian was an advocate for racial justice and the rights of labor. While raising her family, she was also at home in the classroom, on the picket line, or in a jail cell. Marian's husband, Horace B. Davis, who was called Hockey by all who knew and loved him, organized the Fund as a tribute to her. Hockey was committed to creating a Fund to honor "a talented teacher, loved by her students, who was persecuted for her work for peace and freedom." Quoted from The Davis-Putter Scholarship Fund website. The Davis-Putter Scholarship Fund is what it is called today. They helped me with my tuition fees and living expenses and filled in the gaps of other financial needs I had. Everything about my freedom was connected to the movement.

The movement did not put any pressure on me to give back. In fact they were more in favor of me finishing school and then joining. But I wanted to help out now in any way I could especially when I saw on campus the movements that were forming such as the Black student organizations, etc. all of which were part of the larger movement for African American Liberation. The movement was everywhere but I didn't like the narrowness of the movements on campus. My involvement with the National Alliance gave me more satisfaction because I felt it was more real with respect to solving the problems of racist and political repression. The campus movements were more like debates and more on a philosophical basis and a struggle for ideas – which was appropriate for an academic setting but the Alliance was about more than just debating – they were about participating and that was what attracted me. Remember I just came from a prison struggle which was what we were doing for the past 11 years. My mind set was more in tune with the Alliance than with what was happening on campus.

The routine became like this: I would go to school in the morning. I would start around 9:30am and would be on campus until 3 or 4pm participating in classes and going to the library researching and studying. When I left campus around 3 or 4 pm I would go to the Peace Center on North Skinner Street. This was a place started by a lot of groups involved with stopping the war in Vietnam. Now it was being used by other activist groups involved in the civil rights movement. I did whatever they needed me to do. The St. Louis Branch of the National Alliance Against Racist and Political Repression. It had its office in this Center and it was here that I did mobilizing and organizing work on the Wilmington 10 case and other issues. Following is a brief outline of how we came to be and the struggles we were involved in:

When The National Alliance Against Racist and Political was founded in 1973, 44 years ago, our nation was confronted with a new era of racist and political repression. In the decade leading up to our founding convention in Chicago in 1973 all the various strands of the peoples' movement had come under attack. We were founded at a time when, coming hot on the heels of the Civil Rights Revolution, our movement was beleaguered but unbowed by the so-called white backlash and covert, clandestine government repression. The constitutionally guaranteed right of the people to organize and protest was being illegally undermined.

We were born in a crucible of struggle when a dark cloud, like an ominous warning of an oncoming storm, hung low on the horizon and the dusk of twilight was followed by a long night of racist and political repression. First there was a whole train of assassinations of civil rights workers in Alabama and Mississippi; then the murders of leaders such as Medgar Evers, Minister Malcolm X and Rev. Dr. Martin Luther King, Jr., quickly followed by the blatant murders of members of the Black Panther Party. Today we know that these vicious attacks on our movements were more often than not the work of local police, state sovereignty commissions and the FBI. The revelations started in 1971 when "the Citizens Committee to Investigate the FBI" removed secret files from an FBI office and released them to the press. As a result of this courageous act FBI agents started resigning and blowing the whistle on illegal covert actions against people who were simply exercising their rights to organize and protests.

This plus the congressional investigation led by Senator Frank Church made the American public aware for the first time that agencies of government, the FBI and state and local police had moved outside the laws they were sworn to uphold. They created secret and systematic methods of fraud, surveillance, violent force and yes, even methods of assassination (as is documented in the case of the murders of Fred Hampton and Mark Clark). The entire operation was known as the Counter Intelligence Program or COINTELPRO; its founder and author was none other than the FBI Director J. Edgar Hoover.

In the words of Hoover the purpose of COINTELPRO was to "expose, disrupt, misdirect, discredit and otherwise neutralize" groups and individuals who were engaged in constitutionally protected political activity. All strands of the peoples movement were attacked from the NAACP to the National Lawyers Guild, to Black Nationalist groups like the Republic of New Africa, to peace and solidarity movements, from Martin Luther King to Caesar Chavez , from feminist to gay-lesbian to countless human rights groups and organizations we don't have the space to name. No one was spared. In spite of all the various turns of events where the government used agents, hired provocateurs, stool pigeons and carefully shielded assassins to destroy our movements we still continued to fight back. A remarkable example of the resilience of the people was the movement to Free the Soledad Brothers.

The Soledad Brothers were George Jackson, Fletta Drumgo and John Wesley Clutchette. They were accused of killing a white prison guard who had murdered three Black prisoners. Fay Stender, an attorney and activist organized the Soledad Brothers Defense Committee (SBDC). The SBDC organized a wide variety of political activists and celebrities such as Jane Fonda, Marlon Brando, Julian Bond, Tom Hayden, William Kunstler and Angela Davis. Angela emerged as the leader of the movement, in 1970, when the California Legislative Black Caucus initiated an investigation of the Soledad Prison.

Shortly thereafter, on August 7, 1970, Jonathan Jackson, 17-year-old brother of George Jackson held up the court room at Marin

County Civic Center and temporarily liberated three San Quentin prisoners, and in an attempt to bid for the freedom of the Soledad Brothers he took Superior Court Judge Harold Haley and three female jurors hostage. During the attempted getaway everyone was killed except Ruchell Magee and one of the jurors.

Because Angela Davis had purchased one of the guns she was charged with "aggravated kidnapping and first-degree murder in the death of Judge Harold Haley." Aware of the trumped-up nature of these charges and the fact that she was already a target of a vicious anti-communist campaign in the state of California Angela decided not to surrender to the authorities. Thus, she became a fugitive and the third woman in U.S. history to be placed on the FBI's most wanted list. Angela later wrote, in her autobiography, that while she was a so-called "fugitive" she hid in friends' homes and moved from place to place at night. On October 13, 1970, FBI agents found her at the Howard Johnson Motor Lodge in New York City. Upon her capture President Richard M. Nixon congratulated the FBI and called Angela a "dangerous terrorist".

Angela Davis with Valentina Tereshkova

On January 5, 1971, after several months in jail, Davis appeared at the Marin County Superior Court and declared her innocence before the court and nation: "I now declare publicly before the court, before the people of this country that I am innocent of all charges which have been leveled against me by the state of California."

Across the nation, thousands of people who agreed with her declaration began organizing a Free Angela Davis movement. In New York City, black writers formed a committee called the Black People in Defense of Angela Davis. By February 1971 more than 200 local committees in the United States, and 67 in foreign countries worked to liberate Angela Davis from prison. At this time Angela insisted that the movement should not be about just freeing her but all political prisoners and so our battle cry became Free Angela Davis and All Political Prisoners. Solidarity movements sprung up everywhere and not only in the Eastern block of socialist countries and Cuba but in Canada, England, France, Chile, Jamaica, Vietnam and in the liberation movements in Africa the demand to Free Angela Davis and All Political Prisoners was persistently raised.

While we don't have the time to chronicle this, perhaps most massive social movement of the twentieth century we must not neglect to point out that this very movement coming in the wake of one of the most repressive and murderous acts of government against the peoples' movement showed us our future in how to build mass movements in defense of the rights of the people to organize and protest against injustice.

Thanks to the mass movement to Free Angela Davis and All Political Prisoners Angela was found not guilty by an all-white jury. Her experience as a political prisoner and a person whom the state was prepared to execute because of her political beliefs has been an inexhaustible source of strength for our struggle and is one of the foundation stones of our movement to end racist and political repression.

When Angela Davis was freed over 45 years ago she posed to us this challenge: Now we need to free all political prisoners; stop the Crimes of Government against our movement and abolish prisons. Thus, the stage was set for founding the National Alliance Against Racist and Political Repression In the Spring of 1973 nearly 700 grass roots organizers, leaders and rank and filers called for the formation of a national organization of organizations, groups and individuals based on united, organized struggle. Coming out of that historic convention here are some of the campaigns we initiated, struggles we organized and victories we won.

☐ We filed the first petition with the United Nations calling attention to the plight of political prisoners, particularly the victims of COINTELPRO in the Black Panther Party, Dhoruba bin Wahad, Geronimo ji-Jaga, Assata Shakur and others. Dhoruba's conviction was reversed March 15, 1990 and he was released without bail. Geronimo's conviction was vacated June 10, 1997 and he eventually received a $4.5 million settlement for false imprisonment from the City of Los Angeles and the U.S. Department of Justice. Geronimo died in Tanzania at age 63, June 2, 2011; he spent 27 years in prison. Assata Shakur, and Pete O'Neal, also COINTELPRO victims have been in forced exile for over two decades and there are many other Panthers mentioned in our U.N. petition who are still languishing in prison, some have died in prison. Also included in our petition was the cases of Indigenous leader and political prisoner Leonard Peltier and Lolita Lebron one of the five Puerto Rican Nationalists. Leonard Peltier has been in federal prison for over 42 years. He and the Panthers are the longest held political prisoners in the world. There is much that remains to be done here.

□   We intensified our national/international campaign to free Joan Little, who was a 21-year-old Black woman accused of killing her jailer Clarence Alligood (white, age 62) who tried to rape her in her jail cell. She was facing the death penalty. Joan Little was the first woman in U.S. history to be acquitted even though she used deadly force in resisting sexual assault.

□   We launched a massive campaign that freed Johnny Imani Harris from death row and prison.

□   We stopped attempts by the state of Mississippi to execute Mayor Eddie James Carthan on trumped up murder charges.

□   We were a part of the successful campaign that stopped the ultra-right from turning Missouri into a right to work state in 1978.

□   We were a part of the movement led by the Amalgamated Clothing and Textile Workers Union boycott of J.P. Stevens products. This boycott was successful in forcing the J.P. Stevens owned textile mills to recognize the union in North Carolina.

□   We successfully campaigned for extension of the Voting Rights Act of 1964 in 1984 by submitting tens of thousands of petitions, by demonstrations and lobbying Congress.

□   In alliance with the National Committee Against Repressive Legislation, the Center for Constitutional Rights, the National Conference of Black Lawyers, the National Lawyers Guild, the Amalgamated Meat Cutters Union, the Southern Organizing Committee, Clergy and Laity Concerned and others we successfully campaigned against several omnibus crimes bills that were designed to criminalize the peoples movement.

□   We called and held the first National Peoples Hearing on Police Crimes in Los Angeles, CA, in 1981 with Congresswoman Maxine Waters addressing our forum. Out of the hearing we developed our first model legislation for civilian control of the police.

☐   We launched the most massive campaign since the Free Angela and All Political Prisoners campaign to free the Wilmington ten.

Who were the Wilmington Ten? The Wilmington Ten was Rev. Ben Chavis, eight young Black men (Willie Vereen, Wayne More, Marvin Patrick, William Wright, Reginald Epps, James McCoy and Jerry Jacobs who were still in high school and a white woman (Connie Tindall). They were convicted in 1971 of arson and conspiracy. The NAARPR took the case of the Wilmington Ten up at our founding convention and subsequently begun a national and international campaign making it a *Cause Celebre*.

The 1970s, coming in the wake of Dr. Martin Luther King's assassination, was the beginning of what became known as the white backlash responding to the gains of the Civil Rights Movement of the 1960s. The government's response to the ghetto uprisings (called race riots) that occurred on the eve of King's assassination was punitive, violent and repressive.

In 1969, just a year after the murder of Dr. King and the riots, there was an attempt to integrate the high schools of Wilmington, N.C. The city used this attempted integration as a pretext for closing Williston High School, the pride of the African American community. Black teachers and coaches were laid off and students transferred. The school administrators refused to meet with parents and students.

There were no preparations for these abrupt changes. Tensions sprouted up giving rise to clashes between white and black students. There followed arrests and expulsions.
 In an effort to exploit these racial tensions the KKK and other white supremacists began patrolling the streets in an attempt to intimidate and terrorize African Americans. Consequently street violence broke out between the Klan and African American men. Also students decided to boycott the high schools. This occurred in January, 1971.

In Feb. 1971 the United Church of Christ sent Rev. Ben Chavis, director of their Commission for Racial Justice, to Wilmington, N.C. to ease tensions and work with students and the community for a peaceful and just solution. Rev. Ben Chavis advocated non-violence in the manner of the late Dr. King; and upon arriving he immediately proceeded to organize the students and the community. There were regular meetings with discussions on the history of African American freedom struggles and the need to organize a boycott. Within a week (on Feb. 7, 1971) Mike's Grocery, a white owned business, was allegedly fire-bombed and the responding firefighters claimed they were shot at by snipers. Rev. Chavis and the students were peacefully assembled at the Church. A riot broke out in the community, lasting 'til the next day and claiming the lives of two people.

On Feb. 8, 1971 the Governor Robert Scott called out the National Guard. They forced their way into the Church, alleging that they found ammunition. At the end of the day there were two deaths, six injuries and $500,000 in property damages. Rev. Ben Chavis and his nine co-defendants (mentioned above) were arrested and charged with arson. Based on the false testimony of two black men, the Wilmington Ten were tried, convicted and sentenced to a total of 282 years.

In November, 1978 the U.S. Department of Justice filed a petition in Federal Court stating that it had uncovered evidence that clearly demonstrated that the Wilmington Ten did not get a fair trial. The DOJ petitioned the court to either overturn the convictions or hold a hearing on the governments findings. This plus the continued pressure of our movement led Governor Hunt of North Carolina to reduce the sentences thus rendering everyone except the Rev. Ben Chavis eligible for parole. Finally, after 40 some years of struggle the Willington were pardoned.

The NAARPR was also involved in the J.P. Stevens boycott which was a struggle to get union recognition for textile workers in North Carolina which had become a right to work state so it was a very important struggle. On November 30, 1978, thousands of people from across the United States took place in the boycott called, "Justice for J.P. Stevens' Workers Day." In 74 cities across the country, citizens took a stand against one of the largest textile companies who had consistently violated labor laws and attempted to squash their workers right to organize through rallies, press conferences, marches, and more.

More than 3,000 people in New York City alone marched on the company's headquarters, a move that was endorsed by Governor

Hugh L. Carey and his city council. Protests were even occurring in smaller cities, such as Albany, New York, where Secretary of State and Lieutenant Governor-elect Mario Cuomo declared, "to shun the products of J. P. Stevens as you would shun the fruit of an unholy tree."[2] Across the country, protesters urged consumers to stop using the textile giant's sheets, their staple product because "insisted [consumers] should not 'sleep' with the products of a company that had repeatedly violated labor laws and was guilty of racial and sexual discrimination against its workers." [Minchin, Timothy J. "'Don't Sleep with Stevens!': The J.P. Stevens Boycott and Social Activism in the 1970s." Journal of American Studies 39 no. 03 (2005): 511-543.]

The local person who worked with us on the boycott was Jim Anderson, who was the Regional Director of the Amalgamated Clothing and Textile Workers Union (ACTWU). Jim taught us some very effective tactics that can be used in a consumer boycott. We would go into a store selling J.P. Stevens products, fill up the shopping carts roll them up to the cashier and leave the loaded carts for the stores to unload. We nominated Jim Anderson to be a member of our national board. He accepted the nomination and was elected to the NAARPR executive board in 1979. With Jim and other workers such as Lou Moye, Kenny Jones and Dough Lincoln were elected, and they were all from St. Louis, Mo.

Then there was the very important struggle to free Nelson Mandela that we took up. We had free Nelson Mandela petitions that we needed to get signed to present to the United Nations Anti-Apartheid Committee. This was a nation-wide campaign which was part of a world-wide campaign to free Mandela. Since he was a political prisoner in South Africa we used him as an example to show that our country was going in the same direction.

We had many Black people in jail for the same reasons Nelson Mandela was in prison. Angela Davis had been one of those people and the movement had freed her. She challenged us to continue to look at others who were also imprisoned as a result of political repression like Geronimo Pratt, Dharuba bin Wadad, Assata Shakur, and host of others who had been leaders of the Black Panther Party, the Soledad Brother Fleeta Drumgo, as well as Hurricane Carter and other victims of racist frame-ups. We had our work cut out for us. We were getting a lot of traction around the Wilmington 10 case because Reverend Chavis was a highly respected minister in the United Church of Christ and so we were able to mobilize a lot of churches and community organizations and civil rights organizations to his defense. There was really developing a truly national campaign. Of course Angela Davis was one of the spearheads of the campaign to free Reverend Chavis and the Wilmington 10 and that added much needed militant support. I was having the time of my life; organizing and working with these people and going to school and pursuing my academic career at the same time.

The more I got involved in the movement, the more unclear I became about what I wanted to do academically. I was having a problem seeing how becoming an anthropologist would be helpful in building the movement. I didn't want to just be a professor confined to a classroom advocating radical social change. I had no problem with people who were comfortable doing that – I just didn't want to do that.

A strange thing happened. I continued to go to school and study and do work towards my degree but I had no ambitions at all to become a part of the academic community. What I really wanted to do was become an organizer. I started relating to people who were going to George Warren Brown school of social work at Washington U. I found there a group of radical social workers, led by Fred Smith, who were into Saul D. Alinsky.

Alinsky, the guy who wrote the *"Rules for Radicals"*; was an icon in the whole social worker movement. He had the slogan that all politics was local and that we bring about great systemic changes by first working in local communities. He wrote the book for community organizing around various issues like rent strikes, housing conditions and tenant unions, unemployment issues, environmental and educational issues. Whatever the community needed the organizers had to be ready to organize around those issues. This was the way to fight for social reform and revolutionary changes that would ultimately lead to fundamental systemic change. It seemed like it was perfect for what I perceived as my mission except for one significant item: Alinsky and his followers didn't come out for socialism as a viable alternative to capitalism. I found them in their outlook very similar to Bernstein and the Social Democrats who see revolution as an endless cycle of reforms.

I became involved with the George Warren Brown people and joined the National Association of Black Social Workers. Alice Windom who was an outstanding leader in that organization and a phenomenal community organizer became my mentor. I went to her to learn about community organizing and when she found out what I was doing with the Alliance and the Wilmington 10, she said she was glad I came to her for information about organizing but it seemed to her that I was already in the mix and she suggested that she join with me in my causes. We worked together for many years and have a relationship to this day. Here is what Alice Windom taught me: if you want to organize a community then your first obligation was to be a member of that community. And, she said people who are organizing everyone but their neighbors are not organizers.

The quintessential organizer begins with organizing his/her community. She said that I should be profoundly and intricately knowledgeable about the economics in my community. Where do people work? Who owns what? Not just homeowners but also businesses that people own. What health facilities are available? What educational institutions are there? And how are they servicing the people? What municipal services are delivered to the people from picking up trash to getting water and natural gas. All of these things are important because you will find out that oppressed people will have living problems in all of these areas. Services to poor, oppressed people are grossly inferior to those in rich areas. Although we are the majority in the ghetto and might, occasionally, have the most votes we are never the most politically powerful, and this reality is reflected in the quality of the services we get.

Public education is one of the most critical services. How are the educational needs in poor and oppressed communities being met or not met – mostly not met? What is the relationship between the teachers and the parents? How do the teachers view educational reform that will improve the quality and accessibility of education for the masses?

And what about the slum lords? Who are they? Do they represent companies or particular individuals? She told me there was a group in St. Louis a group known as Civic Progress which consisted of Budweiser, Monsanto Chemicals, Ralston Purina, McDonald Douglas and Emerson Electric. These are some of the richest most influential corporations in America with headquarters in St. Louis. Civic Progress is an association of these rich corporations which basically run the City. They affect the distribution of wealth because they are the wealth. If you are to be a community organizer you must find out what they are doing in your community. She was saying that you have to look at plant closing such as the closing of General Motors that displaced thousands of workers. How did this impact the north side of St. Louis where mostly African Americans lived? How would it affect homeowners, public hospitals and schools? Now we are talking about a huge tax base being eradicated which means there will be cuts in municipal services. Schools and community centers will be closed. Homeowners will be losing their homes. Community organizing means addressing all of these issues and bringing people together in an organized way to fight for economic justice and their political rights. It was very interesting that even while Alice and I were having these discussions I found myself involved with these issues.

We were, for example, engaged in an intense struggle to stop Missouri from becoming a right to work state. We united with the Coalition of Black Trade Unionists, the A. Phillip Randolph Institute, SEIU Local 50, United Auto Workers, the Teamsters, the Black Social Workers, Congressman Bill Clay and numerous churches from various denominations. During the development of this struggle I graduated from Washington University and immediately got a job as field secretary working for the American Friends Service Committee (AFSC).My position with the Friends enabled me to really work with Herschel Walker to push the NAARPR in the direction of becoming a mass organization. Herschel and Alice showed me how to do this by reaching out to other organizations to join us in a united fight against racist and political repression.

The results were absolutely amazing; within a couple of months we went from being a small group of about dozen people to over 200 members. And with an active executive board of about 30 members. I learned from Alice the basic principles of grass roots organizing and I learned from Herschel that Communists never lose sight of the need to fight for the hearts and minds of the workers and the racially and nationally oppressed and must therefore, never pass up an opportunity to educate workers about who they are as a class and how to fight to advance their class interest politically as well as economically. Here I called upon my prison experience and organized a Marxist-Leninist study group for the more militant rank and file workers around us. These workers were not members of the Communist Party yet but 90% of them would become members.

The fact that we were a Black and Left led organization engaged in a mass, broad based coalition of labor, churches and community organizations put us in a position to approach grass roots leaders, rank and file leaders in the labor movement, peace activists, youth organizations (in the community and on campus), women's organizations and churches. Just to give a concrete idea of how we built our alliance let me just mention the people and the organizations they represented who were on our local executive board:

Alice Windom	Association of Black Social Workers
Jim Anderson	Amalgamated Clothing and Textile Workers Union
Yvonne Logan	Women's International League for Peace and Freedom
Coraminita Mahr	Black Leadership Training Program
Rev. Sterling Belcher	Emmanuel Lutheran Church
Rev. Bill Stickey	St. Stephens Episcopal Church
Lew Moye	United Auto Workers, Chrysler Plant
Sylvester Raymond	UAW, Chrysler Plant
John May,	UAW, Chrysler Plant
Pam Talley	Student Activist and Nurse
Eldora Spielberg	Quaker
Wale Amusa	All African Peoples Revolutionary Party Her-
Herschel Walker	Communist Party
Zenobia Thompson	Registered Nurse
Leo Fichtenbaum,	Communist Party
Laura More	Women's Group and part of the Gay-Lesbian community
Linda Lincoln	Home Maker
Dough Lincoln	Construction Worker
Marva Thomas	Practical Nurse
Jay Ozier	Community Youth for Jobs
James Robinett	Young Workers Liberation League (YWLL)
Bob Williams	Social Worker/Community Organizer
Kenny Jones	CBTU and an Iron Worker

Loretta Horton   YWLL
James Starks   Worker and former Black Panther
Sen. Gwen Giles Missouri Senate

All of these people were organizers, some were young and inexperienced like me but most were veterans and a few were seasoned like Herschel. They were also black and white, left and center united in the struggle against the ultra-right and racist, anti-worker inspired attempts to turn Missouri into a right to work state. The proposed right to work legislation was on the ballot by a referendum initiative known as Amendment 23 and in the election of 1978 we, united with labor and the entire progressive community, gave it a resounding defeat. Our alliance emerged from this struggle with a healthy working-class base (of over 200 members) and a group of young, dedicated community activists, many of whom later joined the Communist Party.

Following hot on the heels of the defeat of "right to work" the General Motors plant (employing thousands of workers) closed. The biggest and broadest coalition we had just built to defeat the "right to work" amendment could not stop this plant closing because in the wake of victory that coalition was now coming apart. Alice told me that this was inevitable due to the fact that the coalition came together around the single issue of stopping Amendment 23. Still we fought hard along-side progressive trade unionists to build a labor/community alliance to stop the plant-closings; but the craft dominated Central Labor Council of the AFL-CIO and most of the African American labor leaders simply would not step up.

For example, Homer G. Phillips hospital, the hospital I was born in, was about to be closed. After General Motors closed their plant and moved out of the City immediately there was talk in City Hall, mainly the Mayor, about closing Homer G. Phillips. But Homer G. Phillips was also a plant in that it employed well over a thousand people and had a nursing school (called Annie Malone) associated with it. It was the largest black administered hospital in the world. It was founded by an African American attorney, Homer G. Phillips in the thirties and employed mostly black workers. It had the largest alumni of African American doctors in the United Sates and the world. And they wanted to close it.

Alice said to me: "keep on doing the wonderful work you are doing on the Wilmington 10 and keep getting petitions to free Nelson Mandella and keep working with the National Alliance to stop political repression but your main challenge as a community organizer is staring you in the face right now" – that was the Mayor's call to close the Homer G. Phillips hospital. She said, "Look at the North Side of St. Louis and tell me who is organizing against this proposed atrocity."

I told her Action (a militant left-leaning, activist organization) led by Percy Green and the well-respected community activist Ivy Perry were opposing closing Homer G. Also the Black Social workers, Congressman William "Bill" Clay and the Coalition of Black Trade Unionists are all opposed to it being closed. A number of Black aldermen like Freeman Bosley and Clifford Wilson were all opposed to the closing. I told her there was a lot of opposition in the African American community to this closing. But she insisted I had not answered her question which was – what is the organization that is organizing the people against the closing of the hospital. Alice said I just listed a group of organizations that were opposed to it but none of the groups I named was actually in the community organizing any kind of mass protest.

I was not convinced so I said what about Congressman Bill Clay? He has raised his voice against Mayor Conway and has challenged him on the closing of Homer G. Phillips hospital. I pointed out that he probably represented one of the most powerful communities, which is his district that encompasses the largest African American population in the City. She said: "tell me who is hitting the pavement or knocking on doors to organize the people to protest by marching on City Hall demanding that the mayor cease and desist. Show me people in action on the streets opposing this closing," Alice demanded. She had me there. There weren't any people there. She said this was our challenge and we have to do it.

I told her that there was another part she wasn't considering. I mentioned that Civic Progress was too big and powerful to stop. They would throw money at everyone and get the hospital closed. How do we organize against them? She said I was probably right but that wasn't how people fight for social change – giving up before they even get started. She said win, lose or draw we have to fight. We have to look at it from the point of view that even if we lose the people will learn a lot about what it will take to fight back against these cut backs.

Budget austerity programs are not a new phenomenon of the 21st century – they were doing it in the early 1960's and during the Vietnam war. Then like now we were up against tremendous odds. When poor people fight rich people most of the time they will lose but her point was that each time people lose they gain a little more strength and understanding for the need for more radical measures. They get a chance to measure their capabilities against the capabilities of their opponents and they learn how to fight in new ways. Sure, enough I followed her advice and we organized the Ad Hoc Committee to Save Homer G. Phillips Hospital.

We formed a picket line around the hospital to prevent trucks from coming or moving equipment out. Some trucks got through so we slashed their tires and at night we pulled out their carburetors. We set up a tent city on the lawn. We went door to door asking people to come out and give what time they could. At first we were able to get 200 to 300 people from the neighborhood and we were able to surround the hospital. We even had hospital workers who were willing to help like Zenobia who was a registered nurse there who hollered out the window asking how she could help. I told her to throw some beds out the window (I was half joking) and then someone said Frank she is throwing out beds. We used those beds to barricade the entrances of the hospital. Alice said this is the type of thing you must do to let people know you mean business. We made national news and were the top story of all the local news organizations. Congressman Bill Clay sent key members from his staff to work with us on the picket line. For 17 days in August in 1979 we held the picket line, Pearlie Evans from Congressman Clay's staff was there every day and so was Herschel Walker, Alice Windom, Senator Gwen Giles, Alderwoman Boykins, Coalition of Black Trade Union members Lew Moye, Kenny Jones, John May, and Alliance members Pam Talley, Walle Amusa and Leo Fichtenbaum and members of the Communist Party.

As I've already mentioned above the Quakers hired me as a field secretary. While I was mostly working with Alice, I was also working with the Quakers and tried to get them to join us but this was not really their style yet they didn't stop me from participating.

Many of the trade unions were supportive like AFSCME, who had workers in the hospital; but also the late Bill Stoghill, President of SEIU Local 50, UAW Local 25 – the Coalition of Black Trade Unionists, Cassel Williams, the first Black president of the large IAM local. Harold Gibbons, International Vice President of the Teamsters union openly supported us but he could not bring the entire Teamster organization to support us.

This magnificent structure was Homer G. Phillips Hospital

There was also a Black shop steward with the Teamsters, we called Brother Mathews, who supported us. Gus Lumpe also with the Teamsters (editor of the Missouri Teamsters newspaper) and his wife Sheila supported us. We could not get the central labor council out on our side. There were personalities like the late Dick Gregory, Civil Rights activist Rev. Charles Coen with the Black United Front and Minister Farrakhan of the Nation of Islam who came out for us. The Muslim support was cautious yet ever pre-osent. Then there was the local CORE (Congress for Racial Equality) group who wanted to lead us in our frustration not lead us out of

it. They were problematic allies and mainly functioned as a Trojan horse for Civic Progress. Angela Davis, as leader of the National Alliance Against Racist and Political Repression, also came out and supported us unconditionally.

The Ad Hoc Committee to Save Homer G, Phillips was led by Walle Amusa, Pam Talley, Pearlie Evans, Senator Gwen Giles, Herschel Walker, Lew Moye, Kenneth Jones, Jay Ozier, Ora Lee Malone, Laura More, Alice Windom, Gwen Jackson and her daughter Carol Jackson Leo Fichtenbaum and Frank Chapman. The main mission of this ad hoc committee was to stop the closing of this major institution which was almost like a sacred institution to African Americans and the fear was that if they were successful here, others would certainly fall like dominoes – which is what happened. Our fight was not about the personalities or the big guns who came to the front lines. We got our greatest dividends from organizing the people.

We reached tens of thousands of people. We became topics of conversations in everyone's homes. And it really showed the shameful extent to which the African American community in St. Louis was being disregarded and trampled upon by Civic Progress and the powers that be, including City Hall.

Every African American institution in St. Louis, every African American leader of any import came out – a black leadership roundtable was started by Congressman Clay. The African American community was indisputably united in keeping this hospital open. It wasn't just about saving jobs or careers or keeping this hospital with the largest alumni of Black doctors in the world or having the largest nursing school training thousands of Black nurses – it was critical to the health of the African American community which had enormous health problems and would now reach a critical stage from being ignored. In every kind of way it adversely impacted on the African American community while the white power structure only considered the budget considerations.

When we say the African American community in its entirety was opposed to the closing of Homer G. Phillips, this also meant the organized crime elements within the African American community. Something I had completely overlooked. I had completely forgotten about the fact that I was in prison with most of the organized crime elements in North St. Louis. And some of them were occasionally involved in the movement.

For example, Sam (for obvious reasons I can't give you his real name) was a friend of mine (in organized crime) and during the

Homer G. Phillips struggle he called me over to his place and asked me how they could help. They were prepared to help in whatever way I wanted them to help. And, some of his relatives who were in the political arena were also out on the picket line with us and I was not even aware of that until he made me aware of it. He kind of said to me whether you like it or not we go to hospitals too. "We are very much concerned about this hospital being closed. We don't want it closed any more than anyone else. We haven't been bought off by Civic Progress – we can't be bought off – We make our own money...." What he was fishing for was did I want some help in straightening up the picket line – stopping the movement of equipment and supplies going out of the hospital – getting more people involved. What did I want him to do?

While Sam was talking I was thinking in my mind – do I want to do this? Do I want him to get involved with what I was doing – what stared me right in the face was the fact that I was on parole on a sentence of life and 50 years. And already I am in violation of the parole by talking to him. That's what crossed my mind. I was in prison with his brothers and we were friends and I had respect for him because he had done some work with Rap Brown and had been supportive of the Free Angela Davis campaign and had been supportive of me – off the record.

I told him the best way he could help me would be to not help me. And if he wanted to do something to save Homer G. Phillips I couldn't stop him from doing that but I wasn't giving him any advice. I thought the best policy from this point forward would be for us not to talk about this anymore. Frankly, we could not have an association at this time, public or private. And I was not just thinking of myself. I was also thinking about the movement and we already had a confrontation with law enforcement so we didn't need one because we were connected with any racketeering or anything like that.

That was my answer and I strongly suggested that whatever he does in terms of supporting the Homer G. Phillips struggle not to tell me about it as I did not want to know. He looked at me kind of puzzled and said, "Okay – its your call. I respect your position. I understand, but I had to ask and I hope you understand why I had to ask." I said, "Yes I understand on several levels, the friendship with your family and the fact that this affects everyone in the community. It's just that politically we can't move in concert on this...." And that is how it ended. In conclusion, I thought, so we had gangster elements on both sides – one I could talk to and one I couldn't. I could talk to Sam because he was in the neighborhood. The other gangster was Civic Progress and I couldn't talk to them and they were the most formidable because they had the money and resources to stop us. They were already getting busy getting with Aldermen and people in our ranks.

So-called Civic Progress started buying everyone out. They bought out Black politicians. They separated the Aldermen and bought out city hall. Congressman Clay even ran against Mayor Conway to highlight the issue and galvanize iron clad support. Had we gotten that we may have been able to get more of the white working-class communities on our side as well as the trade unionists. Civic Progress was operating behind the scenes proving that money talks and bullshit walks. The aldermen started disappearing as supporters. A handful stuck with us but we were unable to reach that critical mass. Our numbers started dwindling – our highest number of people we had was on the 17th day – 500 people – that was the day they sent in helicopters and alerted the national guard and deployed hundreds of police officers who came out to break us all up because we had a human barricade around the hospital.

Senator Gwen Giles and Pearlie Evans told me that I could not get arrested because it would mean a parole violation and they didn't need me back in prison. She said, "I am a state Senator and they won't arrest me and I disagreed and that was when she told me that she and I were getting into her car and I was to come with her as this was not about me going to jail. She said, "We are making our point – no one will see you as abandoning this and we have all talked this over and you have to get into the car." After seeing how determined she was and making my ego take a back seat I told her I would go with her. She was right it would have been totally pointless for me to continue and be arrested. I would be facing finishing out a sentence of life plus 50 years. I left with her and the hospital was officially closed that day. It took them another year to get the equipment out and today it is a senior housing facility.

1970's as the Age of Repression.

And Why Would We Consider the Year 1979 as Some Kind ff Turning Point?

There are two things we have to look at, I think. One is that the 70's was characterized by the rise of a new movement on the right and that movement was about defending the rights of white men which had been, according to them, totally undermined by the Civil Rights movement. According to these new styled racists the Black Freedom Movement had brought about affirmative action programs that placed unqualified African Americans, other racial minorities and women in jobs and in colleges at the expense of qualified white men being excluded and displaced.

Now, I don't think I am over simplifying their position. When you get rid of all the fluff and rhetoric I think that was fundamentally their position that the quota system which said for example that a certain number of minorities and women had to be employed, allowed internship –the enforcement of these quotas was, according to these reactionaries, denying the rights of white men to equally compete. In other words, their claim was that the quota system nullified competition and therefore was an attack on one of the fundamental pillars of democracy.

That in essence was their argument and that was what their move-ment was about. It was a movement to get rid of affirmative action programs and to undermine all legislation that put affirmative ac-tion and poverty programs in place. For example, CETA programs that allowed minorities to be trained as electricians so they could better compete for these jobs. They wanted all of these programs removed because they were giving minorities and women power over white men that they should not have. And so different right wing foundations, think tanks, etc. began drafting legislation and putting them on the ballots in different states as propositions – the point of these propositions were to eliminate affirmative ac-tion. They also started this movement in the courts in U.S. Steel Workers Union, et al vs. Weber. (Brian Weber was 32 years old, and worked as a laboratory assistant at a chemical plant. His company, Kaiser Aluminum and Chemical Corp, had a policy of allowing whites and blacks into a training program on a one to one basis, even though there were many more blacks than whites. This came from a collective agreement with United Steelworkers of America. Weber did not get in. More training would have led to a pay raise. Weber claimed this violated the Civil Rights Act of 1964 Title VII. The company and the union argued it was pursuing affirmative action to remedy historical disadvantages among blacks.) What they were also saying in terms of the workplace was that affirmative action was destroying seniority which was binding under union contract.

The attack was everywhere, in the courts, in the ballot box and legislatures. It was ridiculously called the "new civil rights movement". They had the gall to say they were fighting for the civil rights of white men. That movement got its steam in the 70's and became the central part of the platform of the right whose titular leader was now Governor Ronald Regan of California who they were going to be running for President of the United States. This was the same Ronald Reagan who tried to get Angela Davis executed in California. The same Ronald Reagan who supported the black list of his fellow artists when he was the President of the Actors Guild. It was the same Ronald Regan who supported the Right to Work laws all over the country. Reagan was organically connected with this defend the rights of white privilege, anti-union movement.

The radical right (as they were called back then) was also out to destroy the trade union movement. They were putting right to work propositions in state after state. They were trying to turn states that had been historically strong trade union states into right to work states.

The other thing they were pushing was the reinstitution of the death penalty. In Furman v. Georgia, the death penalty had been ruled by the U.S. Supreme Court to be unconstitutionally applied to African Americans in particular in that it was discriminatory in its application to blacks and poor people. There were guidelines set forth in Furman v. Georgia that said that state statutes (on the death penalty) as they stood did not meet constitutional requirements so they had to be rewritten in order for the death penalty to become legal. In state after state they brought the death penalty back. The 1970's became a period in which large numbers of executions took place. It also became a period when the anti death penalty movement soared to new heights. All across the country this was happening. Texas was outstanding in executions once the death penalty was reinstituted. Governor of Texas, George Bush executed a record number of people.

You also had omnibus crime bills one after the other, Senate Bill 1 which they introduced year after year in the Senate with different numbers. In the '70s we went from S1 to S13. We were able to stop these streams of repressive legislation for a while. All these omnibus crime bills created harsher sentences and draconian anti-drug laws, it was setting the stage for what we now call mass incarceration; that is, setting up a legal system designed to fill up the prisons.

All progressive elements in the movements and liberals were opposed to these bills. Most of the Democratic Party opposed them but ultimately caved into the ultra- right plugging away until things turned around by the end of the 70's. This avalanche of repression under the guise of law and order started in 1970 with passing of the Federal RICO statue. We felt this was a blow to the movement because the FBI could come to your organization and seize and impound your files – all they had to do was say they suspected racketeering. In the late 70's the movement started losing this fight.

Most significantly what was going on in the 70's was, in general terms, the de-industrialization of America. An updated study needs to be done on this. This meant plants closings – basic industry – steel mills, auto plants, coal mines, public hospitals. A situation being created where massive unemployment was taking place over night. For example, in Dearborn, Michigan, they closed down the plant and 30,000 people were unemployed overnight. In St. Louis, General Motors, 10,000 people over night. Cleveland, Los Angeles, New Jersey, Youngstown, Chicago, all across the nation. Let's take Chicago as an example.

Wisconsin Steel in Chicago. Wisconsin Steel, owned by International Harvester, was sold to Envirodyne in 1977 and by 1980 the Chicago plant was closed and about 2,000 or more workers were laid off. You had 2,000 workers thrown into the street and the last paycheck they were given before the plant closed – bounced! A man we knew who was also a member of our Alliance named Frank Lumpkin organized a committee of those steel workers to fight for them getting their severance pay and other entitlements. That fight lasted at least a decade before those workers finally got a multi-million dollar settlement. They didn't get compensated for things like losing their homes, health care bills that might have been unpaid. This is a microcosm of what was happening to millions of workers across this country. Remember while this deindustrialization was going on, they are also trying to destroy the unions. Nothing was more powerful in undermining and weakening the trade unions than plant closings. UAW, United Steel workers these unions became diminished overnight and their dues income was destroyed over night. This needs to be assessed in detail particularity by revolutionaries and progressives. This took place in the 70's and still persists today. Where once stood smoke stacks there are now dust bowls.

That is why we say deindustrialization created the material basis for the Age of Repression. Instead of the government addressing the mass unemployment and rapid deterioration of social conditions it instituted austerity programs and proceeded to establish a more rigorous regime of repression. These were the things that characterized this period. We talk about racism but there was also racist repression.

During the 70's Senator Frank Church convened a congressional hearing where tens of thousands of papers were brought to congress to show them the detailed extensive operations of the COINTELPRO under J. Edgar Hoover. It was demonstrated through uncontested evidence that the FBI and the CIA were engaged in illegal surveillance of the Civil Rights movement, the Peace Movement and the Labor movement. That they were involved in situations with the Black Panther party that led to people being murdered, for example the Fred Hampton and Mark Clark case in Chicago. People being imprisoned, for example, the Panther 21 in New York. People being forced into exile, Pete O'Neill and Assata Shakur were examples of that. Consequently, we have undeniable evidence that Panthers like Dharuba Bin Wahad were illegally framed up and put in prison by the FBI. They created false evidence and was using illegally obtained evidence.

My point here is to demonstrate what we mean by the Age of Repression. We mean that the democratic rights of the people to organize and protest were seriously curtailed by the illegal actions of our government. It was a repression unlike Jim Crow. Jim Crow was public and legal, this was illegal and clandestine. While Congress exposed it and we take our hats off to Senator Church we have to say that the right wing gained so much political power in the 70's in gaining control of the Congress and taking control of the executive branch by defeating President Carter and electing President Regan – nothing happened. It was not like Watergate – no one was prosecuted in this scandal even though people's lives had been lost and some had been falsely imprisoned. There was no move to prosecute anyone who were apart of this giant network of illegal activities J. Edgar Hoover had created. Hoover died in 1972 and COINTELPRO died with him but it would take years of litigation in state and federal courts before even a few people would get exonerated.

These things not only affected my life, they affected the life of our people of our country. We are not being melodramatic when we say that the Civil Rights Movement, the Peace Movement and the Trade Union Movement and the Women's Movement did not lose their momentum or their appeal to the American people because of internal problems within those movements. We learned from the Church hearings that the Civil Rights movement in particular, but all progressive movements in general were systematically undermined by the government. And that many people in the government, elected officials we sent to Congress did not know these things were happening. We had 2 governments going on, an ostensible one that seemingly operated in the open and an invisible government that was clearly about the business of repression. We are still assessing how that crippled and mangled Democratic institutions and torpedoed our movement.

When I look back none of us saw 1979 as any kind of historical turning point. Yet it was the beginning of an era in which the ultra right would take over the helm of government and force their extremist agenda upon the nation. In Missouri we did indeed fight back.

We won the struggle to defeat the ultra-right in their attempt to turn Missouri into a right to work state. We helped to build a mass campaign to defeat the anti-union, fascist right-to-work gang and scored a resounding victory. We as Marxist-Leninists and organizers of the masses went into this fight with the understanding that to defend the right of workers to organize into unions against the capitalist bosses was defending a fundamental democratic right that constituted the bedrock of all progressive struggles for democracy. The Alliance Against Racist and Political Repression, the Coalition of Black Trade Unionist (CBTU); and also Black union leaders and the rank and file in the United Auto Workers (UAW), the International Association of Machinists Union, and the Amalgamated Clothing and Textile Workers Union (ACTWU) and Service Employees International Union were all in the forefront of this struggle. It was a great moment and the most valuable lesson we learned is that labor united with the African American community can be an unbeatable alliance in fighting the ultra-right.

It was a lesson learned but soon forgotten in the dirt and blood of battle to save Homer G. Phillips hospital. The Black trade union leaders were not able to reap the benefits of this lesson by moving their respective unions into action to save Homer G. Phillips. When the African American community needed the help of organized labor most of the white union leaders were unresponsive. Jim Anderson (ACTWU), Gus Lumpe and Harold Gibbons (Teamsters) and some white leftist rank and filers (mainly Jerry Tucker from UAW) were the exception.

We duly noted how racism and racist attitudes weakens working class solidarity and then proceeded to fight for solidarity anyway. We continued then to present to the Central Labor Council black and white workers fighting for union representation. As black organizers we also worked with the Teamsters union to organize black warehouse workers. Gus Lumpe, the editor of the Missouri Teamster newspaper even acknowledged our contribution by featuring an article thanking Walle Amusa and Frank Chapman for helping in organizing a warehouse. But by far the best act of solidarity we did was with a white coal miner out of Stearns, Kentucky. Anne Braden was my mentor and in this part of my organizing saga. Let's start from the beginning.

St. Louis in 1979 was where I learned how to organize door-to-door, on the streets, block by block and through progressive organizations, unions, churches and community based organizations. I've already talked about struggle against the closing of the Homer G. Phillips hospital. What I didn't talk about was the impact these struggles had on the NAARPR national office and national board. We had people on our national board who represented all of the various strands of the movement. When I think about it, historically speaking, these were some very remarkable people.

For instance, Ann Braden who was strictly speaking probably the most undisputed white woman shero of the South. Unlike Anne Braden Lilian Smith who wrote *Killers of the Dream* was that rare case of an middle class Southern white woman being liberal, who gathered up the courage within herself to speak out against racism. *Killers of the Dream* was a book of essays about racism and the great hypocrisy of American democracy, that congenital blood stain of the republic that declared liberty and justice for all. You had the foremost champion of democracy on earth, the government of the United States preaching to the world about freedom, justice and equality but at the same time as Lillian Smith pointed out, having within its borders a vast section of the country known as the South wherein Black people were being publicly lynched and publicly humiliated by open legalized racial discrimination. Discrimination in everything, discrimination in hospitals where people are born – black hospitals and white hospitals; and even discrimination in grave yards – people could not be buried in the same places. From birth to death there was discrimination in the South and it was legal. So Lilian Smith took a moral stance that it may be legal but it was not moral. Her courageous book stated that it was morally wrong the way African Americans were being treated in the South and it left a horrible stain on our democracy – or our claim to be a democracy.

With Ann Braden it was a difference in approach. For her it was not only morally wrong, the laws and the customs of the South needed to be defied. She didn't put the burden on African-Americans to defy them, she thought white people should. She saw wrong and did something about it. She and her husband Carl were homeowners in Louisville Kentucky and they sold one of their homes to a black family in an all white suburb in Louisville Kentucky in the mid 1950s.

One cannot begin to imagine the uproar this started. First of all, the Ku Klux Klan immediately started burning crosses and tried to

blow people up and gunshots were fired. Ann Braden and her husband Carl united with some other white people and some African
Americans who were friends of the Wade family; they got together
and organized an armed self-defense. They went to the home and
set up a citizen's armed guard to protect this black family from
being terrorized and killed by the KKK. For this they were vilified
by the establishment and were called communists and outside
agitators. Anne was from the South, born and raised. Carl Braden
was a Southern trade union leader. They were vilified in the press
as communists and Carl Braden was charged with sedition, convicted and sentenced to15 years in prison. After serving 8 months
Carl was released on bail pursuant to a U.S. Supreme decision.
Shortly thereafter all charges were dropped.

Out of these struggles came the Southern Conference Educational Fund which was an inter-racial organization in the South
even as the civil rights movement was taking off. Black listed and
driven out of mainstream journalism Anne and Carl started their
own newspaper and called it *The Southern Patriot,* which had the
distinction of being the only militant pro-working class and civil
rights newspaper in the South. These people had been fighting
for black people to buy homes and live where they wanted to as
US citizens without fearing for their life or the legal consequences
even during the gathering storm of the Civil Rights movement.
When the Civil Rights movement finally broke out in Montgomery
Alabama with Rosa Parks, Ann Braden was one of the pioneers of
the movement and she readily joined. She and her husband became good friends with Dr. King and many of his close associates
and fellow civil rights organizers like Reverend Fred Shuttlesworth
and Reverend C T. Vivian. Both Ann and Rev. Fred Shuttlesworth
became leaders of our National Alliance.

Then there was also people like the late Judge Claudia Morcom,
who was a pioneer and advocate for black women in the law. She
was one of the first black women in Detroit who became a member of the bar. She worked with the National United Defense Committees to free Angela Davis as a lawyer. Later she became a judge
and she continued her involvement in the movement. She was
also one of the people who went down South to Mississippi in
1964 as part of the Freedom Summer to register people to vote.
She was also a colleague of Viola Liuzzo who was a white, working
class woman from Detroit that was murdered in 1965 while she

was riding in a car with a black man in Alabama. Also Lenox Hinds who as our General Council also represented Assata Shakur and Nelson Mandela and was the Executive Director of the National Conference of Black Lawers. Stephanie Peltier, the wife of Leonard Peltier served on our Executive Board as did the Vietnamese peace activist and scholar, David Truong. These were the kind of people who were on our national board and with whom I had the honor to join on the board in 1979.

I was elected to the Board in 1977 when the NAARPR had its National Conference in St. Louis. In 1979 Coraminita Mahr, Walle Amusa, Zenobia Thompson, Lew Moye, Kenneth Jones and Dough Lincoln in the wake of the save Homer G. Phillips struggle all became national board members from St. Louis. We were getting more attention and they started asking me to become a leader. I can't tell you how important that was for me. I was fresh out of prison (less than five years) and I was among these legendary figures of the civil rights movement about whom I had read about but never thought I would be sharing with them a membership in the alliance. I never thought they would become my colleagues and I one of them. It was almost like a dream and I was really on cloud 9. They started talking to me about becoming a part of the national leadership and asking me to do things.

One of those things I was asked to do which I remember distinctly was - Ann Braden asked me to come with her to speak with a white coal miner in Sterns Kentucky – the Blue Diamond Coal mines where they were having a fight to have unions. This strike came about as a result of 20 miners being killed in a hot mine that exploded and caved in on them. That sparked the strike for safety committees for the mines that coal miners could be a part of. It was a very desperate fight with state troopers and National Guard and shots fired back and forth.

I could not believe Ann Braden was asking me to go with her – I explained that I was still on Parole and she suggested I speak with my parole officer to get permission. I ended up lying to the parole officer who was a nice lady out of Clayton Missouri who never gave me any trouble. It wasn't a complete lie, I did have family in Kentucky but not in Sterns Kentucky. I told her I was visiting family there and I did not. The only family I visited was my working-class family.

Back to the coal miners. As it turned out I went to Sterns with a white coal miner named Darryll. He told me it would be best if I came into town unannounced and unknown. He could not be responsible for my safety. I asked Ann, why me? She explained I needed first hand experience there so I could report back to them about what was going on. Since I had been involved in several major struggles such as the struggle to save Homer G. Phillips and stop repressive right to work legislation it was thought that I had developed some important connections with trade unionists, textile workers, auto workers, and teamsters. It put me in a unique position to champion the cause of these miners in Kentucky which was a significant state for the Coal Miners Union. Anne thought the Alliance could build a national support network of community and labor. That convinced me that I might be able to play some role. The mere fact that she was asking me to go and that Charlene Mitchell our executive director agreed, I could not say no.

I went to Sterns and it was one of the most interesting experiences in my life. Here I was an African American in this small white coal mining town which was under siege with national guard and state trooper exchanging shots with the coal miners. It was a war zone. The miners were experienced squirrel hunters and knew how to shoot. There was an area near the coal mines where the troopers and guards knew not to go. They were in a stand-off.

I found out from these miners that back in the 20's or early 30s that Sterns was an African American town and most of the miners were Black. But they killed so many of them in the mines that they left and the Irish were brought in. It was such an incredible story I couldn't believe it. These miners had to learn in the dirt and blood of battle that it wasn't just about skin color but it was also about class. Ever since the days of slavery white workers in the South have experienced extreme forms of class oppression. Sometimes under the most horrendous conditions white and black workers united against their common oppressors. The hot mines killed black miners as well as white ones.

The Irish people have an interesting history in the South. Ann Braden, her maiden name was Ann McCarty, was Irish. They have an interesting history dating back to the time of the legendary Molly McGuires who, according to legend, were a group of radical socialists who organized in the coal mines in the later part of the

19th century. They were very conscious of the fact that they needed a union and they were also very much aware of how the mine owners used race to divide the black and white workers. In those types of divisions, the workers always lost. Nobody understood this better than Black workers since they were the hod-carriers of the labor movement.

This took me back to my prison experience because mostly what I met there was poor Black people. I had lots of prejudices about white people and many of those white people stood beside us and fought for racial equality in the prisons. It showed me that people could identify class interests despite race. Here I was seeing it repeated – this time in the so called free world. I saw these poor white people inhumanly treated by the mine owners but willing to work with me, an African American, and the National Alliance to fight the mine owners. I think Dr. King also experienced this same thing when he was organizing the poor people's march on Washington. He took the march to the poor white people in the South. In fact, this is an aspect of the Civil Rights movement that has almost been totally ignored and I don't think that was by mistake. I am so grateful that I had this experience because it is much more valuable than anything I could have read in a book. I saw with my own eyes and experienced feelings of solidarity with the coal miners and other working people regardless of their color.

Darryl came back to St. Louis with me and I got him an audience with the Central Labor Council. This guy could talk – he was a natural born orator. The Central Labor Council in St. Louis was dominated by craft unions and I was amazed he could get any support – but he did. The Teamsters and the United Auto Workers and the Coalition of Black Trade Unionists I expected to be supportive but not the Central Labor Council because they were a conservative, non-progressive group. It amazed me that Darryl was able to get their support.

Once I saw him speak I could see how. He was very powerful, even though he was not well educated but he had a strong sense of justice and the ability to articulate that in words. I was so impressed with him I asked him to come to New York with me to the national conference of the National Alliance Against Racist and Political Repression. I wanted him to give the same speech to them and I wanted him to get their support in other cities and open the door to nationalizing the coal miners struggle in Sterns Kentucky. Also, it could raise much needed money because the union was running out of money – the strike fund was nearly depleted.

Given that reality Darryl was more than happy to come to New York and the National Alliance Board was happy to put him up and pay for him to go to New York. He came to New York and he spoke and the meeting was at the Martin Luther King Labor Center. The union that gave us the space to hold our convention was Local 1199 – which was the health care workers union. The speech he gave at that convention was even more powerful than the one he gave at the Central Labor Council. He knew in New York he didn't have to win anyone over – he knew he was among allies. His message was how we could help the coal miners to deepen and broaden the struggle for more support throughout the country. He also pointed out that the Rockefellers were the primary owners of the Blue Diamond Mines in Eastern Kentucky. He said they had been running those mines for a long time and that really lit the audience up. Now they were determined to have the Rockefellers hear from them because most of the people in the audience were from New York. He also talked about the racial issues and the necessity for black and white workers to work together in the fight against the rich and powerful.

That was the climax of that story. We did a lot of things at the convention in New York in 1979. We came out for the struggle nationwide to save public hospitals. We recommitted ourselves to the struggle to free Nelson Mandela and the Wilmington 10 and all political prisoners and all of the members of the Black Panther Party who had been framed and thrown into prison by the FBI unjustly and who were now also fugitives and exiles as a result of the FBI's counter intelligence program. It was an illegal operation that consisted of the FBI, the CIA and local law enforcement agencies. It was designed to undermine and destroy the African American civil rights movement. It was founded and fashioned by J. Edgar Hoover the director of the FBI.

The people who were imprisoned as a result of this program, we adopted their cases. Assata Shakur who was now in Cuba was victimized by this program. We have two Panthers who are still in exile as a result of this program, namely, Assata and Pete O'Neil.

Assata Shakur was just put back on the terrorist list (in 2014). She was allegedly involved in a shoot out on the New Jersey Turnpike in 1971. The same year she was shot on the highway and Senator Frank Church was holding hearings on the COINTELPRO program. As we pointed above those hearings revealed that the program was illegal and violated the rights of citizens of the US who were engaged in organized protests. The FBI and the CIA disrupted activities and in several cases instigated the murder of people for political reasons. They were political assassinations secretly ordered by J. Edgar Hoover. Advocating revolution is not a crime, at least theoretically, in our country; but the FBI acted as if it was a crime.

In the 1979 convention we recommitted ourselves to our principal to fight against racist and political repression and for the rights of labor to organize and strike.The rights of labor, that was the significance of Darryl at our convention. He added this important element to our cause. The St. Louis contingent thereby made a very important contribution to involve the labor unions in our struggle and we in their struggle.

Also, something else very important happened in New York which sort of catapulted me into the national leadership of the Alliance and into the smiling graces of the Communist Party. The National Alliance board commissioned me to go into New York two weeks before the National Conference to organize a rally to take place on the eve of the conference at the famous Convent Avenue Baptist Church. I had never done any on-the-ground organizing in Harlem so I was not quite sure that I could measure up to the task.

I asked Charlene Mitchell, who was then executive secretary of the Alliance and the greatest organizer I had ever known, did she think I could really get the job done. Her response was, "You better get the job done!" And as I was tightening up, with it written all over my face, she smiled at me and offered some words of encouragement. Main thrust of what she said is that I was learning how to be an organizer and that I had made a good start in St. Louis.

Organizing is a science firmly rooted in practice and so Charlene was saying to me that the same organizing tools and methods I used in St. Louis could also be used in New York. "In fact," she said, "based on what I've seen you do in St. Louis you are a walking community organizer and we intend to use you." She assigned five people to work with me who knew the city in general but knew Harlem in detail particularity.

We put out press statements and flyers announcing that Angela Davis, James Baldwin, Judge Bruce Wright, one of the surviving Scotsboro Boys, Jose Soler, President of the Puerto Rican Socialist Party, Cleveland Robinson (the legendary Black Trade Union leader of New York), Henry Foner, President of the Furrier Workers Union and Anne Braden would be the speakers.

We went on radio talk shows (Black, progressive and mainstream). We met with church leaders (like Father Lawrence Lucas who once hosted the Black Panther Party Breakfast Program), with Elombe Braith, leader of the Patrice Lumumba Coalition, John Henrik Clarke (the Garveyite, Professor icon), district political leaders in Harlem (Bill Perkins of the Harriet Tubman Club), with Harlem Fight-Back leader, Jim Haughton, Harlem labor leader, President Jim Butler of AFSME local 420, Brother Arnold Cherry rank and file leader of the Transit Workers Union. Also we had Maria Ramos to contact and meet with all the Black and Puerto Rican Student Organizations. We met with and got statements from cultural figures like Ruby Dee, Ossie Davis, Louise Patterson and I believe Pete Seeger and Ossie Davis made up the cultural part of the program.

Most importantly I met with the Communist Party District Organizer in Harlem who was very knowledgeable about all the grass roots movers and shakers in Harlem, both known and unknown. I was having the most profound and richest cultural and political experience of my life and I knew it. Ron Tyson, a gifted and brilliant young writer of the *Workers Weekly World* Communist Party newspaper helped us with press releases and weekly write-ups in the party press. We became friends and it is at this time that I met his brother Kevin Tyson who was a tireless foot soldier and we also became friends. The result of our endeavors was a turn-out of nearly five thousand people. We could not get everyone in the church, which holds over two thousand. So we threw the church doors open and turned up the sound system. People stayed for several hours. In three weeks we went through Harlem like an organizing fine-tooth comb, leaving no known stone unturned and finding some that we didn't know about.

Before returning to St. Louis I met with Henry Winston, the National Chairman of the Communist Party. Winston (whom we affectionately called Winnie) was blind as a result of medical neglect he had suffered while in federal prison. He had been convicted under the Smith Act, which was an unconstitutional law that outlawed the Communist Party. I remember when I spoke to Winnie his head seemed to always be tilted toward his right shoulder while his left hand would be rubbing his chin. Two things stood out about this meeting: 1) Winnie asked me numerous and very detailed questions followed up by quick, insightful and dialectically loaded comments that prepared you for the next question. I had never conversed with a person this thoughtful and analytical about organizing. It was very stimulating and I found myself reliving things as I was describing them. It was very exciting. 2) When we finally stopped I suddenly realized that this conversion left me thoroughly exhausted. All I could think about was going home and resting.

When I came back from New York we were invigorated and we started developing ties with the labor movement which had not been seen in a long time in St. Louis. I started writing articles against apartheid for the The St. Louis Labor Tribune. I started doing book reviews for the Missouri Teamsters. We recruited into our ranks, iron workers, construction workers, auto workers and a few teamsters. At least a third of our local branch, which consisted of about 200 people, consisted of rank and file leaders and members in the trade unions. There was at least one or two trade unionists which were white union workers and one of them was Dough Lincoln, a rank and file construction worker and a leader of ACTWU by the name of Jim Anderson. Then there was black rank and file union leaders like Lou Moye, Kenneth Jones, John May and a white auto worker named Steve Holland.

It gave us a very strong and powerful chapter and it made an indelible impression on Charlene Mitchell, our national executive director and on the national leadership of the Communist Party like Jim Jackson who was one of the intellectual leaders of the party. Jim and Henry Winston who were national leaders of the Communist Party were both Black. They asked me to really consider moving to New York and becoming part of the national leadership of the Alliance. I told them that I had just gotten married and I have a step daughter who is in elementary school and is only about 6 or 7 years old. I further stated that I have a young wife who is just now graduating grad school and receiving her Masters in Urban studies and who doesn't have a job. I am working for the American Friends Committee and earning only $800 a month. My wife didn't expect me to support them on that so she was looking for a job. I was told by the Party if I went to New York they could guarantee me that my wife could get a job. Until that happened they would subsidize me by paying our rent and they would also help us in securing housing all of which would be set up by the time we got there. They told us we needed to come right away – in a few months.

So this discussion continued back and forth between us. I made another trip to New York by myself but I kept my wife abreast of everything that was going on. She was truly an amazing woman because she told me if I wanted to go to New York and it was important to advancing the struggle of the movement then she would come with me. I suggested I go to New York first and get established and then call for her. She said that wouldn't work be-cause we already spent too much time apart already. She said if I went to New York she would have to come – she was not going to be left behind. We discussed leaving her family and she said I was her family now and Coralita was my daughter. I commented that she appeared to have a stronger position than I did on this and she replied she wasn't stupid – she knew I would be going to New York as I was intoxicated with the movement. She said, "I know you are going and I am determined that you don't go without me."

I found this unbelievable and kept exploring all of our options so that we wouldn't get into one of those situations where she would blame me for making her come to New York. Consequently, I said, "What about your career and the connections you have here and all of the resources." She looked at me dumbfounded and said – "You don't get it – I don't love my connections, I love you and I would not be happy here while you are there." She said her degree was good throughout all of the United States, not just Missouri. In addition our friends are committed to helping us when we get there. Finally, she asked me why I wanted to go without here? That questions hit me right between the eyes. I realized then that I didn't want to go without her. In reality I did not want to go without her and Coralita but thought they might be a hindrance to me doing the things I wanted to do as an organizer. I thought professional organizing as I understood it was not something that is compatible with family life. She hit me in the head with that comment and I humbly admitted to her that I didn't want to leave without her. We left for New York, after we wrapped things up, in a U-Haul truck driven by brother Walle Amusa, a brilliant young chemist from Nigeria, who was an integral part of our movement that we had recruited into the Alliance.

REFLECTIONS ON THE PASSING OF THE SEVENTIES INTO THE EIGHTIES

Looking back, we see the seventies as clearly a moment when repression took a sharp turn due to economic and social conditions aggravated by massive plants closings and the austerity budget cuts. We see the seventies also as a prelude to the emergence of neo- liberalism. By 1976 the federal budget was hogtied to the Wall Street Barons and the Military Industrial Complex. While military spending sky-rocketed budgeting for social programs plummeted.

The government played Robin Hood in reverse. I remember that everyone in the peace movement was talking about the huge sums of money being spent by the government to build up the nuclear arsenal to keep up with the Soviet Union and to carry out wars of aggression against developing countries. There were public forums and debates about guns vs. butter. The Vietnam War was over but the cost of that war and the preparation for future wars of intervention in Chile, Nicaragua or any country that defied U.S. imperialism was economically penalizing the poor, the working class, and the nationally oppressed Black and Brown peoples. One obvious result of this bourgeoning military budget was its virtually wiping out of the last vestiges of LBJ's antipoverty programs. Those job training programs like CETA (Comprehensive Employment Training Assistance), and the Youth jobs programs over the summer months were all wiped out in a flash under President Jimmy Carter. Carter was hailed as a peanut farmer from Georgia who became President. The Black and poor people in the South were chanting: "We don't want no peanut pie; Jimmy Carter's got a New South Lie!"

With Jimmy Carter we had a pro=austerity program president who, unlike his successor Ronald Reagan, was not a warmonger. So, when I went to New York in 1979 to assist Charlene Mitchell as her Associate Director of the National Alliance Against Racist and Political Repression (NAARPR) I had no clue of what lied ahead for our organization and me personally. We had beat back the right to work ballot initiative with a broad and militant workers-community alliance. But shortly thereafter the single largest plant (i.e. the GM plant employing 10,000 workers) in the heart of the Black community (in North St. Louis) closed. Plant closings hit our communities like a hailstorm instantly laying off tens of thousands of workers and resulting in the closing of public schools and hospitals. What I didn't know was that Ronald Reagan the right-wing extremist who backed right to work laws and the racist driven white backlash against affirmative action was going to be elected President in 1980.

I arrived in New York in the early winter of 1979. In the Summer of 1979, the ordeal of Joan Little ended with her freedom. This case came about in 1974 when Joan Little (a 24-year-old Black woman prisoner) killed a white jailer (named Clarence Alligood) who tried to rape her. Angela Davis had played a great galvanizing role in building the movement to "free Joan Little" by emphasizing sister Joan's right to self-defense and by pointing out that she had "truly been raped and wronged many times by the exploitative and discriminating institutions of this society." Joan Little's victory was a great boost for our movement and made all the more real by the fact that one of her lawyers, Jerry Paul, was also a member of the national board of the NAARPR. We believed that we had a good tailwind that would push us into even more victories in the Wilmington Ten cases. And we were right for we did win some measure of freedom for Rev. Ben Chavis and others involved in the Wilmington Ten cases.

But what I didn't know was that two veteran civil rights workers, Maggie Bozeman (51) and Julian Wilder (69) would be convicted of voter fraud in Alabama and given the maximum sentence of 5 years. After the passing of the Voting Rights Act in 1965 Black people living in the Black belt counties in Alabama and Mississippi were frequently charged with voter fraud and throughout the South there was an attempt to criminalize Black elected officials. But Albert Turner in Sumpter County Alabama and our Alliance folks (in Birmingham, Rita Anthony, Judy Hand, Colonel Stone Johnson and Scott Douglas knew how to fight back and they did. They engaged people in organizing a mass defense campaign to defend those charged with voter fraud and they organized people in the struggle to extend the Voting Rights Act. In 1981 Ronald Reagan was getting sworn in as President and Eddie James Carthan, the first elected Black Mayor of Tchula was forced to leave office after trumped charges and a two-year jail sentence. I knew then that here were two events with grave implications for our movement for Reagan was the spear-head of a new ultra-right movement whose stated objective was to crush the Black liberation Movement, coral and destroy the labor movement and up the ante for counter-revolutionary, counter-insurgency movements everywhere. The persecution and expulsion of Mayor Carthan represented the beachhead of extending into the eighties the new era of repression aimed at totally dismantling the Black Liberation Movement economically, politically and culturally. The attack on Mayor Carthan was part of a broadside frontal attack against all the gains of the Civil Rights Movement. In every area of life. In every government institutional structure policies were instituted to serve monopoly capital by dampening class struggle and pumping up national oppression. Unions were both forced into retreat and abolished (e.g. PATCO the air traffic controllers union was the first union to be busted

Under Reagan) and the AFL-CIO along with so-called peace movement groups was tricked into counter-insurgency programs in Southern Africa and throughout the world. These political practices were designed to pump hormones into a dying capitalism prior to the theory of neoliberalism laying claim to them. Neoliberalism is not a new mode of production replacing capitalism/ imperialism, it is a new mode of discourse that rationalizes the social savagery of monopoly-capitalism in its dying stage.

I witnessed these hormones being shot into the blood stream of monopoly-capitalism in the seventies with President Reagan's trickle- down wealth program which promised that the workers would get benefits by sacrificing their gains so the capitalist bosses could prosper in order for everyone (in the long run) to prosper. We saw increased racist and political repression not only in Alabama, Mississippi, North Carolina and other areas of the deep South increasing with the erosion of the Voting Rights, with racist frame-ups and railroading Black and Brown people into prisons under the new draconian drug laws. We saw liberal and conservatives alike argue that welfare was subsidizing the vestiges of slavery thus proving the basis for a united front of liberals and conservatives for the abolition of welfare. We saw the rebirth of the Daniel P. Moynihan Report which said "at the heart of the deterioration of the fabric of Negro society is the deterioration of the Negro family..." By placing the Black condition of inequality within the deteriorating structure of the Black family the Moynihan Report makes the consequences of oppression the cause of oppression. In other words, the Moynihan Report was a source and one of the component parts of the neoliberal ideology that blames Black people for being responsible for their own conditions of oppression. These ideas rationalized and justified the rise of the prison industrial complex, deregulation, privatization and budget cuts that erode and destroy social programs for Black, Brown and working-class people.

What Black people are responsible for is that despite 250 years of the auction block of slavery, 150 years of racist discrimination and national oppression and genocide they have through struggle survived. Even when hope appeared on the horizon, as it did with the historic victory of Harold Washington winning in the Mayoral election in Chicago in 1983 it often came with bitter setbacks and sometimes out and out defeats. Harold Washington would not have won without a firm alliance with the Mexican community and the Chicano and the Puerto Rican Liberations Movements.

Key to this Black and Latinx unity was an outstanding and brilliant Chicano, working class leader name Rudy Lozano. Harold said it himself that Rudy would become Deputy Mayor but before that could happen, he was assassinated. We worked with Rudy's wife Lupe for a few years trying to get a congressional investigation into his murder. This tragic murder of Rudy was followed a few years later by the sudden death of Harold Washington. Our movement was devasted but not defeated. The struggled continued in the Latino communities with emerging leaders like Jesus "Chuy" Garcia and Luis Gutierrez. In the Black community there was great difficulty in maintaining the progressive movement heralded by the election of Washington. In these memoirs we cannot do justice to analyzing the causes of these setbacks, but we felt obligated to mention them in passing. In speaking of the political trauma that impacted our movement in the eighties, I must mention one that leaves me baffled and angry even to this day. And that one is when the Philadelphia PD dropped two one- pound bombs of

Tovex (a dynamite substitute) on a building occupied by members of an organization called Move. The bombs hit a gasoline powered generator on the roof of the house causing a fierce fire that engulfed 65 nearby houses. Five children, ages 7-13, and six adults were killed.

I went to Philadelphia a few 24 hours later knowing and feeling outrage that Black people had just been brutally murdered, massacred by a white Police commissioner (Gregore Sambor) in a city that had just elected its first Black Mayor, Wilson Goode. After the massacre we called him Mayor No Goode. I went to see for myself what these mass murderers had done. I remember standing at the edge of the block looking at the debris of burned down buildings and I was very angry and choked up with emotion. How could the Mayor have agreed to this? Why was Black Philadelphia not in open rebellion? I didn't know John Africa or Ramona Africa (a survivor) or any of the five children and six adults murdered. But I knew that I was angered and made bitter by the fact that a lack of collective out-rage on the part of our people was painfully missing.

This was a bad omen, a sign of a new era of ruthless relentless repression and police tyranny that would draft the police crimes of the sixties. In fact, what happened ten months later was a precursor to what would follow the audacious criminal acts of the police and public officials. A duly appointed commission found that "No Goode" and his police commissioner had acted "recklessly" but not criminally. No one was criminally charged. The Mayor "No Goode" was reelected and the people were taxed about $45 million to rebuild the neighborhood for the next 15 years. Shortly after the fire-bombing of MOVE in Philadelphia we moved the National Alliance office from 27 Union Square West to 125 West 119 th Street in Harlem. He seems like as soon as we set foot in Harlem we were working at first with the progressive district leader Bill Perkins of the Harlem Harriet Tubman Democratic Party Club on a case involving the murder of a young Black scholar, Edmund Perry who was murdered by some decoy cops on 110 th Street. Perry, a 17-year-old Black youth had just received a scholarship award to go to college.

Harlem was outraged, we united under the militant leadership of the late Elombe Brath's Patrice Lumumba Coalition, Jim Bell of the

Coalition of Black Trade Unionists, Harlem's own Labor leaders Jim Butler of AFSME Local 420 and Jim Haughton of Harlem Fight Back and our own Communist Harlem leader Charlene Mitchell, we pulled together that same night (April 30, 1987) over 2000 people to march on the 126 th Street Harlem Police station. It was a militant and spirited march but the demand for justice was narrowed down to firing and charging the killer cops.

These were busy and brutal times for our people and our movement. White youth mobs in Benson Hurst and Howard Beach Brooklyn were attacking Black men for just being in their neighborhoods. Again, we had mass demonstration and marches chanting "No Justice, No Peace". Murders were being committed and the police and prosecutors were just sitting on their asses. And then came 1989 with the most vile, racist frame-up since the Scottsboro cases of the thirties. The Central Park Five case involving five teen age kids, four Black and one Puerto Rican who were charged with raping and assaulting a young white woman jogger. It was like all of the lynch mob antics of the Jim Crow era were back to haunt us and take from us all the hard-won gains we had made as a people. It became clear now that the criminal justice was indeed the New Jim Crow.

For me 1989 was that moment of truth in the struggle where we had the opportunity to stand up and fight back with some of the true freedom fighters of Harlem (like Elombe Brath, and Michael Warren) who were never confused about which side they were on, who militantly defied the powers that be, the prosecutors, Gov. Cuomo , Mayor Koch, the police thugs, and the mass media and advanced the struggle against impossible odds.

Also, in 1989 the NAARPR was stretched beyond its capacity. From the mid-eighties to 1989 I visited and wrote letters far more political prisoners than we could help. I remember visiting Black Panthers Dhoruba Bin Wahad, Nuh Washington and Anthony Bottom and how sad it was because all we had the capacity to do at that time was to give moral support and publicize their cases. The same situation confronted us in dealing with the Leonard Peltier case. As a national organization by 1989 we were definitely in a state of decline. In my personal life I was also in a state of decline. Let me just note in closing that the so-called fall of the Soviet Union and the subsequent political chaos it created on the left also took its toll on our movement and me personally. In 1989 we no longer had a powerful friend, as far as I could tell, to aid us in making the international community aware of our plight as a people.

I had read about the Judas Time during the McCarthy era when political cowards went before Congress to denounce communism and collectively wrote a book called the "God That Failed" but I never thought I would live to see such treachery in my life time. The imperialists aided and abated by revisionists and renegades defeated twentieth century socialism in the land of its birth. It was a great day for traitors and a sad, regrettable day for revolutionaries. Yet the damned don't cry. We were challenged to rise above a trivial and cowardly past that had been forced upon us by our enemies, to move on to the rebuilding of a new revolutionary movement. I believe we will meet that challenge. We must for socialism is a historical necessity. I believe the struggle continues and that victory is certain.

New York, New York

To me New York City was legend and reality. I read so much about it and knew people who had been there and I had nothing but admiration for it. I considered New York to be the cultural, intellectual and radical hub of the USA. In the 1950's I was influenced by the beatnik culture and people (the Holy Barbarians) like Jac Kerouac, Alan Ginsberg, and a very talented and genius of a writer named Leroi Jones who later changed his name to Amiri Baraka.

I thought Baraka and James Baldwin were to the sixties what Alain Locke (author of *The New Negro*) was to the twenties (i.e. The Harlem Renaissance), the spiritual spear-head of the Black Renaissance in Harlem. For me Baldwin's *Nobody Knows My Name* and Jones' *Blues People* and *System of Dante's Hell* was the opening shots in what was to become the greatest blossoming of artistic/ literary geniuses ever witnessed in Harlem and New York City.

There was the launching of *Freedomways* in 1961 by Esther Cooper Jackson, Paul Robeson and W.E.B. DuBois, which created a much needed cultural forum for the Negro Freedom Movement then emerging in the South. In the pages of *Freedomways* I learned about such writers as Loraine Hansbery, Claude Brown, Alice Walker, Kenneth Clarke, Shirley Graham John Oliver Killens, Ed Bullins, Jean Carter Bond, Ron O'Neal, John Henrik Clarke, Ernest Kaiser, Nikki Giovanni and the list goes on. But I will never forget that through *Freedomways* and Esther Jackson in particular I became friends and comrades with James E. Jakson (a brilliant Black Marxist-Leninist and courageous freedom fighter who was my intellectual mentor).

Harlem was considered to be the cultural capital of Black America. This was the home of the Harlem Renaissance where you had a flowering of African American genius never before seen in this country. Modern Jazz, Bebop had its birth in Harlem, NY at Minton's Playhouse with Charlie Parker, Dizzy, Thelonious Monk and others. You name a great artist or great intellectual in the African American community and at one time or another they lived in Harlem. Dubois, Paul Robeson, as well as great thinkers and organizers like Hubert Harrison, Marcus Garvey (Universal Negro Improvement Association, the most massive African American organization in the history of America), such was phenomenal Harlem. And out of it came Adam Clayton Powell one of the great political icons of the 20th Century, the first African American congressman to fight for Civil Rights on the floor of Congress. A Phillip Randolph the father of the Sleeping Car Porter's Union who was a socialist and one of the editors of the *Messenger* magazine (Chandler Owen was the co-editor). Randolph was a great labor organizer and leader. He was the one who came up with the idea of the March on Washington long before it happened in 1963.

So here I am in the place where African Americans had really made their mark on every aspect of American culture and social life. This was the legend, history and culture of it.

The reality of Harlem is that when I got there, it was, in the words of Kenneth Clark, a dark ghetto. There was also in Harlem widespread unspeakable poverty. The protest movement in the 60's was always uptown in Harlem and one of the leaders was Jesse Gray who gathered up a huge sack of rats and mice and took them to City Hall and let them go. That was his way of dramatically proving that Harlem had lots of rats. Rumor has it that he made some comment to the effect that the rats had better friends in City Hall than in Harlem.

There was also Jim Haughton who had been in and around the Communist Party but who broke with them and started a group called "Harlem Fight Back". Harlem Fight Back was an organization that fought for Black people to have jobs in construction. He was demanding affirmative action from the unions. What spurred this on was that they were trying to build a huge building in Harlem called the Harlem State Office Building.

The people of Harlem immediately noticed that on the construction site there wasn't even one black person. Not even gophers. So, Harlem Fight Back began to wage struggle to get black workers on the site – their position was that if no black workers were working on that site they would shut it down. They were able to rally thousands of people and shut it down. They made it such that the only way the City could build that building was to negotiate with Fight Back and the City did what it had to do. These kinds of things had already taken place by the time I got there.

A leading member of the Party had died right before we got to Harlem and we were promised his apartment. The first day we got there we found out that there was a problem with the will and everything was tied up in Probate Court including the apartment. Members of his family had taken it over and they were hostile to the party. So we had moved all of our furniture and belongings to NY and we had nowhere to go since we learned all of this the day we arrived. I don't know why we weren't told earlier and I was so disgusted and angry with the situation because I felt we had been treated poorly. How could you have people come a thousand miles believing they had a place to live and not tell them.

Charlene Mitchell who was then the executive director of the Alliance felt bad. She offered a room in her apartment that we could stay in until we could find suitable housing. We had no choice. We had 3 people, my wife, myself and step daughter living in a room just big enough to hold one bed and a dresser. All of us had to sleep in the one bed. I could not deal with that. So I told Charlene, I can't do this and asked her if she had somewhere I could stay. She told me I could stay downstairs with the widow of William L. Patterson (one of the great legal minds of Harlem and one of the writers who wrote the Petition to the UN entitled *We Charge Genocide;* he was a legendary civil rights lawyer in Harlem.

So there I was in his room sharing an apartment with his wife Louise Patterson who was 75 years old at that time and a cultural icon of Harlem in her own right. I agreed to do these arrangements – I didn't see any other choice. I left my family with Charlene and I lived in the Patterson apartment. This went on for months while we looked for housing and my wife looked for a job, even though she was promised a job. She ended up having to scramble to get the job without any real help. She did a long shot. She went to the Urban League and applied for a job and they sent her to the housing development corporation (HDC) in lower Manhattan. She got the job. They had an opening and she had the academic credentials and she used some of her movement experience and they were impressed with that. When she got the job she was so excited; we went out to dinner and the next day we went to look for an apartment. Charlene and the Party were willing to lend us some money so we could get suitable housing. We started hunting and found a place in the Bronx off of 161st St., next to the Grand Concourse and two blocks from Yankee Stadium and a big beautiful park. I really didn't think we would be able to get it but we negotiated and negotiated until we finally did. Someone else was also trying to get the apartment. Something happened to them so the owner came offered us the apartment if we could get one month's rent, one month's security and a deposit.

We came up with the money with our savings and the money we could borrow. My wife was making a nice salary – almost ten times what I was making with the Alliance. We were very happy with the apartment. We moved all our stuff in from storage. Within a month or so we were in the apartment and she had seen a few paychecks. We thought we had it made. She was also in the Teamsters and I was able to get Teamster benefits as well. That is how our life got established in NY.

I dove right into my work. Coraminita was right there with me and she also agreed to head up the local branch of the Alliance. We were working on the Wilmington 10 case night and day. We were also working on the Johnny Imani Harris case. He was a young black man who was accused of raping a white woman in Mobile, Alabama. He was facing the death penalty and was on death row. We were desperately working to get a stay of execution which we were able to do. We were also involved in the struggle to free Nelson Mandela and pushing the petition campaign across the country. We always invited the African National Congress to all of our events and we were solidly involved in the South African movement. We worked on Black Panther Party cases like Geronimo Pratt and Dharuba Bin Wahad – he was part of the Panther 21. We were involved in a petition campaign to the Justice Department and Congress to extend the voting rights Act. We were fighting some cases in Alabama – two senior citizens – Maggie Bozeman and Julia Wilder – These women were facing criminal charges for voting fraud in Alabama. The racist elements in Alabama had used this as a scare tactic to scare people from voting. We used this case to expose this and to promote our cause to extend the voting rights act.

During this time Charlene Mitchell was the Executive Director of the Alliance and I was the Associate Director. Alice Windom and Herschel Walker taught me about community organizing and Charlene Mitchell taught me and a host of other people on our national executive board about organizing nationally and internationally, and she was a real genius at it. I talked about the historic mass campaign to Free Angela Davis and All Political Prisoners but what I failed to mention is the undisputed fact that the pivotal organizer and leader of this campaign was Charlene Mitchell. She had been in the movement since she was a teenager and was mentored by some of the best Communist leaders in America. I can hardly express in words what it felt like to be working beside this great woman who saw way more in me than I ever saw in myself. She taught me that being a Marxist-Leninist, revolutionary requires at least two things: consistent study of the science of Marxism-Leninism and to be constantly engaged in the struggles of the working class masses and all progressive struggles to advance democracy, to end racial and national oppression and economic exploitation of all workers.

Finally, we were also involved in JP Stevens Boycott and getting union recognition for the Textile Workers Union at the JP Stevens plant in North Carolina. NC was a right to work state so this was a big challenge not only for union recognition but also to move people to organize to repeal the Taft Hartley Act – the right to work laws. This was the overall character of my work for the next ten years from 1979 to 1989. What activities I became involved in to carry out this work was amazing. I became a member of the Human Rights Committee of the World Peace Council so we could go to various countries around the world to organize support for all of these cases.

In 1981 I came off parole and I was able to get a passport. In 1982 I started to travel. The Peace Council decided to send me to the Soviet Union because we really wanted to take advantage of the political situation between the US and Soviet Union. US was accusing the Soviet Union of massive civil rights violations harking back to the Stalin era. They had a massive campaign to free Solzhenitsyn who was on an island that they called the Devils Island of the Soviet Union. It was not clear what crimes he had committed. Did he speak out against the government? The Soviets had accused him of working as a spy or working for the CIA. Amnesty International said he was being persecuted because of his political beliefs. I didn't really know how much of it was true but I knew my country was repressing, killing and jailing people of color on a mass scale. What we did know was that the US was no angel. And we were going to challenge our country – if they were going to be for human rights half way around the world then they needed to be for human rights here. Our government had people in jail for allegedly violating laws when all they really did was protest injustice, people were being denied the right to organize or protest the policies of the US government.

So, we had our political prisoners too. We challenged our government to address the issue. When I was in the Soviet Union for almost a week, I was very careful not to say anything that could be interpreted as me being hostile to the people of the U.S. our issue was with our government and its racist policies and human rights violations. We mainly addressed non-government people. We went into factories and talked to workers and we talked to students. We were being hosted by the World Peace Council. We attended state dinners and things like that as guest of the Soviet Union. There were no discussions about what our country was doing wrong at these dinners and government functions.

The only times conversations or presentations about the wrongs of our government took place was at meetings organized by the World Peace Council which involved people from all over the world, mainly developing countries. It was an attempt to create peaceful dialogue based on mutual respect between the Soviet Block of socialist countries and the capitalist West. It was not just about human rights but also about nuclear proliferation – the goal was to have peaceful coexistence between Socialist countries and Capitalist countries. Of course, this discussion was taking place in the midst of a big war in Afghanistan; and the residual heat from the Vietnam War was still going strong. The war was over but there were still a lot of ill-feelings. The Vietnamese and the U.S. suffered great losses. You might say rather than being a time of healing and mutual understanding there were still hostile feelings and distrust.

I came back from the Soviet Union with mixed feelings. I didn't feel like we had accomplished much. At the time I didn't understand the ability of the World Peace Council to get information out internationally, so I had difficulty gaging what had actually been accomplished other than a tour to create good will. I learned that there was a real genuine fear on the Soviet's part that they would be attacked by NATO countries – the US and its allies – the NATO alliance. This fear was not just among the politicos it was also among the people. The people were telling us to go back and talk to the American people and your government and let them know that the Soviet people don't want war. They showed us anti-war monuments they had built. We saw one in Kiev in the Ukraine where a fire had been burning since the end of WWII. They told us it was in memory of the millions of people who had died in WWII. They lost 20 million people in that war. Some areas they did not rebuild because they wanted a reminder of what war does. We talked to veterans of WWII who had been at the siege of Leningrad – they did not want another war. World War II had done two things to the people. It had made them not want war and to become paranoid toward their neighboring countries because they feared that those would be the countries the US would turn against them – that they could be pawns in another aggressive war. They remembered how Hitler had used Poland and they were looking at how the US was presently using Poland to whip up anti-Soviet propaganda and undermine peaceful co-existence.

We had the opportunity to talk to people who had actually been in the war. They made sure we talked to these people. On the other side of it, they took us to nurseries to see the children and Yalta which was a resort for retired workers – Russia's Miami. Many of these retired workers were WWII Veterans. That really impressed us.

When I went back to the USSR in 1983 they were involved in Afghanistan. There was a war fever but it was put in an interesting way. Helping a third world colonized country to achieve its national liberation and possibly to have a Socialist Republic like in Vietnam. Whatever the intentions were, we knew that was something that the US and others would not permit to happen. There was now another hot war coming out of cold war rivalry.

Those of us at the Peace Council could see that this would be the Soviet Union's Vietnam. We also believed that the people of the Soviet Union were not fully informed of their countries foreign policy. I saw this building in Moscow – huge building – it might have been a famous hotel in Moscow and on the top it was a huge sign in neon lights. I asked my interpreter what it said and he said it read: "In solidarity with the people of Palestine". I asked him if they had anything like that anywhere else. He told me they had signs for solidarity with the African National Congress, with the Cuban people and these signs expressing solidarity were all over the Soviet Union – that's public. My interpreter was an intellectual and had a high position in the Communist party – he explained that what was not seen in the 5-year plan that was shown to the Soviet people was the aid sent to national liberation movements in Asia, Africa and Latin America.

What they didn't know was the amount of money being sent to support these organizations while the people were waiting in line for food and other necessities. He said, "This is hurting our economy." He thought it was bad foreign policy. I argued with him that the Soviet Union was the first socialist country in the world; that they have been embargoed by the West, attacked and invaded by the Nazis and their borders violated. Hence their foreign policy was part of their defense – if they defend these anti-colonial struggles that weakens the enemies of socialism and expands the socialist camp.

Here was a Party intellectual telling me that it was a problem if you were a Soviet citizen standing in line for bread while money was being given to these national liberation organizations. He wasn't a prophet but he was right. Socialism eventually started a down turn. I don't rule out the impact that the CIA and other organizations and the cold war tactics had on their so-called collapse, but I believe that this foreign policy also had a crucial impact. This was also a time when Soviets had started allowing foreign credit cards to be used and the smell of consumerism was in the air. There was obviously dissatisfaction in terms of the availability of consumer goods and services – by US standards most of the Soviet Union was living in poverty.

These are just the patchwork observations of a partisan for socialism who never spent more than two weeks in this vast land that gave birth to the first socialist republic and I dare not present them as anything more than that. The problem I have with a lot of my American comrades is their arrogance when it comes other countries and particularly the then existing Soviet Union. I use to be amazed how some comrades would become absolutely livid whenever Stalin's name came up and how these same people were quick to find fault with almost every aspect of Soviet life. How could you be a Communist and yet be in lock step with anti-communists who not only attacked Stalin but every leader Soviet prior to Gorbachev? It made no sense to me then or now. In fact, I think a lot of us, coming out of a country steeped in the mire of racism and anti-communism, are so lacking in moral and intellectual aptitude that we are incapable of grasping and developing a proper attitude toward other countries fighting for their freedom from capitalist, imperialist domination. Given our own history of a retarded development of socialism, white chauvinism, recalcitrant racism and the inability to address the national question we are hardly in a position to set ourselves up as the judges of the Soviet experience or any other revolutionary movement. Focusing on what went wrong with the Soviet Union should, in my opinion, be accompanied by focusing on our failures as well.

I remember when Perestroika and Glasnost was first advanced the leadership of our Party embraced it. I was a part of the leadership then and I, along with a few others did not embrace it. Those who were keen on anti-Stalinism and weak on the national question eagerly embraced Gorbachev as the great socialist innovator. And when it became clear that beneath the progressive cloak was the dagger of betrayal the same champions of Perestroika ran like rats from a sinking ship. My point is this: If we are going to cry that socialism was betrayed then those in our ranks who were a part of that betrayal should also be exposed. Otherwise kill the noise!

The second time I went to the Soviet Union I did not return directly to the US. I went to Eastern Germany, Denmark and came back by way of Italy and then to the US. When I was in Germany for 3 or 4 days and those people were very efficient. I didn't see any poverty in East Germany. They did have in Dresden war torn buildings and every anniversary of the bombing of Dresden thousands of people came out for a national mourning. The schools were nice and clean and the kids seemed happy and healthy. I asked why there was such a marked difference in living conditions between Germany and the Soviet Union.

My interpreter in Germany was a woman whose name was Maria. She said that East Berlin was a showcase. The Soviets put so much time and money into it because it was so visible and they were trying to show people that socialism was working. I also met the African American cartoonist Ollie Harrington while I was in Germany. He had been a cartoonist for the Communist newspaper *The Daily Worker* in the 30s. I had seen his work and he was really a very sharp political cartoonist – they could be real gross or real funny but always carried a very powerful message for peace and the fight against racism. I spent 2-3 hours with him and I had dinner with him and he mentioned he had read my articles about my prison experience. He was full of a thousand questions about the US. He was a Harlemite and when he found out I was living near Harlem he exhausted me with his questions. This was very special to me; seeing Ollie in East Germany and going to the mass in Dresden, it was a very emotional experience. The mass was a symphony played in commemoration of the relentless bombing of Dresden during World War II.

I think that Germans are probably among the most musically gifted people in the world. I began to see a connection between German and African American music. For example, some of the great African American musicians like Charlie Parker used German music in their compositions. Like his composition 'Donna Lee' was nothing but a Bach Fugue. I am listening to these people play and I could hear Bud Powell, Charlie Parker and others. I learned that German people loved Jazz. Ollie Harrington was full of stories about this. I learned that the founders of Blue Note records were two Jewish refugees from Germany, Alfred Lion and Francis Wolf. The guy who funded Lion and Wolf was Max Margulis, a renown Communist writer. I couldn't believe my ears. Ollie was an ardent lover of Jazz. He explained that Lion and Wolf were refugees from Nazi Germany. He told me about the German guy who published all of Scott Joplin's music – 'Maple Leaf Rag,' 'the Entertainer.' He told me about Schumer, a great publishing company in NY that lasted through the '80s was founded by Germans. That led me to think that we have all heard of Bach and Mozart but didn't really appreciate the amazing talent of the German musicians. Imagine if I had been there longer than a few days. I started thinking about when I was a student learning the piano it was all from German musicians and my background was heavily influenced by Bach. I was glad I went to Germany.

Denmark was uneventful, and I was in Denmark for over a week. They speak English and Danish there. I saw lots of McDonalds and

American soldiers there. I was in Copenhagen. Culturally it was interesting and the people loved music. I saw Reggae musicians playing in public and I heard that they had good jazz clubs there. The Peace Council was having long meetings because Regan and Gorbachev were meeting and there were disarmament talks going on. The Peace Council meetings were long and boring and I went to the bar.

My time in Denmark was spent going to boring meetings and getting drunk. They probably have an interesting cultural life there but I didn't take advantage of this opportunity to meet anyone interesting there. I remember that when I was leaving they gave me an horrendous bill that was outrageous. I was glad the Peace Council could pay it. I did meet an interesting Black man named A.C. Byrd who was a member of the Peace Council. I had never met anyone who was so well versed in international affairs and who knew so many international people. He also liked to drink and we spent many hours in the bar and had some magnificent bourbon-driven talks.

Encounters with the U.S. Peace Movement

National Anti-Imperialist Movement In Solidarity With African Liberation (NAIMSAL). This was my first contact with the anti-imperialist side of the peace movement. It was at a fundraising dinner
in Chicago that I met Ronelle Mustin and Tony Monteiro. Ronelle
was the local leader and Tony the national. I was particularly impressed with Monteiro, for he seemed to know everything I wanted to know about the struggle in Southern Africa. He educated
me and turned me on to the Marxist-Leninist African revolutionaries such as Amical Cabral, Augustino Neto, Toivo Ya Toivo, and
Samora Machel. Tony use to describe the Southern Africa Liberation movements as national in form and revolutionary in content.
Ronelle Mustin on the other hand was the organizer for NAIMSAL
with the mass approach, at least in Chicago. In building the anti-
apartheid movement Ronelle worked with elected officials, Pastors (church leaders), and community based organizations. As an
organizer

I was only marginally involved with NAIMSAL. The Alliance supported their boycott of the oil companies and other actions of
solidarity aimed at defeating apartheid. I thought the pathway to
peace in Africa was overthrowing apartheid. When the U.S. Peace
Council had its founding convention in 1978 Michael Myerson invited me to join and run to be elected to the national board. I did
and I got elected. During the convention I ran a workshop on racism and the peace movement. And that is where I met A.C. Byrd.

I had many encounters with A.C. Byrd. One time was in Spain
where they were having a human rights conference in 1986 or
1987. Byrd was an African American in a US peace movement
that was mainly dominated by white people. Even though the US
peace council was better than most because they at least had a
number of African Americans and other people of color in their
national leadership. The leadership of the peace council as far as
I know was always multi-racial. The importance of this to me was
brought home by Byrd, on the one hand, and Michael Myerson on
the other. Michael Myerson was a veteran organizer on the left

who was actually raised in the Communist Party. He was Jewish in the cultural sense of the word but not in the religious sense. Myerson wanted me to do some writing on behalf of the peace council wherein I would address the race question. He put it quite bluntly – talk about the racism in the peace movement. Byrd thought it important to be critical, he also thought the best criticism would be more persuasive for the Peace Council itself to promote more African Americans into leadership roles. He said to me that if they were going to preach to the rest of the movement about racism they should preach by example. I don't think Myerson disagreed with that because he promoted me as a leader in the US peace movement as well as Gus Newport, former Mayor of Berkeley and others.

I think Mike Myerson was a sincere opponent of racism. But he had a problem with the aggressive way that AC Byrd approached the question. I have to admit now looking back in a practical sense AC Byrd was much more aggressive than I was in terms of calling out the racism in the peace movement. He really felt like the peace council was being a bit self-righteous in talking to the rest of the peace movement about racism instead of addressing their own. We became friends and in a gentle way he let me know I was not helping matters by writing this pamphlet that I wrote on 'Racism in the Peace Movement.' He told me that all the white people in the peace council love your pamphlet – it makes them feel like they are doing something. A lot of black people in the council are asking themselves: But what are they doing?

At the time I didn't really want to hear that. Given the hindsight of history I think AC Byrd was right. The problem with the US Peace Council was that it was more a part of the American peace movement than it cared to admit and a lot of the racist tendencies that existed in the America peace movement also existed in and was shared by the US Peace Council. Because the US Peace Council was a left-led organization these half measures in the fight against racism was even more hypocritical and I was a part of this hypocrisy.

The US Peace Council historically had talked about the importance of black and white unity being the bed rock of any progressive movement in the United States. In the Communist Party organization, Black people were represented at every level from the national leadership down to the district organizations. The Party had a reputation for advocating for African American equality. When you look at how they were acting within the US peace movement at this time in the 70's and 80's, it's almost as if they had abandoned their earlier principles. The US Peace Council was basically carried by the Communist Party so they were in large part responsible for the leadership of that organization.

AC Byrd more than anybody I met in the peace movement taught me that in the international arena Black people were often undermined and not fully supported in their struggle against racism. The nuclear arms race was often used as the excuse to side track the question of racism and national oppression because peace was more important. And, he taught me that in spite of themselves the peace movement had stereotyped us into positions where we were supposed to be about civil rights and racism in the Southern United States and that was it. When we got into the international arena we were not considered to be as important as the broader issues of war and peace. I continued to work in the U.S. Peace Council because it recognized its short-comings and was committed to the fight against racism and apartheid.

I remember raising some of these questions with my friend and mentor Jim Jackson, who was an African American and a brilliant Marxist-Leninist theoretician, and he simply said Byrd was not a Communist but a Nationalist. However, this in no way invalidated his stance against racism. I felt like, okay, we agree, now what are we going to do about it? No doubt we were stumbling but we were stumbling forward.

On the other hand, Gus Newport made outstanding contributions by actually acting out as a Black leader in the peace movement. Newport stood head and shoulder above Byrd and Jackson, as a leader in the Peace movement and as an ambassador for African Americans. When he was the Mayor of Berkeley he was probably the only elected official in the United States, Black or white, that openly sided with revolutionary movements in Africa, Asia and Latin America. I noticed that at these international conferences, organized by the World Peace Council, Gus Newport was obviously the most respected and honored leader from the U.S. delegation. I believed that respect was earned, for Gus Newport was always a consistent fighter for peace and socialism and today, although he has passed his eightieth birthday, he still stands tall and strong in the struggle. After Denmark I returned to the New York via Italy. I was in Rome for a day for a connecting flight but that day was a great day. I stayed in a hotel called the Forum. I could look out the window and see the Coliseum and it was eerie because I had read about it in books but now I could see it outside my window.

The whole international experience was incredible. This wasn't the only trip I made internationally; there were several. In 1987 and 1988 when the struggle for Nelson Mandela was intensifying I began to appreciate even more the importance of international struggles in relation to our struggles here at home. We could not have freed the Wilmington 10 had it not been for the international struggle. For example, when I was abroad on many occasions I was able to get petitions signed. Like in the German Democratic Republic hundreds of thousands of people had signed our petitions for the Wilmington 10 from little kids to national leaders. When we were in Prague at a World Peace Council meeting I was able to secure the signatures of the Supreme Court Justice of India and British parliamentarians as well as parliamentarians all over Europe.

There was a Vietnam delegation in Prague representing the new Socialist Republic of Vietnam. To the person each of them signed the petition. They were political figures that signed on and some of those who had been military personnel asked me if it would be okay for them to sign on because they didn't want to cause any problems since our country had been at war in Vietnam and they had been on the opposite side. I was in Madrid Spain at an international human rights conference that consisted of trade union organizations, women's organizations, political leaders and parliamentarians from all over Europe and again, as long as I could stay on my feet I was able to get signatures.

At the end of the day I could see where this international campaign was very important. We also used it to garner support for political prisoners like Leonard Peltier, a native American who had been framed by the FBI in the late 1960s as a result of his participation in the Wounded Knee struggles. Johnny Imani Harris who was a young African American in Mobile Alabama who had been falsely accused of raping a white woman and was sentenced to death in that state. He was on death row and we were able also able to get thousands of signatures from these various countries asking the Governor of Alabama to exonerate him and get him off death row. Brother Harris not only got off of death row but was eventually freed from prison.

Also David Troung, who was a South Vietnamese scholar that lived in Washington D.C., was accused of spying and was facing espionage charges. We believe his prosecution was a direct result of the Vietnam war and he was not a spy. He was an antiwar activist against the Vietnam war. He had some contacts with the South Vietnamese where he had relatives and he had relationships within the country but not such that he was a spy. He was a professor of South Vietnamese studies – he did not have any access to national security information. He talked to South Vietnamese people about his job and his life in the US but to call this spying was a long stretch. He was not accused of passing on any classified national security information. Basically, he was being accused of complicity just because he had personal as well as educational ties to South East Asia. The government accused him of using his educational research as a cover for spying. He was eventually convicted and sent to federal prison for five years but we were able to garner for him a lot of support from the international community. I believe his sentence would have been much harsher, like 20 years had we not been able to get mass support and use it to apply pressure on our government. I visited David while he was in prison, it was an emotionally trying moment for me to see this very gentle and humanistic person subjected to the cruelties of prison life.

We also learned a great deal about the importance of international support in our efforts to free Nelson and Winnie Mandela. At this time Winnie Mandela was banished to one of the Bantustans and Nelson was on Robben Island. The international support to free these two icons was overwhelming and like nothing I had ever seen. The Alliance had no problem getting support. Our contribution to that struggle was small in comparison to the international community. For example, in the Soviet Union millions and millions of people from factory workers, sports people, artists, Olympic greats and leaders had all signed the petition to free the Mandelas – not to mention the ordinary citizens. Everywhere you turned in the Soviet Union there was a tremendous outpouring of support for Mandela – this was true in all of the other socialist countries that I had visited like, Czechlovakia and the German Democratic Republic. The support was overwhelming and when I got back to the United States and I carried 10,000 signatures to the United Nations Anti Aparthaid Committee – most of which came from America – I felt like we were not a major part of that struggle because alongside of those 10,000 signatures were millions coming out of the Soviet Union and other Socialist countries. I knew why in those countries the leaders were calling for the freedom of Mandela but our country was not. In 1987 the United States considered him a terrorist.

I need to mention also that every year from 1979 to 1988 we submitted thousands of signatures to the UN Anti-Apartheid Committee on behalf of Nelson Mandela. I came to know my way around the UN. After some of these presentations before the Committee I started hanging out at the UN Lounge; I hung out at its large circular bar with people from all over the world – and all of them had this tremendous amount of respect for the South African freedom fighters who were an official part of the UN. I spent many hours there drinking with Johnny Makatini who was one the leaders of the African National Congress in the United States and a representative to the UN.

My drinking had gone from bad to worst. I would go to these affairs where they would have alcohol, whether it was a union meeting or a mission to the UN party or a fund raising party for the African National Congress – no matter what the occasion I drank until I got embarrassingly drunk. My colleagues and comrades began to speak to me about my drinking and told me that if I was going to continue to drink on these occasions then I needed to stop coming. If I chose to come, then I needed to stop drinking. I had no control and I couldn't tell them I couldn't stop so I quit going to the functions. This was the beginning of a period where I stopped going to a lot of things because I could not handle my drinking.

Up Close and Personal

Now we come to that part of my story where I make myself vulnerable. In my first writing of this section I went into a lot of graphic detail about my struggle with alcoholism. It's a very depressing, heartbreaking story of me being a wrecking ball in my own life and the life of others. My drinking rendered me unstable and reckless. It made me subject to one of the most degrading forms of human bondage known to the human race.

While I have every right to disclose to my readers the wretchedness of my own life I have no right to disclose the pain and misery of others who were affected by my sick deeds and needs. I have no right to make them vulnerable. That's one aspect of the problem of intimate disclosure, of what I did to my love ones.

The other aspect is subjectivity. I am giving you only my side of the story based on my experiences. Doesn't matter if I admit all my wrongs or not I can't presume to speak for those who were wronged. Both of my daughters, Naima and Jamilya, but especially Jamilya have been very adamant about this.

What I can say about myself is that by 1984 I was turning chronic alcoholic and everybody knew but me. I was functioning in terms of showing up for work. And almost miraculously I maintained the respect of the workers, mainly because when I showed up to fight that is precisely what I did.

1984 was a turning point in my life in many ways. One was my marriage was falling apart. As I have indicated earlier this was the period where my drinking was starting to get out of control. My wife and I were constantly bickering and fighting over different things. Mainly over me not being available. I would sometimes be gone for 2 or 3 days engaged in a drinking bout and also I was slacking up in terms of my movement activities. I continued to show up at the office to do my work with the Alliance. I continued to go on organizing tours in different parts of the country, but I was drinking through all of this. Even had a drinking partner – the person who was supposed to be assisting me in my field work ended up being my drinking partner. Sometimes we would go into Birmingham where we had a very vibrant Alliance chapter. Before we would get into the business meeting we would get juiced up the night before and would come to the meeting hung over and the remarkable thing is that we were able to get through these meetings. Mainly because I think the comrades there really understood us and helped us. I am sure we were not the only problem drinkers in their lives. They helped us get the work done while suggesting to us that we could get more work done if we slowed down the drinking. We started doing the work first and then drink. We would always finish the work up a day before our flights were scheduled out, right before we left we would have a chilling out period where we would do some heavy drinking. Then we would fly out.

This pattern followed us around wherever we went. When I would come back home from these organizing tours I would be exhausted between the work and the drinking. I would come home and collapse and would be no good around the house for sometimes 2 or 3 days unless, of course, I had a drink. My wife suggested that we get marriage counseling because I was grouchy and having emotional flare ups and she was doing the same thing because she was sick and tired of my crap. Things for a very long time kept going downhill. I agreed that we should see a marriage counselor. I remember the counselor was charging us $45 a session and by the time I got in the third session she made a suggestion – she didn't really want to do anymore sessions unless I was willing to get help – going to AA. I said I didn't think I had a drinking problem like that and I could stop whenever I wanted and the issues with my wife were not alcohol related. We weren't getting along because of her attitude about my work and I didn't know how to deal with that. The counselor said: "That wasn't what I was hearing – I am hearing you have a serious drinking problem and I can't take the counseling any further unless you get help." I said OK we will get a counselor who will help.

My wife asked me to at least try but I wouldn't so we found another counselor who was part of our political organization and somewhat of a friend. He agreed, reluctantly, because he was friendly with both of us but he was a professional psychologist. He didn't like to counsel people he knew but because of the friendship he would give it a try. After a few sessions , he said the same thing as the previous counselor. The only thing that would save this marriage would be if both of us were willing to make some concessions. He told my wife she should get counseling with someone who could show her how to deal with an alcoholic and that I should get help with my drinking. Again, I refused. And, to prove I was not an alcoholic I went on the wagon. I went on a long dry spell. I wouldn't even drink beer. Every now and then I would smoke marijuana or take some valiums but not alcohol. And things seemed to improve –at least I was coming home and meeting some of my marital obligations.

But during this period I was also growing closer in friendship with Maria Ramos. I first met her when we were organizing in Harlem back in 1978-79. She did security work for the Alliance as well as administrative work in the office. She was an excellent and dedicated worker. when we worked together around the various issues we worked on. She did a lot of the secretarial work in the office. She was an excellent worker and very dedicated. We started hanging out, innocently, after work for cocktails. However, I did go home and didn't stay out all night.

And then it developed where one night I went home with her. We were both tippsy and that was the beginning of the end because we had sex and my wife found out about it and she was very pissed. She asked me what was I going to do. She was not going to live like this. If I wanted to be with Maria I needed to be with her and if I wanted her then stay with her. I told her I was emotionally confused – I felt more comfortable with Maria but obligated to her – so I was torn. She said, "I will make it easy for you – I will give you one year – you can do whatever you want – after a year, if you haven't made up your mind about staying with me I will divorce you. I am only doing this because I love you. If you don't come back in a year forget it." I said what if I don't go for that deal and she said the only way we couldn't do it is if I stayed now. She wasn't going to go in and out of the relationship. I couldn't have Maria as my good time girl and her as a wife. I did something real crazy I moved to a separate apartment by myself. I didn't move in with Maria – I thought if I got by myself I could come to a resolution of this problem.

It was a two bedroom apartment and I stayed there for several months. All I was really doing was putting myself in a situation where I could drink more and not be bothered by her or Maria. Maria found where I lived and she told me she would help me but I would have to come out of that apartment, because I was going downhill in the apartment, and stay with her. But I didn't know how she would help me. Basically, I don't think she realized the extent of my alcoholism. She thought she would just be organizing my life and since we both worked in the office together she would be with me most of the day and then most of the time when I was in town. I moved in with her and I cut back on my drinking, once again. I started just drinking on the week ends with her, and it seemed we were developing a relationship. We fell in love. Then she got pregnant. I asked her why she wasn't using protection and she said because she wanted to have a family. I felt trapped – time passed and she started showing and I went through a change – I convinced myself that maybe this was what I needed. Maybe if we had a child and got married this would force me into straightening my life out.

By this time, a year was just about over. I told my wife I wanted to get a divorce and she agreed to a no contest divorce – she wished me all the best and gave me a divorce – but she still wanted to remain friends because she still had feelings for me yet she was willing to let me go. Now Maria and I are together, and I went through all of these changes to get my life in order. I tried to measure up and cut back but every now and then I would go on a binge. Maria got me involved with LaMaz classes and then the baby was born. I remember I went to the hospital that day and I was with her the whole day.

All that stuff I learned in LaMaz classes didn't mean anything. I fell apart. I did not want to go through this. She had her legs in the air and they were talking about centimeters and the doctor kept telling me I had to stay and they put me in a gown. She begged me to stay with her. Reluctantly, I stayed and the baby wouldn't come out so they had to do a Cesarean. When they pulled the baby out of her body, I was standing there in a state of shock when the doctor handed me a baby – I looked at her and asked the Doctor why she was so white. The doctor told me they are all like that – she will get browner. Sure, enough when I went back to the nursery she had some color. That was my first daughter, Naima. Something happened to me when I went through this experience that I thought had transformed me. I saw the miracle of birth and she was so beautiful she had me beaming with a smile. I fell in love with my daughter right away. For a while – maybe a year – I came home every night and tried to be a father and helped Maria as she recovered from the hospital. I got special time off from my job and when she was a year old I took her to my job with me and everyone fell in love with her, including my ex-wife, Coraminita. Coraminita really wanted me to be happy so she was happy for me when Naima was born. I felt really fortunate to have all these beautiful women in my life.

I nursed Naima when Maria had to wean her off of breast-feeding. I learned a lot of biology and I also learned about the powerful attachment between the woman and the child. I was emotionally and physically grounded in this relationship for almost two years. Then, Maria became pregnant. She wanted me to go through the LaMaz classes again. All of sudden I was feeling stressed and worried about how we were going to manage with two children.

I started drinking. I don't know what happened I just started back and this time it got real bad. Now I am doing ridiculous stuff. By this time, its quite evident I can't have just a few beers. I was drinking alcoholically. Maria went to my friends in the union movement. I wasn't working with the Alliance because it wasn't paying enough to support a family. Now I was working for Local 1199 – the largest health care workers union in New York. It was a very powerful left-led union. Their main union hall was named after Martin Luther King and I was happy to be there and they paid very well. I was making about $37, 000 a year, which was more than double my salary with the Alliance.

Maria went to my union comrades and told them I wasn't coming home and if I did come home I was drunk and argumentative. She was afraid something was going to happen to me. The person directly over me, Marcio Garcia, he was a part Puerto Rican and Cuban and he asked me if I wanted to go to Cuba and stay there for six months to deal with my alcoholism. I told him "Hell No". I don't need to leave my family that long. He told me I couldn't stay in the union and get paid the money they were paying me while I was destroying myself and my family. He told me I would have to either go to Cuba or a rehab. I chose rehab and they sent me to Rhinebeck, New York while Maria was pregnant with our second child.

This place was unbelievable. I was there in the Summer and it had a swimming pool and I had my own private room. They had pool tables, pianos – all kind of recreational facilities. They also had AA meetings from 9 am until 6 in the evening. Around 8 in the evening you had free time up to 10pm where you could watch TV or do co-educational things where we could socialize – play cards, etc. We got up at 7 am and had breakfast and then had prayer and medication until 9 am until we went into therapy. Everyone was assigned a counselor to help you put together a program of recovery. I stayed there for 30 days.

I can not tell you what I learned there because I wasn't into it – I was into the socializing. I played piano and flirted with some of the woman there. When I went to meetings I intellectualized them and showed off my intelligence. But I didn't learn anything about staying sober because I didn't want to learn anything. I wasn't convinced I was an alcoholic. I couldn't explain why or how I started but I could always know when I stopped – I was able to stop. So, I had my own program. I was not convinced that AA or any kind of recovery could do more for me than I could do for myself.

I came out of there after 30 days. Maria came to get me and she was very pregnant and starting into her 9th month. My union gave me a stack of checks. I had over a thousand dollars in checks and Maria and I went home. I looked good and she was happy and she thought it was over and that I had conquered the monster and she didn't have to worry about me getting drunk again. For 30 or 40 days, she didn't have to work. I went to meetings and went through the ritual. I can't tell you what happened at those meetings. I sat down, listened and left. I heard people talking about the program but none of it resonated with me, I was different than them. Then came the baby. Once again I am in the delivery room and I have the gown on with the little cap and I am watching her agonize having this child. Again, it ended up being a C-section. It was almost identical except this time instead of going to the nursery to see the baby I went to a nearby bar and got drunk.

The hospital beeped me on my beeper and when I called them they said there was a problem with my child and I needed to get there soon. I went crazy and thought maybe she had a disease and she was going to die. The hospital wouldn't tell me what was wrong – only that she was critical and I needed to come. I ran to the hospital – there had been a problem with her breathing but by the time I got there it had been resolved. Now she was doing fine. When I got to the hospital Maria did not realize how drunk I was and she handed me the my daughter. I almost dropped her and kept telling Maria to take the baby back but it wasn't registering with her. Finally, I told her I was drunk and she grabbed my newly-born baby girl. I apologized, and Maria took me back to her room where she was recovering from a C-section and told me to lay down in her bed until I could get myself together. She said I was sick too and needed to get myself together before I could get out of there. Shortly after that I passed out in the bed with her. When I came too she was there with a towel wiping my head and crying and telling me how much she loved me and that I had to pull through this for her and the kids. I was saying she was absolutely right and I wouldn't do this again. She told me to go home and stay there until she could get there.

For a moment things seemed to get better. I got real busy in my union work. Even while I was in the cups and hanging out in Harlem I continued to stay connected to the movement mainly through my work with Local 1199 as a union organizer and my involvement with community organizing. When David Dinkins, the first African American Mayor of New York, was running for that office 1199 assigned me to work out of his campaign office in Harlem so that we could become an integral part of his field operations. As in any campaign our principal task was first to get people registered to vote and then on election day to get them out to vote. However, as soon as I hit the ground in Harlem and started connecting to people I realized that the Dinkins' Campaign was more than just an election campaign, it was a movement led mainly by African Americans, organized labor (for example, Local 1199, SEIU, District Council 37 AFSME locals, Transit Workers Union and District 65 UAW), Black Nationalist formations such as the Patrice Lumumba Coalition, the Black United Front and the organized left (which at that time was mainly the Communist Party, USA). In the main this movement was a merger of the Black Liberation Movement and the various left-led sections of organized labor. It was not a movement financed by any section of the grand bourgeoisie of Wall Street. It was at its core a progressive and unifying movement that brought together African Americans, Puerto Ricans, Dominicans, progressive whites and all the various strands of the peoples' movement.

Our office was right there on 125th Street a few doors down from the Apollo. Every day but Sunday I dressed up in a suit, white shirt and tie to go to work for the Dinkins Campaign. No matter how late I stayed up the night before drinking I pulled myself up and went to work. Finally, I just stopped drinking as we went into the final stretch of the campaign because I really didn't want to mess this up.

On that final day we had our car-pool people and on the ground people organized and ready to get out the voters. We had our poll watchers in place and our phone bank set up. I came into the office at around 6am and by 8am we were on the ground running. We dispatched people in cars to check all the polling places to make sure people were there and that they had whatever they needed. We had the phone banks fully staffed so people could make and take calls. We had teams of people on foot who could go and knock on the doors of seniors to make sure they get to the polls and to encourage everyone to come out and vote. I basically functioned as an administrator, making sure that everyone was doing what they were supposed to do when they were supposed to do it.

It was a day of exciting mobilization of tens of thousands of people in Harlem alone. We got people to the polls by every necessary means, including carpooling. At the end of the day about an hour before the polls closed they were predicting a victory for David Dinkins, for the African American Mayor of New York City. Harlem was in an uproar, it was celebration time. People were literally dancing in the streets and every bar was full of happy people. I drank that night and I didn't go home. I did not pull through for my family as I had promised Maria. My drinking got progressively worst, so much so until I had to go to a rehab again. This time I checked myself in.

Lost in the Sauce

In 1990 I'm in California at a halfway house that was managed and owned by a Mexican gentlemen by the name of Arturo Rivas – we called him Art.

Art Rivas was a man in his mid-fifties recovering alcoholic and drug addict who operated a half-way house in Pacoima – a small city in the San Fernando valley and its only claim to fame is it is the city that Richie Valens, an icon in the Chicano Rock & Roll movement of the late 1950s, grew up in – he died in a plane crash with Buddy Holly and J.P. Richardson February 3, 1959. I knew Richie Valens was a genius of a musician and composer, but I would have never appreciated him as I do now, having lived in Pacoima for over a year.

Shortly after I started living in this half-way house I was hearing that Nelson Mandela was coming to town. I was sober and had not had a drink in months – almost 6 months. I heard he was going to speak at the LA Coliseum. I remembered some of my old ANC friends, Shirley Williams and her husband Trevor who were there in the LA area. I tried to get in touch with them to see what was going on. They put me in touch with Congresswoman Maxine Waters and a number of African National Congress members and I was invited to work with the committee. So, I thought this was my chance to get back involved in the movement and maybe that would help me deal with my drinking problem. At least it would fill up that hole in my life where I was feeling like I had thrown away everything and was becoming a hopeless drunk.

I thought I had found a solution to my life. I would deepen involvement in the movement and all would be well. I really had problems with AA – I had philosophical problems – basically I didn't believe in God – I was an atheist. I could not see past the atheism. How could I be a part of a fellowship that was God centered and I was an atheist? At that time I was ignorant to the fact that there were atheists in AA – all I could see was this irreconcilable conflict. They described the disease of alcoholism that I was drawn into but I saw them as pushing at best a religious solution to a problem that had nothing to do with religion. I disqualified my-self from AA and started looking toward getting back involved in social movements and political struggles as my way of getting a new start – a comeback – a path to sobriety.

I jumped in feet first – head first into the work of the committee around Nelson Mandela. I started giving a lot of time to that and I knew some members of the Communist Party there who were very much involved also in the preparation for Nelson's arrival. I had been kind of like estranged from the party at the time given my drinking bouts – I was estranged from everyone. They didn't care I had a drinking problem – they wanted me to be involved in the party because they felt I could make a contribution and they needed me so to hell with my drinking problem.

They were understanding because I wasn't the only Red who got drunk – they had experience with this issue over the years. They encouraged me to participate in AA or do whatever it took to get sober while still being politically involved. They opened the door and invited me back in. I worked with them and the ANC commit-tee and we basically were doing things like making arrangements for Nelson to speak – making sure word got out to the community – we wanted people who were involved in the anti-apartheid strug-gle to be in a leading role but wanted to reach out to all of the community as we saw it as a way to get others involved who had not been previously committed to the struggle for social justice.

We did a lot of work in South Central in the African American community. We were amazed to find out that a lot of people not involved in our movement knew about Mandela and knew about his struggles in South Africa and held him in high esteem. After all those years of working against Apartheid we were seeing the result and seeing the impact we had on the communities until Mandela actually came out to speak.

There was no political, social or religious organization in the Af-rican American community that did not know about Nelson Man-dela and didn't hold him in high esteem and supported him in his struggles. Those who had been reluctant to support him and speak out like the NAACP were now speaking out with a boldness that was unbelievable.

The problem was that people for many years were afraid to openly support Mandela because he worked with Communists. The Communist Party was an integral part of the ANC. And so, that was a problem for them. Nelson refused to denounce those Communists like Fidel Castro who worked with him in the struggle against Apartheid – in fact he embraced Castro. Mandela also embraced Gadaffi even though Quadaffi wasn't a Red; he was, however, anti-imperialist and he sided with Mandela against Apartheid.

When we finally had the rally it was the most magnificent thing I had ever seen. I thought when Angela Davis got out and they did the rally in Madison Square Garden with 10,000 people – I thought that was phenomenal. But here we had Mandela in a stadium that seated a 100,000 and it was full and people were sitting on the playing field in chairs and all of the bleachers were filled up. You had all kinds of cultural groups there. Like Andre Crouch (gospel singer), Two Live Crew – rappers – Jazz Artists everybody was there and we loved this man. When he came on the stage people stood for several minutes – it felt like forever. They were cheering and jumping up and down hollering Nelson Mandela – Nelson Mandela.

I had never seen anything like it. It was the most exhilarating experience I have ever had and it is difficult to articulate. The organization I was involved in (the Alliance) had played a good role in getting this man's freedom. When we took those petitions to the United Nations calling for his freedom we didn't realize what impact we were having. Sometimes we thought we didn't have any impact and we were giving in to cynicism because we didn't see the results of all of the work we were doing. But here we had a living example of our work: apartheid had been defeated – the most racist and fascist regime since Adolph Hitler had been defeated – what a joy! It's in moments like this that one's faith in human beings and humankind is reinvigorated and one realizes that all of the sacrifices made, and lives lost in the struggle were not in vain.

After that victorious celebration I was back into unemployment and back into the routine of living in a halfway house of recovering alcoholics and back into going to meetings every day, as required. Back to the monotonous routine of the meetings, and all of that stuff – I wasn't into it. I had greater issues on my mind. I was now thinking about the next phase in the movement and where do we go from here. Where is the South African movement going – will they really be able to get their freedom and defeat the banks and large corporations who had a choke hold on South Africa – did they really have a chance to win freedom? This occupied my mind all of the time and I did not think about AA and the 12 steps of recovery. I was working the program intellectually and I discussed things with my sponsor. He didn't have me working the steps or doing other things. We would meet and have coffee and talk and share personal problems and just basically celebrate that we didn't have a drink that day but nothing was going on inside of me that was any different.

I still had deep and abiding feelings of loneliness. I still had a problem connecting with people and I used the movement to deny my problems. I used the movement to show I could connect with people and show that I was involved in the issue of racism in our country and community problems and how to address the social change. I kept feeling justified to say that I was okay and dealing with people. Yes, I was dealing with people but I was not dealing with myself. I had a problem – I could not stop drinking and being active in the movement was not a solution to my drinking problem. I used the movement to not deal with my drinking problem. So eventually I ended up saying to myself maybe I am not an alcoholic. Maybe I can drink and still be responsible to my family, to society. Why do I have to be different than other people. That put me right back into the cups – right back to drinking. And the way I justified it was the death of my sister, Yvonne and my friend Herschel. My sister had died of breast cancer and Herschel was killed in a car accident while he was delivering petitions for some protesting workers.

When I found out about Herschel's funeral I was actually sitting in my sister's funeral. I was in a lot of emotional pain and all I wanted to do was medicate it with alcohol. But I didn't drink that day. As bad as I wanted to drink I white-knuckled it, as drunks say. I had told Art Rivas that I would return to the half-way house and continue my recovery and I did for the rest of the year.

By the time 1991 rolled around I was planning on leaving California – getting back to the East Coast. The problem was I was broke, and I couldn't get back there without money. I called on my Aunt Rose – my father's sister – from whom I had never asked anything in my life. She always admired me for the things I did after I got out of prison. She always told me how proud she was of me and the changes she saw in my life. I called her up and asked her if she would help me get out of California because I didn't want to be there anymore – I didn't have a job and I was stuck in this half way house. She said she could help me. She sent me a greyhound bus ticket and she said, "I can get you to Chicago and you can get a job and get yourself the rest of the way."

I came to Chicago – I had friends here – Mildred and Willie Williamson – who were also movement people. I called them and told them I wanted to stay in Chicago for a while and asked them if they could help me get a job – and they said they would be happy to – they wanted to see me do better. They had a very nice basement that was fixed up very nice and they basically let me have that for my living arrangements. It was very clean and spacious and comfortable. I had a phone, TV, radio, library of great books to read. Willie he would loan me money to go look for a job and finally a woman by the name of Susan who worked for the American Red Cross – she was a nurse and a good friend of the family – and so she told me they had a job opening for $37,000 a year – back in 1991 that was a good salary for somebody coming from zero.

I took the application and they decided to hire me. My wife, Maria sent me a letter in response to a letter I had sent her – saying that I had been clean and sober for a whole year and she wanted me back into her life and back into the life of our kids and asked me to come home. She said come home Frank we need you. And I said OK. I didn't even think about it. Willie and Mildred were very upset – they didn't think I knew what kind of situation I was going back to and I had just gotten a very good job and a great break. She was a professional teacher and they felt she should come to Chicago and they agreed to help us until we could get a new place. I suggested that to Maria but she didn't want to move. She had a good job and was working on her master's degree. She didn't want to uproot all of that as well as the nice apartment that we had invested in – we even had guests room. She said to me just come home, please.

I went home – I packed up and went to New York. When I got to New York, as I was getting off the Amtrak train – I looked down the platform and there was my little girl Naima running with her arms outstretched to hug me. Maria had Jamilya in her arms. I was very happy and moved to tears. I thought I made the right decision – my family needed me and life was looking better.

Maria let me know right away that there were conditions. She told me that she did not want to take this relationship where it left off. She wanted me to court her all over again as if what happened before had never occurred. There would be no sex and I would have to start all over. I told her she should have told me this before – but then said OK I would do it.

But first things first –I had to find a job and find some AA meetings. I started going to meetings and got a sponsor. Once again I was intellectualizing the program and talking with my sponsor and sharing at meetings but I wasn't really dealing with me. I was convincing them I had changed but I was not convincing myself. It was all about outside issues – once again I was not dealing with me – I was trying to convince those people at those meetings that I was a changed person. I wasn't working my program – taking inventory – not really working on me. I was still seeing my problem as simply being on the outside – I needed to fix things with my family – fix things with my job – fix things with my AA meetings but was not about fixing anything with Frank. I was hiding from myself the reality that what I really wanted to do was drink because that was the only thing that would make me comfortable on the inside. I was still very uncomfortable with myself and still at war with myself. The only thing that would calm that down and give me peace was drugs and alcohol. I didn't know any other way and I wasn't seriously looking for another way.

I got a job working with Acorn – a community activist organization as the director of their political action committee. It paid about $650 every 2 weeks. That was quite a step down form what I would have been making at Red Cross. But it was sufficient with the money my wife was making. But at the time I thought I was just making peanuts. What they had me doing was organizing people I already knew – part of my responsibility was to reach out to unions and community organizations to endorse the candidates we were working with. There was a new city charter that was coming up and a lot of new people were running for city council. Progressives began to push their candidates – all over Brooklyn,

Queens, and Manhattan and acorn was hooked in to all of that. They wanted me to go to unions, etc to get support for their candidates. I remember my first city wide meeting of all the progressive leaders of all the progressive movements when I came into the meeting with John Hess who was the Director of Acorn in Brooklyn – All these people, like Gerry Hudson head of the Political Action Committee for Local 1199, Jim Bell, President of the Coalition of Black Trade Unionists – the UAW people – Cleveland Robinson and many, many others. And my 1199 friends too. When John Hess saw I knew all of these people already – I explained that I met them when I was organizing for 1199 – he had no idea I knew all of them and he was thrilled when he believed they would be willing to work with me – it was incredible. He didn't have any idea that he was getting a PAC committee person with ties like this. They didn't shake John Hess's hand – they shook mine – and they said they missed me and hadn't seen me for years. I didn't realize they had this kind of appreciation for me and it felt good.

Once again it put me on that high plain where I was thinking I could handle all this – I am back – I have my family back and I have this great job – I still had status in the community and I could still deal with my people. And I started meeting new people like Una Clark who was running for city council and who was very progressive. Also Major Owens a great progressive Congressman from Brooklyn and a member of the Black Caucus. Roger Green a black assemblyman from Brooklyn, also very progressive. I am back in heaven.

One day after a political meeting we went to a bar celebrating victory that we had with Congresswoman Nydia Velazquez, who was a Puerto Rican woman we got elected to Congress. We are out celebrating and somebody asked me what I was drinking and I said Jack Daniels on the rocks and the drink was served and I drank it. The thought occurred to me that I should not be doing this but I also thought I could handle this and told myself to look at all the things I had done – I also reminded myself I couldn't do too much drinking because a lot of people were depending on me. So I had a few drinks and left.

When I got home my wife asked me if I had been drinking and I said a few. She was worried but I convinced her I could do this and I was able to convince her to believe I knew the value of moderation. She didn't argue with me and let it go by. Every week I was turning my check over to her and she was leaving me just enough money to get to work. Things were going okay and she felt good about my sincerity. She let it go.

A few weeks go by and I get my check and I remember when I got the check I thought about going uptown to pay back Alice some money I owed her. She ran an after hours spot. She is entitled to her money, I thought. So I cashed my check and I had $650 in my pockets. I am only going uptown to pay Alice some money and have a cocktail and then come home like last time.

But it didn't work out like last time. I went and paid back Alice and she offered me a drink and a toot of cocaine – I refused the cocaine and she convinced me I could have a drink. I had the drink, and when I left that place I was broke. I had a drink, then the drink had a drink and then the drink had me. They had to give me cab fare to get home. I spent the whole $650 in that stinking place with that raggedy floor – it was just a liquor and cocaine station. It smelled like cocaine and whiskey. And I was sitting there and drinking and eventually I had the toot of cocaine. The drinking had started making me groggy and so I took a few toots of cocaine so I could go on with my drinking. I started on that see saw – down with drinking up with cocaine 'til the next day.

I couldn't get to my job so I called in sick and they said okay. They didn't realize where I was headed – my wife did. When I got home she told me to go to a meeting right away – don't go to work or anything – just go to a meeting. I couldn't say nothing because I couldn't say I didn't need a meeting – I had just blown all of that money. All I could say was yes. She said she was going with me and she grabbed the kids and we all went to a meeting in a church basement. They had a special room to take care of the kids. It was a closed meeting and since my wife wasn't an alcoholic she stayed with the kids. The meeting lasted an hour and the only thing I remember about that meeting was a guy said that the reason I relapsed – or resumed drinking – and the reason you did that is because you have an alcoholic brain. Noting else I was involved with mattered because I had an alcoholic brain. I responded thanks for the information and left. I went home and went back to work. I stayed dry for about another month and then I got another pay check and this time it wasn't to go to see Black

Alice it was stopping by a bar on the way home and having a cocktail. It made absolutely no sense but it was what my mind thought and I told myself I will just have a few drinks and go home. I could do that – anybody could do that. I had a few drinks and went home. This time I sneaked in the house –Maria was asleep and I had the money and I put it in the glass on the kitchen table and I slept in one of the other rooms. I got up the next morning – early and I showered real thorough and made sure I brushed my teeth and gargled and gargled and came out and she said good morning. She asked me what time I got in and I told her late and she relaxed when she saw the money. She asked me if I drank and I told her no I just sat around with the guys. She told me she was leaving Thursday to go to the Catskills to visit her mother be back on Sunday. She left Thursday with my daughters. I went to work but from Thursday night 'til Sunday it was a lost weekend for me, I went on another binge.

At that point I became lost in the sauce. I left Maria and my daughters. Since I couldn't stop drinking I figured it was best for me to leave as opposed to creating endless heartbreak and pain in their lives. I got jobs and went back to work for a while for the Musician's Union local 802 – I got remarried to Dorice Smith and tried to start a new life in Harlem – I got involved in the hustling life in Harlem and I worked with people in the numbers racket. I started hustling after hour spots and played music to get drugs and alcohol. I was into a whole different life. I was being pulled down into this abyss of drudgery and pain by the gravitational force of addiction.

My life became enshrouded by the drama of accidents, especially car accidents. But there were other dreadful accidents as well. I fell in the subway tracks one time and almost fractured my skull – I did get a concussion. Doctor said I was very fortunate. I ended up in emergency rooms a lot but none of this carried the message for me to quit. I still kept trying to beat the bottle. I figured there was something I wasn't doing but never figured the something was to put the bottle down. I was looking for a safe way to drink. I thought that everything I gained, I lost – even my last wife Cookie. She got me into her family and her son and daughter and I had good in laws.

It seemed like I was getting my life back together, but it was all fake – I still couldn't stop drinking for no one. I kept thinking that if I got the right woman, the right this, etc. But none of that helped. I had money and relationships. I remember this time when I was in the dry station where alcoholics go to dry out. My wife came to visit me and brought food and a guy in the station saw my wife and asked me if she was my wife and he said I was a lucky son of a bitch to have a wife like that. It just got completely by me.

I took it for granted. She was like my nurse. He was a stranger and had more appreciation for her than I did. Things like that made me think I was really becoming a creep and all that caused was self-loathing but never in the direction of gratitude. I was incapable of gratitude. What I was capable of was – I am really a no-good rascal for how I was treating this woman but I couldn't appreciate her.

I mention this to show how low I had sunk morally and spiritually, and it kept getting worse. I went to see my daughter once and she was graduating from the school of arts in Manhattan. One of her teachers was Natalie Cole's music advisor. It was on 46th and 8th Ave. in the theater district. She took drama and dancing and they were doing the ballet the night of her graduation and she was in the ballet and Maria told me they were doing this ballet and my daughter was graduating and that she would be happy if I came. I said, OK I will come and I went with a friend of mine and I was so drunk because I started drinking before to celebrate her graduating – I was drunk and smelling and when we sat down in the third row in the orchestra section – the whole row moved out and I didn't even notice it. Maria told me all of them moved because of you and your smell – the whisky and the body odor.

What an embarrassment to me and my daughter let alone yourself. My thoughts were that I didn't have to sit there and take this and moved to the back. When I moved I saw people moving back to their seats. When I got to the back Maria told me not to leave – "you can come to dinner with us", she said. When I got outside I felt so embarrassed I couldn't go through with dinner and I left. They kept calling me but I never answered. After this incomprehensible demoralizing incident, I knew I had to stop drinking by whatever means necessary.

Chicago, Coming Back Home to the Struggle

In St. Louis I moved in with my mother and sister Sharon. I was so shaken at the time by what happened in New York at my daughter's graduation/performance that I didn't want to ever see a drink again. I shared the experience with my sister and she said, "Frank you must stop drinking or you will lose everything. Why don't you join up with your friends here who are still in the movement?"

I became active in the movement as well as the Communist Party in St. Louis and started me a cleaning business called Universal Porter Service. Well neither the cleaning business nor my being active in the Party again worked out. The Party had changed. It was no longer even trying to operate as a Marxist-Leninist, revolutionary party. Some of the older comrades in St. Louis were upset with the elimination of Leninist standards but were in no way organized to do anything about it. For personal and political reasons I left the Party in 2009. I was asked to leave the Party because of personal family problems; however, I left the Party willingly and without being expelled because of long standing ideological disagreements.

As for the cleaning business, well it took me back into the life because most of my contracts were with bars and after-hour spots. I tried for a minute because the money was good but I quickly came to the conclusion that I was back on the road to being a drunken bum and so in May, 2011 I pulled up stakes and went to Chicago When I came to Chicago in 2011 I was really just passing through. Leaving St. Louis was not just a matter of pulling up stakes. I had accumulated enough money to go back to New York and make one final effort to sober up among friends and family.

However, an essential part of family, my daughter Jamilya, was in Rhode Island about to graduate. Out of nowhere the idea of going up to Brown University for my daughter's graduation popped into my head. And so, I bought AMTRAK tickets to New York with plans to go from there to Rhode Island. I left St. Louis on a dreary, rainy night on May 3, 2010. During the train ride to Chicago I thought of all sort of things I would do for my daughter to show her how much I wanted her to be happy by giving her some sort of outstanding gift. I started a conversation with someone on the train and we talked for several hours all the way into Chicago swapping stories from our personal lives. However, I did not talk about how I had been a father that my kids saw every now and then, mostly then.

Arriving in Chicago I was informed that the train going to New York was running late, giving us about an hour and a half lay over time. There was either a bar in the AMTRAK station or one conveniently nearby. I don't remember. I told the bartender to remind me a half hour from departure time that I had a train to catch. Well once I took that first drink all bets were off. I forgot about just how alcoholic I was. Once I got started I couldn't stop. In fact, I closed that bar and went and found another one in Greek town. I drank until I passed out. I woke up in Cook County Hospital tied down to a stretcher. I must have been rolled in the bar because all I had left in my pocket was $20 and I had no idea as to where my luggage was. So, there I was lying there wallowing in self-pity and self-loathing, feeling lower than whale shit.

A young Chinese Doctor came to my stretcher, looked at me and said, "Sir you know what your problem is? You are a hopeless alcoholic..." Then she looked at me with caring eyes and said: "Do you want some help? You remind me of my father. He died because he never asked for help." I quickly responded, "Yes, yes, help me please....", in a very humble voice. Like the guy they sung about in the song Ole Man River I was "Tired of living but afraid of dying."

Well, not quite for I wanted Frank the drunk to die because I had come to the point where if I drew another breath I wanted it to be sober. That was my last drink, May 5, 2011. I was 68 years old.

The good doctor arranged for me to go to a 21-day rehab. I stayed there for 45 days. They suggested when I left that I go to a halfway house in Bridgeport and I did. I stayed for the three-month probationary period, and was offered a job as house manager. I took the job and dedicated myself to staying sober by helping other drunks. And it worked. Around 2012, that is my first year sober, I started going back around the movement. I landed in the Chicago Alliance Against Racist and Political Repression. I felt like the prodigal son coming home.

After the fall of the Soviet Union and a massive exodus of the Black leadership of the Communist Party, the National Alliance Against Racist and Political Repression suffered from the loss of membership and resources. One branch after another started to fold up except for the branches in Louisville, Kentucky and Chicago, Illinois. I believe two remarkable women, Anne Braden and Josephine Wyatt had a lot to do with that. You met Anne Braden early on in these pages so it won't surprise you if I tell you that she used the resources of the Southern Organizing Committee and the Southern Education Leadership Foundation to keep the Kentucky Alliance a float.

However, Josephine Wyatt, the heart, soul and brains of the Chicago Alliance is a different matter and you have yet to meet her. My life as an organizer has been influenced in deep and profound ways by women warriors like Esther Jackson, founding editor of *Freedomways*, who made my case and plight in prison nationally known. Then there was the mathematics teacher Claudia Zaslavsky who did an appendix on me in her book *Africa Counts*; by Alice Windom who taught the ABCs of grass roots organizing and by Charlene Mitchell, the great organizing genius, internationalist and communist whom I had the honor of working with for nearly ten years. Through Charlene I worked closely with Angela Davis who was a co-chair and spokesperson for the National Alliance Against Racist and Political Repression. So, Josephine was like the only person I knew who was still alive and carrying the Alliance banner forward into battle, and when she asked me to come back to the movement she talked to me like I had never left. It was definitely an emotional moment for me and my tears inside came out to dry.

Josephine Wyatt joined the ancestors just as she was coming up on 95 this past July 11, 2017. Joining the movement and the Communist Party shortly after World War II Josephine became an ardent and consistent fighter for Black Liberation and Socialism. When Angela Davis was captured in 1971 and put on trial for murder Josephine, like many others in the Black community, stepped up to meet the challenge. She along with Sylvia Woods led the campaign to Free Angela Davis and All Political Prisoners . And in 1973, in the wake of Angela's acquittal, when the National Alliance was founded in Chicago, Josephine was there laying the foundation bricks for the Chicago Alliance.

When I first came back to Chicago in 2010 Josephine, Clarice Durham, Billie and Ted Pearson were the people holding down the fort. Clarice and Ted were the co-chairs and Josephine was the treasurer. They approached me in the Spring of 2011 about becoming the Educational Director for the Chicago Alliance and I quickly said yes. Josephine was so happy to see that I wasn't drinking and that I was eager to get back into doing Alliance work. She would say to me "Frank we really need you to help to build this organization like never before. In Chicago they are killing off our young people or sending them to jail in astounding numbers. And the police are the cutting edge of all this."

As the Educational Director I was mainly doing educational work for new members and there wasn't a lot of new members. Then in March of 2012, a 21-year-old Black woman was shot in the head by a cop. The cop, Dante Servin, said they were making too much noise in the Park at around midnight. So, he got out of bed, got in his car and did a drive by on this group of young Black people, shooting recklessly at them and killing Rekia Boyd. It was a clear-cut case of murder and nothing was being done except the usual routine investigation that always exonerated cops. At the next meeting of the Alliance they made me the Field Organizer to start a campaign to stop police crimes. Everyone agreed and thus began the rebirth of my life as a community organizer.

Our movement has been recognized and is being assessed by the powers that be. That is what the Mayor's apology in the torture cases was all about; he apologizes to the torture victims and admits that the police who perpetrated these crimes were morally and legally wrong. But the Mayor did not set forth a program of action that would bring about any systemic change. They know their system is plagued with racism, corruption and injustice and so do we. The difference is we want change and they don't; we want justice and they are hell bent on maintaining this system of injustice.

Our Organizing Committee To Stop Police Crimes was conceived on April 19, 2012 when the Chicago Alliance Against Racist and Political Repression (CAARPR) met with the late Lew Myers, a radical Black attorney and teacher at Kennedy-King College, to discuss the possibility of having a community meeting on police crimes and torture. Coming out of this discussion was an agreement with

Brother Myers and the Kennedy-King Criminal Justice Project to co-sponsor a Peoples' Hearing on Police Crimes with the CAARPR at Kennedy-King College. Later, on April 23, 2012 we convened our first meeting, and those present were Khalid Abdullah, Jeff Baker, Cherese Williams, Allisah Love, Lamont Burnett, Jesse Caver, Mark Clements, Randy Ryder and Ted Pearson.

I was the newly appointed Field Organizer for the Chicago Alliance Against Racist and Political Repression, and I was responsible for presenting to the committee a plan of work for organizing a Peoples Hearing on Police Crimes to be held at Kennedy-King College on June 9, 2012.

After some detail discussion the various elements of the proposed plan were discussed, amended and approved by the committee. We agreed to develop a Call for united action around the issues of police crimes and torture. We sent the Call out to the affected communities, to various strands of the organized people's movement and known survivors of police crimes and torture. The Call's message was as follows:

> ."...the Chicago Alliance Against Racist and Political Repression calls upon all our sisters and brothers, representing all strands of the people's movements, to join us in initiating a call for A Peoples Hearing Against Police Crimes (i.e., brutality, murder, torture, complicity in vigilantism and racial profiling). The purpose of this hearing will be to provide a public forum where the victims of police crimes and the various organizations fighting against police brutality and torture can present their cases and demands for justice.

> "The facts and evidence are clear; the police throughout our country are out of control. Most striking is their use of brute force when dealing with people of color and progressive movements for social change. This is precisely what we mean by racist and political repression...."

We agreed to reach out to the families of police crimes victims who had been murdered as well as surviving victims of police crimes and torture. We also wanted to mobilize community-based organizations, churches, civil and human rights groups, grass roots leaders and politicians. We did in fact mobilize 23 victims, survivors and their families and several groups and leaders in the community. Those organizations that endorsed us coming out the gate were, the New Jericho Movement, the Committee for A Better Chicago, Campaign to End the New Jim Crow, Arab-American Action Network, African American Police Association, the South Side NAACP and the Kennedy-King Criminal Justice Project in Englewood.

We agreed to reach out to all strands of the movement, to human rights and civil rights organizations, community-based organizations, political organizations and leaders.

Our Organizing Committee to Stop Police Crimes expanded and was immediately joined by Cherese Williams, Mike Elliot, Allisah Love, Larry Redmond, Lajuana Lampkins (torture survivor and mother of a son killed by police violence), Larry Kennon and Bertha Escamilla. And in the following weeks of May and June, 2012 we did reach out and called for an organizing meeting with the victims, survivors and their families for June 29, 2012 and with various organizations, survivors and victims of police crimes and torture to be held at Kennedy-King College on July 10, 2012.

Both of these meetings were well attended (nine families of police torture victims were present at the June 29 meeting and about fifty people (from the community) were present at the July 10 meeting and helped to lay the foundation for our first successful Peoples Hearing on Police Crimes. We called upon the survivors of police crimes as well as community organizations to help us in mobilizing for this hearing. We were also careful to point out that we were not mobilizing for a single event, but to kick off a movement, a political campaign for civilian control of the police.

Shortly after the July 10 meeting we were informed by the President of Kennedy-King College that pursuant to a police complaint we could not have our Hearing on their campus. In two weeks, we had to find an alternative meeting place and get the word out to our people and the community. Brother Lew Myers helped us secure space at Teamwork Englewood, a community-based organization in Englewood.

In the next two weeks we distributed thousands of flyers and knocked on doors and made phone calls to several hundred people. Some of the key organizations that helped us in getting the word out were the South Side NAACP, the New Jericho Movement, the Committee for a Better Chicago, United Auto Workers Local 551 Solidarity Committee, the Campaign Against the New Jim Crow, Occupy the South Side, the Arab-American Action Network and the Criminal Justice Project in Englewood. We canvassed the streets of Englewood getting people to take pluggers and sign petitions.

We held our first Peoples Hearing to Stop Police Crimes at Teamwork Englewood on July 21, 2012 and about one hundred and fifty people came out. The people were wall to wall because the room could only accommodate a hundred people. Nonetheless it was a very successful meeting and it really gave people hope that we could build a movement to stop police crimes through a campaign to politically empower the people to hold the police accountable for the crimes they commit. About 23 people testified about how they, their family members or their particular organization had been police crimes survivors.

This, in broad strokes, is how our movement began over 60 seven years ago and how in the process it became a movement fighting for justice for the survivors of police crimes and torture and for community control of the police.

Many of the people we reached out to and who reached out to us joined our movement. For example, Cherice Williams, Khalid Abdullah, Greg Malandrucco, Kamm Howard, Crista Noel, Marissa Brown, Jonathan Winbush, Sara Ortiz, Annabelle Perez, Emma Lozano, Rev. Slim Coleman, Alejandro Barba, Sarah Wild, Emmett Farmer, Percy Coleman, Valerie Love, Armanda Shackleford, and Jeanette Plummer, Carolyn Johnson, Rosemary Cade, Jeanette Plummer, Anabel Perez, Sara Ortiz, Bertha Escamilla, Martinez Sutton (Rekia Boyd's brother), Kevin Tyson and Darryl Brown (Prison Ministry of Trinity, UCC) just to name a few. And with this new momentum we started to organize for a second peoples hearing and to develop a sub-committee, coordinated, by Crista Noel, Kamm Howard, Larry Redmond, Marissa Brown and Khalid Abdullah, to carry our struggle to the United Nations.

After our first peoples hearing we could honestly contend that the people who are racially profiled, brutalized, tortured and killed by the police were no longer simply a flashing headline or a cold statistical figure; they now had a human face and voice and they do more than cry out in anguish and implore the powers that be to give them justice. These women and men, mothers and fathers, sisters and brothers have ceased being victims and have become the fuel, the fire and the organizers of a growing mass movement to stop police crimes. They are learning in the dirt and blood of battle how to be freedom fighters.

The same must be said for organizations and groups who are victims of police repression as a result of their struggles for progressive social change such as the Committee to Stop FBI repression, the Arab-American Action Network, the New Jericho Movement, the Occupy Movement, Freedom Road Socialist Organization and others who participated in the first Peoples Hearing...and who continue to fight with us to stop police crimes. They too are the fuel and fire of our movement.

Many times, since the first Peoples Hearing on Police Crimes in 2012 we have continuously confronted the problem of setting a date for action, then mustering forces and organizing participation in the action. We have done this because this is a continuous process we must engage in if we wish to build a movement. We started out with less than a few hundred contacts in the communities affected by police crimes, now we have over sixty thousand and that number will grow as we continue to do mass work like we have been doing for the last seven years.

Tabling in the community and rallying people to our cause in community activities in the neighborhoods, canvassing, mobilizing people for protest actions such as the annual Black Friday Boycotts and numerous public forums calling for community control of the police are the means by which we maintain the engagement of our people.

We built our movement with the first peoples hearing in July 2012, the second peoples hearing held at the University of Chicago in February, 2013 and the 500 strong March on City Hall August 28, 2013. Also, in 2013 we filed a complaint with the United States Department of Justice, all these events were bench-marks in the launching of our campaign for an all elected Civilian Police Accountability Council) CPAC.

In 2014 we held a National Forum On Police Crimes and Torture and a mass rally with Angela Davis wherein more than a thousand people participated. In 2016 August 29 we mobilized with Black Lives Matter Chicago, BYP 100, Arab American Action Network, the Chicago Teachers Union Freedom Road Socialist Organization and others 3000 people in one mass rally demanding the end of police crimes and torture and expressing solidarity with our sisters, brothers and comrades in Ferguson, Missouri. When the Chicago Teachers Union marched later in 2016 they put 30,000 people in the streets demanding an end to school closings, community control of school boards and a good union contract and one of the front banners let it be known that they were also supporting our struggle for community control of the police.

The most critical development in the Campaign for CPAC was the mass march of 3000 people on August 29, 2015. It was the largest march against police crimes following in the wake of the murder of Mike Brown in Ferguson. A majority of the march were oppressed Black and Brown peoples and hundreds of Palestinians and Muslims from the Council of Islamic Organization of Chicago. Rasmea Odeh, the legendary Palestinian freedom-fighter, spoke about her racist frame-up, attempts to deport her and the battle for her freedom. Rasmea was facing a trumped-up charge where the U.S. government accused her of lying on her entry application twenty years ago. Other survivors of police crimes who spoke were Emmett Farmer and Martinez Sutton the brother of Rekia Boyd. It was an important day of solidarity involving the CTU, Black Lives Matter, BYP100, Trinity United Church of Christ and others.

These were not mere events or solitary moments of protests. No, on the contrary these were phases, stages or moments in building a movement with a clearly defined focus and political objective. Namely, to get legislation passed creating a Civilian Police Accountability Council (CPAC) that will empower the people to hold the police accountable for the crimes they commit and for their conduct in general.

We demonstrated in every phase of our movement that we win the participation of the people when we go to the people and ask them for their involvement and support. As a result of this mass-approach-mobilizing we have won the support of about 60 organizations including Black Lives Matter, the Chicago Teachers Union, the

Pilsen Alliance (a Latino, community-based organization), Trinity United Church of Christ, Church of the Living God, Arab American Action Network, Assatas Daughters, Black Youth Project 100, Coalition of Black Trade Unionist, Coalition of Labor Women Union, Freedom Road Socialist Organization, SEIU Local 73, SEIU Local 1, SEIU HCII, United Electrical Workers, United Working Families and many more churches and community based organizations . We have also continued to reach out to communities such as Kenwood, Woodlawn, Washington Park, Hyde Park, Chatam, South Shore, Roseland, Englewood, Pilsen, Humboldt Park, Little Village, Lawndale, E. Garfield Park, Logan Square, Uptown and Broadway, Roger Park and some new near North side communities.

Not only do we currently have pending in the City Council our proposed Ordinance for an all elected Civilian Police Accountability Council (CPAC) we have an average of 1000 supporters in 38 Wards. Our CPAC Ordinance was introduced into the City Council chambers in 2016 by Alderman Carlos Ramirez Rosa (35th Ward) and seven other Alderpersons. Most recently, since the newly held city-wide elections for Mayor and the City Council Ald. Rosa (35th Ward) Jeanette B. Taylor-Azeez (20th Ward) and 11 other Alderpersons have signed/endorsed the pending CPAC Ordinance now in the Public Safety Committee of the City Council.

These 13 alderpersons are the end result of the recent city-wide wherein 17 candidates won who had endorsed CPAC. Of course, right after the elections we have been met with hard and hostile attitudes by the Mayor Lori Lightfoot and her cohorts on the City Council, yet we have the ever-growing support of the people and various strands of the peoples' movement. Candidates running with CPAC as part of their platform garnered at least 176,000 votes.

The 176,000 votes for candidates endorsing CPAC is more than a number, a mere vote count for CPAC. It is a number that reflects a qualitative change for the CPAC campaign. Suddenly, we found ourselves thrust into the electoral arena, where we would count our supporters not in terms of people saying "yes, I support CPAC..." but count their votes for a CPAC candidate.

Counting votes and having our candidates win an election opens up a whole new vista for organizing for CPAC. Now we have before us possibilities of working with the various Ward organizations to consolidate CPAC voters and supporters in a given Ward. Also building a base of support in the Ward that signed on or endorsed CPAC is critical in keeping the politicians from selling us out. For the most part our people have not met politicians who won't sell them out and this includes the liberals, progressives and socialists. We must insist that politicians say what they mean and mean what they say. We must continue to push the issue not the politician. Having an organized mass base of CPAC supporters is critical. As the peoples lobbyists we don't have a money filled envelope to push, we have the CPAC supporters city-wide who will ring the bell of the politicians and demand justice.

We have thousands of volunteers who have signed up at our tables. And we don't know exactly how many CPAC supporters we picked up during the elections.

Our greatest organizing challenge going forward is how to turn this mass support we have garnered into organized bases in the Wards and neighborhoods. Can we build Ward committees in the 38 Wards where most of our supporters reside? Well, let's start with the 13 Wards of the Alderpesons who signed on to our proposed CPAC Ordinance. I believe the future of our movement will be determined by our continued base-building efforts in our communities, and since the immediate goal of this base-building is to get CPAC enacted then we must focus on building Ward committees.

The question is sometimes raised about trust, like we are supposed to trust the politicians to deliver on their campaign promises. But politics is not about trust, its about power. And if it ain't about the power of the people then it ain't about nothing. When you break your pact with the people then your integrity is down the drain and the people have an inalienable democratic right, a duty and responsibility to vote you out just like they voted you in.

The way we are continuing to build our movement through the Stop Police Crimes Organizing Committee and our various allies is informed by our organizing experience over the past seven years. The main challenge we confront at every turn is how do we engage the masses in all areas of our work. We now have developed a real sense of our potential and limitations, we are consistently coming to grips with our limitations with respect to time, people and resources. In this regard we are always exploring how to work closer with unions and allies in the communities.

We are learning from all our various activities how to make critical and objective assessments of our successes and failures. Our successes inspire us and raise our expectations, but our mistakes teach the most valuable lessons by the pain and hardships they cause. We have been convinced not by clever arguments but by the hard-knocks of experience what it means to develop a mass campaign to stop police crimes and torture.

We believe that building CPAC committees in the wards is the most effective way of pressuring/lobbying City Council members to support our CPAC Ordinance. This is important because we need to be taken seriously and we need to take ourselves seriously. The field operations and organization required to get people involved in the electoral process, political ward organization and signed up as volunteers in our campaign is challenging, hard grass roots work. But most importantly it is a test of our commitment to build a truly mass movement to end the brutal and murderous police repression that exist in our communities.

The Chicago Alliance Against Racist and Political Repression formed the Organizing Committee to Stop Police Crimes to provide for the masses an organizing vehicle for effective systemic change. We are learning how to fight back by fighting back, we lead by example not by declaration or decree. Our late comrades Josephine Wyatt and Clarice Durham taught us that our job as organizers is not only to set the course of action but to teach ourselves how to steer the ship. Action, keeping people in motion, keeping the people engaged in political action; this is how movements are built, this is how they grow. Charlene Mitchell taught me that we must lead people out of their frustration not in their frustration.

To avoid going down tactical blind alleys always be conscious of our strategy (keep your eye on the goal posts). If you can't see the goal from where you are fighting then you won't know if you're going forward or backward. Keep your eye on the prize and move forward.

In this moment of history, we have known frustration unbelievable. The murder of 17-year-old Laquan McDonald (he was shout

16 times, 14 times while he laid helplessly in the streets) brought about a decisive, abrupt qualitative change, throwing the city of Chicago into a tailspin of a political crisis. This young Black person, who was legally a child, was shot 16 times by a racist, crazed killer cop name Jason Van Dyke. Mayor Rahm Emanuel suppressed the video evidence of this heinous crime for 400 days because he didn't want people to see it while he was running for reelection. After the election was over the Mayor was forced by a court order to release the video. The State's Attorney, Anita Alvarez called a news conference the day before the video was released warning people that it graphically portrayed a brutal execution style murder. Yet nothing could forestall the outrage of the people once they saw the video. In one fell swoop the Mayor, the City Council and the Chicago Police Department were exposed for their complicity in one of the most heinous crimes ever committed by a CPD officer. The city rocked with demonstrations and the shutting down of traffic in the streets for days after a major Black led demonstration of thousands in the central business district. The protestors marched through the streets shouting, "Sixteen Shouts and a Cover-Up!

The demand for justice was paramount so we proceeded to organize an intense campaign to get Jason Van Dyke, tried for murder. He was tried and convicted by a jury (mostly white) of second-degree murder and 16 counts of aggravated assault. He was facing a minimum of 96 years on the assault charges alone. So, what did the Judge do. He decided to throw out all the assault charges out and to sentence Van Dyke just on the second-degree charge. Van Dyke was sentenced to 6 years and 9 months. This sentence was so outrageous that even the Illinois States Attorney General Kwame Raoul filed an appeal in the interest of justice.

On the eve of the Jason Van Dyke trial Mayor Emmanuel said he would not run for reelection. His secret partner in crime Lori Lightfoot quickly threw her hat in the ring.

It was the stark revelation of the city's complicity in a horrid police crime and the spontaneous protest rebellion of the people that led to the indictment and trial of Jason Van Dyke for first degree murder, the firing of Superintendent of Police McCarthy, the electoral defeat of State's Attorney Anita Alvarez and Mayor Rahm Emanuel not running for reelection. The political struggle sharpened to the point where a new Mayor and 15 new members of the City Council were elected. The new Mayor, Lori Lightfoot, is the first Black woman gay person ever elected to this office. She opposed CPAC when she was President of the Police Board but never mentioned it when she was running to get elected or when she headed up the Task Force On Police Accountability created by Mayor Rahm Emanuel. Now that she is the Mayor, just like her predecessor Rahm Emanuel, Lightfoot has introduced legislation designed to undermine or kill CPAC in committee.

Our persistence has helped to stimulate a more open public debate on the question of community control of the police. We are definitely moving in counter motion to the reactionary, white supremacist extremists who want to uphold the status quo no matter the human cost.

Chicago is a Unique Window That Reveals the Horror of Police Tyranny In The United States In The Era of Mass Incarceration

Chicago is a unique city when it comes to torture and police crimes. This is attested to by these facts: Chicago is the only city in the nation that has passed an ordinance providing reparations for torture survivors; Chicago, is the only city opening a Torture Justice Center to provide psychological and social services to survivors of torture and to educate the public. In no other City in the United States is there an ordinance requiring public school students to learn the history of police torture. Chicago is the only city where organizations demanding an end to police crimes and torture went to the United Nations. Our reports to the UN were accepted and CPAC was recognized and endorsed.

This uniqueness stems from Chicago's legacy of police violence and abuse. And this legacy is currently being revealed by the Chicago History Museum with its opening of records, including lawsuits, investigations and reported instances of police brutality.

According to the record more than 200 criminal cases between 1972 and 1991 were tortured into making confessions by a decorated U.S. Army (trained in torture techniques) Chicago Police Department (CPD) officer named Jon Graham Burge. Burge was suspended from the CPD in 1991 and fired in 1993 after the Police Review Board ruled that he had tortured suspects (majority of whom were Black). Because of the statute of limitations Burge and his squad of torturers were never charged and convicted. 2003 Governor George Ryan pardoned four torture survivors who had been sentenced to death.

In 2008 the U.S. Attorney Patrick Fitzgerald charged Burge with obstruction of justice and perjury. He was convicted on all counts and sentenced to 4 years in prison. Yet the Supreme Court of Illinois has ruled that Jon Burge will continue to receive his pension.

In 2009 the state of Illinois passed a law authorizing the Illinois Torture Inquiry Relief Commission. Since 2011 several cases have been reviewed by the Illinois Torture Inquiry Commission. Dozens of cases have been referred to the Circuit Court of Cook County and by April 2016 and a few men were released while another 130 cases have been claimed beyond the scope of Burge and his crew.

Having already paid out $57 million to survivors of Burge's torture and another $50 million defending CPD officers the City decided, under mass pressure from the peoples' movement, to establish a $5.5 million fund for reparations to survivors of Burge and his cohorts.

Going all the way back to the red-hot Summer of 1919 "race riots" or pogroms against Black people the police have a history of unleashing terror on the Black community. But the present crisis of policing in Chicago is deeply related to two poignant incidents of violence. One involving the murders of Black Panther Party leaders Fred Hampton and Mark Clark who were murdered by CPD officers December 4, 1969. These murders were blatant acts of racist repression perpetrated against the Black Liberation movement. And another incident involving the killing of two police officers on February 9, 1982. These officers were shot and killed in Area 2, Jon Burge's jurisdiction and he was the commanding officer.

Burge was outraged, and he immediately proceeded to dragnet the Black community, including mass arrests, shooting pets, handcuffing suspects to stationary objects for days and holding guns to the heads of children. Rev. Jesse Jackson charged that Burge was placing the Black community under martial law, while Renault Robinson, President of the Afro American Police League said Burge's actions were 'sloppy police work" and "a matter of racism."

Jon Burge was allowed, under Mayor Jane Byrne, Cook County State's Attorney Richard M. Daley, Chicago Police Superintendent Brzeczek, to carry out a vendetta against Black people in the wake of the murder of two police officers thus hundreds of innocent human beings were kidnapped, tortured and wrongfully convicted. In fact, City Hall and the Criminal Justice system and the media were in such vigorous support of this regime of terror 'til even the election of Harold Washington couldn't turn the tide. This is how the present racist/repressive style of Chicago policing got started. Now we come to how the people's campaign to end this reign of police terror got started.

In 2012 with the murder of 21-year-old, Rekia Boyd, a young Black woman who was murdered by an enraged cop for making noise in Douglas Park after midnight, there emerged in Chicago a rejuvenated movement for community control of the police led by the Chicago Alliance Against Racist and Political Repression. We called peoples hearings on police crimes and torture and drafted an Ordinance calling for the creation of an all elected Civilian Police Accountability Council.

The reason so many police crime survivors like Emmett Farmer (father of Flint Farmer) and Dorothy Holmes (mother of Ronald "Ronnieman" Johnson) want CPAC is because this is the only pathway to justice for them.

In June7, 2011 Flint Farmer was murdered execution style by CPD officer Gildardo Sierra. The murder was video-recorded showing Sierra standing over Flint Farmer shooting him while he lay helpless on the ground. The other case involves the senseless shooting of Ronald "Ronnieman" Johnson. "Ronnieman" who was killed by CPD officer George Hernandez in October 12, 2014. He was 25 years old and a father of five. On the night of the murder, witnesses have said that police officers did not identify themselves before opening fire on unarmed Johnson, killing him from multiple gunshot wounds. His death has been ruled a homicide. And there was no prosecution.

There is no statute of limitation on murder so when we get CPAC enacted we will be able to reopen these cases.

From the launching of this campaign for CPAC we included the demand for freedom and justice for all the torture survivors. The torture cases like the cases of police murdering us demonstrate loud and clear that we are powerless over what the police do in our communities, so they can murder and torture us with impunity.

The theme of our hugely successful rally with Angela Davis on Sunday, June 17, 2018 was to welcome home the victims of police crimes who've been exonerated or released. These are men and women who were either framed, or tortured, or both by officers of the Chicago Police Department. We estimate that there are perhaps 250 others that we know about, almost all of whom were torture survivors and still in prison. Our welcome home cry was "Welcome Home – Now Let's Free All the Rest"

Most of the 38 people exonerated by Kim Foxx and her Conviction Integrity Unit were people who were framed by corrupt cops, at least one of whom, Joseph Miedzianowski, is now serving a life sentence in Federal Prison for dealing drugs and arming street gang members who were part of his conspiracy to distribute crack cocaine on the streets. Another, Reynaldo Guevara, has had a score of cases that he brought (frame-ups) tossed by Foxx. One ofthese cases involves Juan and Rosendo Hernandez, bette
r known inthe community as the Free The Hernandez Brothers case.

The Englewood Four is one of Alvarez' most notorious cases. She insisted on 60 Minutes that they were guilty even after another man's DNA, a serial rapist, matched the rape kit taken from the victim. The courts ultimately exonerated them over her objections. See https://www.youtube.com/watch?v=bksPvb9KvyU.
Our Chicago Alliance has been working with torture survivors and their families for decades. One case comes to mind and that is the Gerald Reed case.

On October 3, 1990, Gerald Reed, 27, was arrested and questioned regarding the murder two days earlier of Willie Williams and Pamela Powers. He was questioned by Detectives Michael Kill and Victor

Breska at Area 3 Homicide, members of the notorious "Midnight Crew" of torturer Jon Burge. They beat him and kicked him repeatedly and broke a metal rod that was in his right thigh along with the surgical screws that held it in place, causing him excruciating pain. The rod had been surgically placed years before to repair his thigh bone, which had been shattered by a gunshot.

It was clear to Reed that the beatings would continue until he agreed to confess, and he did. He repudiated the confession at his trial and has proclaimed his innocence ever since. There was no other material evidence against Reed at his trial. Gerald Reed was convicted of both murders and sentenced to life in prison without possibility of parole.

But that did not stop the torture. For 27 years Reed has repeatedly requested medical intervention to fix the horrible and excruciatingly painful damage done by his torturers. He has been unable to walk. Finally, last year, he was taken from Stateville Correctional Center to Dreyer Medical Center in Aurora, where Orthopedic Surgeon Steven I. Rabin performed the first step required to repair the terrible damage to his thigh bone and ease his suffering. Dr. Rabin made it clear that a second, follow-up surgery, was necessary to improve his condition and end his pain, along with physical therapy.

Gerald Reed was returned to the hospital at Statesville in January where he waited for the second surgery. Dr. Rabin, however, had a heart attack and was unable to complete the task. Gerald Reed stayed in the hospital at Statesville for over ten months. He has had minimal physical therapy and is still suffering from serious pain in his leg.

The Illinois Torture Inquiry and Relief Commission held, in a decision rendered on June 18, 2012 and further amended on March 19, 2014, that there was a "preponderance of evidence" that Reed had been tortured and forced to confess. Yet more than 5 years later Gerald Reed remains in prison and in terrible pain as a result of being tortured by Chicago Police.

December of last year Gerald Reed's conviction was overturned and the Judge ordered a new trial. The special prosecutors have pressured him (Gerald) to take a deal of time served. He would be released but his conviction would stand. Gerald is innocent and is demanding release without conditions.

So, after 29 years here we are, still pleading in the courts for an innocent man. The system wants Gerald dead and we want him free. We will win, Gerald will be coming home. There seems to be a race in this case between time and catastrophe. We must bring Gerald home!

As we rise to every new dawn in our struggle we start out with the conviction that we will carry the day because our comrades Josephine Wyatt and Clarice Durham still lives in our hearts and our deeds.

My Life as a Testament to Triumph over Tragedy

People, smash the ancient charm
Of a too lethargic slumber:
With the most terrible of awakenings
Spread alarm to grinning crime.
Lend an ear to our voice
And leave the darkest night behind.
People, take hold of your rights,
The sun shines for all. --Francois Babeuf

I want to talk about the difficulty of this enterprise of writing a biography when you are doing it about yourself – you are locked into subjectivity. I want to do a short view long view type of thing in terms of what this means for me and what it can mean for the community and the people who become a part of it – particularly African Americans but also for those who struggle for progressive social change here and throughout the world.

My memoirs are really an extended commentary about the things I have been involved in as a prisoner, as an organizer without really much reflection on what it all meant. I want to touch on this for just a minute because I had developed some perspective while in prison on how to work with people to bring about change in the criminal justice system and society. Being locked up with a life and fifty- year sentence provides a great incentive to work with others, with jail-house lawyers, prison pastors, educators, civil rights groups, militant political activists of every stripe as well as intellectuals and publicists.

I worked with all sorts of people, all of whom I have mentioned. I also worked with prisoners of every kind of political persuasion you could think of – prisoners who thought they were Nazis to prisoners who thought they were Black revolutionaries and Black nationalists. So even before I got out of the joint I had a sense of how multi-faceted the struggle is and has to be.

In the process of working with all of these different people in and out of prison I learned that dogmatism serves very little purpose.

I became a communist when I was 23. I am still a convinced Marxist-Leninist. I don't think we can afford to not work with other people if we insist that our ideas are the only valid ones. We have to be open to uniting and working with people on things we can agree on. I found that to be very practical when working on the issues of prison reform. There were professors who believed that education inside the prison could help prisoners to re-socialize and make them valuable members of society. In working with them the whole entire point of us working together was the belief that bringing education into the prisons at the college level would have a powerful influence in rehabilitating prisoners, so they could become productive members of society again.

We could agree on that and a condition for that agreement was not that they be Marxist or I be a Republican or Democrat. Professor John Dahm was a Republican but he believed in this proposition as strongly as I did. In fact he was able to get a block grant from the Law Enforcement Assistance Association because they trusted his conservatism. In working on it together we never made our different ideologies a bone of contention – we stuck to the broader agenda. So that gave me some hope. If we could do this in prison then surely there would be greater possibilities of doing this in the larger society.

While in prison and when I came home I found that the people who fought the hardest and the most consistently and vigorously were people on the left – old school communists from the 1930s and 1940s and the new developing communists who, like me, came in the wake of the sixties. These comrades had a mass/democratic approach, I think, that was not unique to their time and era. Many of them worked closely with churches, labor unions, and women's organizations. They didn't walk in declaring they were Communists or revolutionaries. They came in as fellow workers and oppressed people recognizing there was the struggle for justice and the need to join it.

Seeing that the super-exploitation and national oppression of Black people is the bedrock of political reaction and white supremacy, communists have always recognized the centrality of the struggle for Black liberation. In the process of engagement or involvement they earned the love and respect of the people. And these were the people I learned from once I got out of prison. I found myself working with church people, trade unions, women, gay people and to me that was the movement. As that movement builds and grows and struggles against the injustices that are perpetrated against minorities – all people outside the 1 % and their flunkies-- people began to draw conclusions and make decision on how to fight for the future.

I think more and more people are beginning to see capitalism is very destructive. In fact the new title for capitalism is vulture capitalism meaning that our country is run by the banks and that we have seen the greatest transfer of wealth in US history take place in the last 8-10 years. But, what does this have to do with socialism or what the political future of the American people is? I believe that we will find our way through the practice of the science of Marxism-Leninism. Which means consciously building a revolutionary party of class conscious workers dedicated to uniting the working class and the racially/nationally oppressed peoples in the fight for democracy and socialism. I think on these issues that we have to practice our way into correct thinking. And we have to learn to work together on those things which are important, like the environment, climate change, peace instead of war, ending racial and national oppression – these are things that if you took a poll today the large majority of the human race would want to change.

The question of socialism is becoming eminent. The contradiction between socialized production and private appropriation has sharpened to the point where poverty is spreading among the people like a disease epidemic. No one wants the present economic crisis we have today but there are those today, and I mean both the Democrat and Republican Parties, who are leading people in their frustration instead of trying to lead them out of it. We need to build a Party firmly rooted in Marxism-Leninism. We need to build a broad militant coalition of the people to take power from these reptile representatives of the culture of predatory capitalism. Both factions of the ruling class party don't want to do anything for social progress – they only want to make the rich richer and the poor poorer – and their arrogance is unparalleled. The only time in history you might find this type of arrogance is before the Civil War when the slave holders in the South assumed such arrogance that they attempted to impose slavery on the whole country and used the US Supreme Court and the Congress to do it. The Dredd Scott Decision and the Fugitive Slave Act-- all took place before the civil war. Basically, what the slave holders were saying to the American people then is what the Republican Party today is saying to us now and that is if they have to destroy democracy to keep their wealth and power then so be it.

We can learn some lessons from our history because in the scale of human history the Civil War was only yesterday. That is why we can see movies like, *Free State of Jones* and *Birth of a Nation* and it can be extremely relevant to what is going on today, because we have unresolved questions. I think the main lesson is that we cannot move forward as a country and as a people until we politically resolve this question of democracy versus plutocracy, of slavery versus freedom, of national oppression versus the right of self-determination and capitalism versus socialism. And key to this whole struggle is the fight against anti-Black racism, which is the hard core of white supremacy.

I agree with Marx when he says that white workers cannot be free as long as they view enslaved Black workers as a pedestal on which to stand and as long as Black labor is sold and branded. That is as true today as it was then because capitalism is still exploiting and robbing workers as a class of the fruits of their labor. Today we are not sold as chattel but we are still branded by the system with the vestiges of slavery. The purpose of racial antagonism among workers is to keep the white supremacist robber-barons of capitalism in power. The problem with racial antagonism is that it works. The solution lies in uniting the proletariat with the nationally and colonially oppressed people in the struggle to overthrow capitalism/imperialism.

What has been our experience, looking back over my own life? I, as a Black person have been in situations where my life was at risk based on this racist, apartheid system here in America. While in prison they put a white person in a cell with me who was poor working class, just like I was a poor working class but he hated black people, or thought he did. The reason the warden put him there was to do some harm to me. No matter who killed who it was a lose-lose situation. The several things I had going for me to keep Billy Joe and I from attacking each other was we were both prisoners and neither one of us liked the warden and we were both poor working-class people and didn't neither one of us like the rich.

What happened was that we were locked in a struggle against the warden to improve the conditions of the prison and because we were locked in that struggle we were able to talk to each other and in talking to each other and uniting against the Warden we found our common interests. The reason he was a Nazi was he had been sold a bill of goods that the way to fight his oppression was to stand on the backs of others – he could be a racist – he could be better off as member of the master race.

Socialism for white workers based on the continued economic exploitation and colonial/national oppression of people of color around the world is the fascist lie being repeated and being drummed into the heads of white workers of Europe and America. But it is a lie that can never erase the reality that under capitalism all workers are forced to sell themselves into economic slavery for some part of the working day.

We will grow progressively in the direction of extending and expanding our democratic rights to the extent that we unite and fight together to overcome these obvious and gross injustices that are making all of us suffer. I can't base my freedom on the greater suffering of someone else. We either hang together or we will be hung separately. I think my life is an example to be used by whomever wants to use it to show that there is never a situation where hopelessness is an option. I had life and 50 years in prison which means I am supposed to still be there, but here we are.

Just the other day we saw where people were incised by the fact that an African American man who was murdered on the streets under the eyes of a video camera by several police officers attacking him and choking him to death. People were angry because the police officer who did the choking was not charged – would not even be brought to justice for the crime he committed on video. Over twenty years ago we were incited by the video-recording of the beating of Rodney King but today we have the police committing murder on video and in a few instances there have been uprisings and in virtually all instances protests exist the beginnings of mass resistance to police crimes.

According to the Malcolm X Grassroots Movement people there had been nothing this gross (committing murder of Eric Gardner while being video-recorded) since the Rodney King case in 1993 but unlike the King case, there was not an uprising in the ghettos or Black districts of the people where tanks and soldiers could go in, circumscribe the rebellion and squash it. What happened was that people of every creed and color came out into the streets of New York, Chicago, Miami, Los Angeles – all over the country – most of whom were white – and protested this. They could not call it a race riot. They didn't come out to loot or create a pretext where the governor could call in the national guard. They came out to demonstrate their right to protest and interfere with business because they made it very clear that this wasn't the America they wanted. Black lives do matter. The way the prosecutors used the grand jury system outraged Americans not just Black people. A lot of the white protesters came from the Occupy Movement. Black youth assumed the leadership of these demonstrations.

Here we are again, there is new hope on the horizon – the same hope I saw when I was in prison. When I was in prison I saw new hope with the freeing of Angela Davis. Now I see the same thing around the Michael Brown and Eric Gardner situation. I see hope with the uprising of the Black youth and the outrage of the American people. This is not the 1960's, the 1970's or the 1980's. This is almost a quarter into the 21st century and these young people have much more in the way of tools to work with in terms of organizing and mobilizing people than we did in the 1950's and 1960's. We didn't have social media – there was only the ruling class dominated media and the media of a marginalized counter-culture and the organized left.

Since Travon Martin these young people have developed a culture of protest and rapidly evolved into a movement. And they are being attacked on all sides by the ruling class. They are being courted by the Democrats and some of their corporate connected charities. Ideologically some are being driven by notions of utopian socialism or abolishing the police and prisons this side of revolution and therefore betray a misunderstanding of the relationship between the state and revolution. Some of the thinking of our young Turks are confounded by a misunderstanding of the concepts of class, race and gender that denies class struggle as the driving force of history. But these disagreements or ideological differences should not stop us from uniting with these young people for when all is said and done we must work with them as progressive and revolutionary forces in the making who are destined to see further and visit tomorrows that we will never know. We must show them and teach them not to make the mistakes we have already made for them.

There was class struggle before there was a class analysis. According to a class analysis, workers are capitalistically exploited regardless of their race, sex or sexual orientation not because of it. Capitalism absorbs and uses all previous modes of production (ancient society, slavery and feudalism) and the oppression of women which goes back to the very beginning of class societies. Capitalism gave birth to and institutionalizes racism and new forms of sexual exploitation and oppression. All of this can be subsumed under class analysis, but Scientific Socialism doesn't stop with a class analysis, no not at all. Having discovered and laid bare the laws of class struggle it points out that the self-emancipation of the working class is the first stage of ending all inhuman oppression. Class analysis is a description of the problem and class struggle is the solution.

From the standpoint of Marxism-Leninism, i.e. modern revolutionary science rooted in class struggle, every new youth movement must confront the guardians of bourgeois ideology who reside in what DuBois called the 'Halls of the Elms' (Universities). In the past I believe this was done in a most thorough way by the Young Hegelians Ludwig Feuerbach, Karl Marx and Fredrick Engels. As communists we are still grasping and developing the principles of scientific socialism Marx and Engels discovered. I believe we must fight for an understanding and application of these principles in the present struggle for Black liberation and socialism. And this is why I joined three years ago the Freedom Road Socialist Organization. I believe that they understand and fight for these principles. I believe they are amongthe Marxist-Leninists of the 21st Century destined to carry the torch of revolution forward.

But the most incredible thing about our youth is they continue to learn and stay engaged against the status quo. I believe that because they stay engaged on one level or another they will advance the movement far beyond our past achievements of 50 years ago. Hope springs eternal, there is a whole new range of possibilities that just opened, and I am glad I lived to see it. Someone once asked Marx when does a revolution happen and he responded, "when it happens". As a process revolution is always happening but we don't see it in the slow quantitative changes, the forward and backward movement of piece meal reforms, the accumulation of grievances and injustices. We see it in the qualitative leaps which always come suddenly. We see it in what is new and developing with Black Lives Matter and the pockets of resistance springing up all over the country. We see it with the workers at the point of production challenging their bosses and with the Chicago Teachers Union pressing forward as a militant leader of the trade union movement, uniting the fight for jobs with the fight for justice.

Here is what I want to say to those who think it's all about the educator either giving or denying enlightenment to the oppressed nations and masses of people in the colonies under imperialist domination. The educator must be educated by the revolutionary masses who throughout history have never ceased to struggle against oppression. When we don't take into account the fact that the history of all hitherto existing civilizations is the history of class struggle, the now hidden now open struggle between the oppressor and the oppressed we develop a one-sided notion of progress because we tend to see the oppressed as comatose, docile masses stuck in their misery and suffering. We fail to see the revolutionary side of their misery and therefore fail to see that it is precisely the oppressed who are the engine of human progress. No matter what nonsense and lies the oppressors teach in the academies and halls of so-called higher learning there will be uprisings in the colonies and the oppressor nations. The slaves will remain restless and aching for that moment when they can seize the time and take power.

We are in the upswing of a new movement, so let us not scratch our heads wondering where it is going to go or how long it will last. It is our duty as revolutionaries to consciously intervene and become part of the headlights of this movement, so it can see where it is going and sustain itself until we get the job done. Ours is not an exact science, we can't predict time and place of occurrence when it comes to social movements but what we do know is that anywhere and everywhere injustice exist there is struggle. History teaches us that human beings will never give up fighting for justice – that is a constant fact. That is why our National Alliance Against Racist and Political Repression chose the slogan 'Freedom Is A Constant Struggle.' over forty-five years ago.

A Short Epilogue

A few twenty-four-hours-ago some young students from De Paul University asked me when did I join the struggle and it made me think: First I was born in the struggle and then I joined it. I did not choose to be born Black and working class in America and I didn't choose to be born into oppression, hunger and destitution and to be born into a family that fought for survival and against the daily insults and assaults of racist repression. When I was a child back in the 1950s if I saw the police and it was after curfew then I ran and so did the other urchins of the ghetto.

When I was a teenager I saw the burned, beaten and murdered body of Emmet Till in the centerfold of Jet magazine and that's when I first realized that I was in a struggle for personal survival and like it or not in the struggle for the survival of my people. In different phases and stages of life I as a Black person and a worker was always realizing that I was in the struggle for a better life than I was being served.

My life has always been in the dirt and blood of battle I have had to be in since I was born. So, I didn't just up and join the struggle one day in a sudden fit of humanity and love for others. I was always a working-class warrior on my way to becoming class conscious and a freedom fighter on my way to becoming a Black liberator. It's been like this for me because the struggle is my life.

Mandela's first autobiography was entitled the *Struggle Is My Life* and that is the one that I like the most because its focus is on struggle as the gift of life. Or like the Filipinas put it. RESIST TO EXIST! Our comrades in those African countries then colonized by the Portuguese created the slogan A LUTA CONTINUA! (i.e. "the struggle continues"). On his dying bed when Karl Marx was asked "What is life?" He answered: "STRUGGLE!" Peradventure struggle is the law of life but as we have seen from the example of my own life it is also a gift of life that is always giving.